AF506283

THE STRUGGLE FOR FORM

THE STRUGGLE FOR FORM

PERSPECTIVES ON POLISH AVANT-GARDE FILM 1916–1989

EDITED BY KAMILA KUC & MICHAEL O'PRAY

WALLFLOWER PRESS
LONDON & NEW YORK

A Wallflower Press Book
Published by
Columbia University Press
Publishers Since 1893
New York • Chichester, West Sussex
cup.columbia.edu

The images included in Chapter 1 are reproduced by courtesy of the
Themerson Estate and GV Art Gallery, London

A complete CIP record is available from the Library of Congress

ISBN 978-0-231-16982-0 (cloth : alk. paper)
ISBN 978-0-231-16983-7 (pbk. : alk. paper)
ISBN 978-0-231-85065-0 (e-book)

Columbia University Press books are printed on permanent
and durable acid-free paper.
This book is printed on paper with recycled content.
Printed in the United States of America

c 10 9 8 7 6 5 4 3 2 1
p 10 9 8 7 6 5 4 3 2 1

CONTENTS

ACKNOWLEDGMENTS

It is in the nature of books of this kind that debts of many different sorts are incurred. We first would like to thank Yoram Allon at Wallflower Press for his immediate enthusiasm and support for the project, which he has sustained throughout its rather lengthy production, and, not least, for his patience.

For important help in the early stages, thanks are due to Paulina Latham and Marlena Łukasiak at the Polish Cultural Institute, London; Marcin Giżycki; Ryszard Kluszczyński; and Łukasz Ronduda. We would also like to mention Agnieszka Wolak for her hospitality in Warsaw and her continual support and friendship. Others who often gave practical help and advice or offered critical discussion were A. L. Rees, David Curtis, Daniel Bird, Ilona Halberstadt, Michael Maziere, Kuba Mikurda and Ben Cook.

In particular, enormous gratitude is due to Adam Wyżyński and Krzysztof Berłowski at the National Film Archive, Warsaw, whose enthusiasm in locating materials went far beyond any professional duty, and also to Jasia Reichardt at the Themerson Archive, London, who gave her enormous support and in a generous spirit provided excellent stills of the Themersons' films.

The same is offered to David Curtis and Steven Ball at the British Artists' Film and Video Study Collection, Central St Martins, whose knowledge of the subject was extremely important and whose assistance with documentation and film viewings was crucial.

Michael O'Pray would also like to acknowledge the early financial support for travel in relation to the project of the Research Committee of the School of Architecture and Design, University of East London. Kamila Kuc would like to thank Urszula and Mariusz Dragan for their hospitality during extensive research visits at the National Film Archive in Warsaw.

Of course, we owe much to our contributors for their hard work and commitment, with little remuneration, as is the way more often than not these days, and we offer enormous thanks to them. We would also like to acknowledge the contribution of the magazines Lux Centre, *Undercut* and *PIX* in granting permissions to reproduce essays, without which the project would have been impossible.

NOTES ON CONTRIBUTORS

MARCIN GIŻYCKI is a film and art historian, critic, filmmaker, photographer and educator, and the Artistic Director of the 'Animator' International Animated Film Festival in Poznań, Poland. He teaches in Poland and the US and has published seven books and made a number of documentary, experimental and animated films.

MIKOŁAJ JAZDON is a film historian and Professor in the Department of Film, Television and New Media at Adam Mickiewicz University in Poznań. He is the author of books about the documentary films of Krzysztof Kieślowski and Kazimierz Karabasz and the editor of the first book on contemporary Polish independent cinema. He wrote several booklets for the DVD collection of Polish documentary classics ('Polska Szkoła Dokumentu'), and was the scriptwriter and the interviewer for a TV series about recognised Polish documentary filmmakers ('Sztuka dokumentu'). He is also the programmer of Klub Krótkiego Kina, a weekly programme of screenings and public meetings with film directors, and an artistic director of the International Documentary Film Festival OFF CINEMA in Poznań.

RYSZARD KLUSZCZYŃSKI is Professor at the University of Łódź and the Łódź Academy of Fine Arts. He published widely on video art, multi-media and avant-garde cinema. His current interests revolve largely around cyber-culture. He is an art critic and the author of many publications on Polish avant-garde and experimental film.

KAMILA KUC is a film and art historian and curator. She completed her PhD thesis in the history of Polish avant-garde film at Birkbeck College (2012) and is currently authoring a manuscript based on her thesis for Indiana University Press. She is a co-editor of the first Polish collection of Laura Mulvey's most influential essays (ha!art) and is also co-editing the first in English companion to Walerian Borowczyk's films for Berghahn Books. She teaches art and film history and theory at University of Brighton, Hertfordshire and Kingston.

MICHAEL O'PRAY was Professor of Film in the School of Art and Theory, University of East London. He has published widely on avant-garde film and animation and edited *Andy Warhol Film Factory* (1989, translated into Japanese in 1991); *The British Avant-Garde Film 1926–1995: An Anthology* (1996); and, with Jayne Pilling, *Inside the Pleasure Dome: The Films of Kenneth Anger* (1990). He also wrote *Derek Jarman: Dreams of England* (1996, translated into Korean in 2004); *The Avant-Garde Film: Themes, Forms and Passions* (2003); and *Film Form and Phantasy: Adrian Stokes and Film Aesthetics* (2004).

JONATHAN L. OWEN completed his PhD on Czech cinema at the University of Manchester, UK. He has worked as an Associate Research Fellow at the University of Exeter and a Teaching Fellow at the University of St Andrews. He is author of the monograph *Avant-Garde to New Wave: Czechoslovak Cinema, Surrealism and the Sixties* (Berghahn, 2011) and has contributed various book chapters and articles, including to the journals *Framework* and *Canadian Slavonic Papers*. His research interests are East European cinemas, East European avant-gardes, animation, cult cinema and co-productions.

A. L. REES is a research tutor in Visual Communication at the Royal College of Art, London. He programmes and writes about artists' film, video and digital media. A new and updated edition of his 1999 book, *A History of Experimental Film and Video*, was published by BFI/Palgrave Macmillan in 2011. Other recent essays are in *Iconics* (Japan), *Millennium Film Journal* (USA), *Sequence* and *MIRAJ* (London).

MATEUSZ WERNER, born 1970, PhD, is a philosopher of culture and film critic. He lectures at UKSW University in Warsaw. He is the editor of the philosophical quarterly *Kronos*; author of the book *Facing Up to Nihilism: Gombrowicz, Witkacy* (Warsaw, 2009), on the phenomenon of nihilism in literature; and editor of *What Does Kieślowski Tell Us Today?* (Warsaw, 2008, in Hebrew) and *Polish Cinema Now! Focus On Contemporary Polish Cinema* (London and Warsaw, 2010; Seoul, 2012). He has recently edited a collection of Pier Paolo Pasolini's essays, *After Genocide* (Warsaw, 2012), and contributed to international film magazines such as *Cahiers du cinéma* and *Close Up* (Italy). He is a member of FIPRESCI and the Polish Filmmakers Association.

INTRODUCTION

Michael O'Pray and Kamila Kuc

This book was conceived as an introduction to a film avant-garde that, despite its almost mythological reputation, especially around the Film Form Workshop, we felt was sorely under-represented in the English-language literature on avant-garde film. The selection of writings gathered here range in origin from the early period of Polish cinema, the opening decades of the twentieth century, to roughly the late 1980s. This cut-off point for obvious reasons seems appropriate and not simply an art historical device. The end of the Cold War and collapse of the Iron Curtain in 1989 was one of the most important and profound moments of the last century, involving changes of the most fundamental kind, at all levels of the old Soviet bloc countries: political, social, economic and cultural. The moment was a seismic one which transformed the structures, mechanics and attitudes in these countries, in ways that are still being felt almost twenty-five years later, and certainly in Poland.[1] It should be added that this event also, and perhaps unpredictably, had enormous consequences for the so-called Western countries, outside the Soviet bloc.

We have made no attempt here to address the political aspects of the history of the Polish avant-garde between the end of World War II in 1945 and the establishment of an independent Poland in 1991. However, as is to be expected, the political situation plays a role in many of the essays, from the political differences operating in the Polish adaptation of Futurism early last century (see chapter 2, by Kamila Kuc), to the impact of the Thaw on avant-garde film in Poland after Stalin's demise and the introduction of a more 'liberal' Soviet regime in 1956, announced at the twentieth Congress of the Communist Party of the Soviet Union (see chapter 4, by Marcin Giżycki).

Mikołaj Jazdon's piece also has at its core the impact of State censorship and ideology in documentary filmmaking from 1945 to the 1970s in Poland. It needs to be added that Giżycki's essay is especially important in rectifying the mistaken view that the Polish film avant-garde only re-emerged with the appearance of the Film Form Workshop in the 1970s. As he points out, with the Thaw and the resulting collapse of the official Socialist Realist aesthetic, Constructivism and other art influences made themselves felt, leading almost immediately in 1957 to innovative abstract avant-garde films by figures such as Andrzej Pawłowski and Mieczysław Waśkowski and experimental animation by Jan Lenica and Walerian Borowczyk. This strong avant-garde animation proved enormously successful at foreign festivals and also, importantly, reasserted the centrality of animation that had been developed but rarely fulfilled in the early Polish avant-garde, discussed in Kamila Kuc's essay. The radical forms and context of the Film Form Workshop in the 1970s were political, as Ryszard Kluszczyński's meticulous study shows.[2] Similarly, Jonathan Owen's piece on the Polish émigrés has as its background the part played by the restrictions of State ideology and censorship on those who, like Jerzy Skolimowski and Borowczyk, consequently departed for the West in the 1960s.

Our historical cut-off point also means that the complexities, political, cultural and otherwise, of Poland in the post-war period remain in this collection largely in the margins. But as Piotrowski points out in his magisterial study *In the Shadow of Yalta*,[3] the bloc countries cannot be reduced to some homogenous whole, as they often were from the other side of the Iron Curtain in the West. Rather, all of them were quite individual, especially in their artistic and cultural practices. Furthermore, relations and artistic exchanges between other bloc countries and with the West itself differed enormously from country to country, as was the case in, for example, East Germany, Hungary and Czechoslovakia compared with Poland. For example, at the famous *Film as Film* show in 1979,[4] which was a history in many ways of the avant-garde in its more formalist guise, Poland was the only bloc country included, represented by Waśko, Robakowski, Bruszewski and the Themersons. Members of the Workshop did show abroad, and there was some exchange between Britain and Poland in the 1970s, fostered by the British Council. Interestingly, two further connections of a somewhat accidental nature also provided a British connection with Poland, one very specific and the other a wider phenomenon. The specific was the presence until their deaths of the Themersons, who had lived in London since the beginning of World War II, for much of the time ignored in film circles (see chapter 1, by A. L. Rees), and the more general was the wide presence of a Polish community, which had stayed on and settled down in Britain after the war.

The study of the relationships between the Polish avant-garde film and that of other countries deserves another book, and we might add, so do almost all the topics discussed here in individual essays. Once again, the aim, one that can never be neutral, was to provide no more than a topography, a general layout of the terrain of the Polish avant-garde film that might be particularly useful for those readers first approaching the subject.

We were very aware, of course, of the important work done by Polish film historians, especially Ryszard Kluszczyński and Marcin Giżycki, in the post-war Polish film and video tradition. We have used and very much built on their immense knowledge of the area. Outside Poland, writing on this pre-1991 Polish film avant-garde has been rather sparse and scattered, existing in the few catalogues devoted to the international avant-garde film scene and in the magazines and journals attached to this scene.[5] Interestingly, Kluszczyński's writing in 2000 on the Workshop is in part a response to the dismissal of the 1970s movement by some Polish critics and historians.

No attempt has been made to trace the important individual artistic careers of many of the Workshop members who were already going their separate ways by the mid-1970s. More importantly, perhaps, after the collapse in the 1970s of the European avant-garde film festivals at which there had been an opportunity for filmmakers and audiences to see international work, there was very little Polish work in distribution and available for screenings in Britain. This is an opportune moment to mention our exclusion by and large of the video art that was being established in Poland around the time it was in Britain, in the mid-1970s. Video was a new art media that, as its main adherents showed, demanded different methodologies, ideas and forms of practice. It was beyond the book's limits to cover it in any way that was not simply perfunctory. It needs to be said that, unlike in Britain, Polish filmmakers were quick to include video as part of their practice without forfeiting film itself, as can be seen in the work of Robakowski and others. In fact, the Film Form Workshop was quite unique in that from its very beginnings it embraced other art forms – photography, theatre, poetry and performance – all of which played an important role. The multi-media aspirations of the group led to a diverse range of practices within it, especially video, not found anywhere else at the time.

Some remarks are needed perhaps in relation to our use of the term 'avant-garde' in the book's title. The main contenders for the 'avant-garde' these days are 'experimental film', denoting a kind of method, and 'artists' film', which describes the practice(s) in question according to the maker's status. 'Avant-garde', on the other hand, asserts the relation of the practice(s) to something else, usually to what is perceived as the mainstream, the conventional and the status quo. While it seems uncontroversial to apply 'avant-garde' to the film discourses around Futurism and the work of the Themersons in the first few decades of the last century, its appropriateness in describing the Film Form Workshop's output in the 1970s is perhaps more debatable. However, the term was used in Poland during the latter period, with variants, namely 'neo-avant-garde' and the 'pseudo-avant-garde'. If an unstable term, 'avant-garde' persists in resurfacing. What was at stake in Poland in the post-war period was whether the films produced were in an antagonistic-cum-critical relationship to the State, and, as the terms used imply, for some the output was simply a new (neo) contemporary reworking through of an older avant-garde, that of the inter-war years, but for others, detractors of claims for a vanguard position, it was a pretence, not the real thing (pseudo). Kluszczyński's piece on the Workshop is in part a response to these criticisms of the Workshop as a pseudo-avant-garde.

A problem identified more recently with usage of 'avant-garde' is its implicit universalism, so that work falling into the category is deemed to have a value historically determined by a largely Western tradition, one that recognises no differences between the various societies and their different political, social and cultural constitutions and traditions. In Poland, and in the other Eastern bloc countries behind the Iron Curtain, the 'status quo' was different in each country, as well as being characterised generally as being different to that of Western countries. For this reason, applying 'avant-garde' to 'émigré' filmmakers like Skolimowski and Borowczyk is less controversial, though not without, we are sure, some objectors. The relationship between the State and art in general in countries behind the Iron Curtain was quite unique and complex, as writers like Piotrowski have argued. The history of the post-war film avant-garde in terms of its relationship to the communist State is another area for future study.

Finally, the book is composed of different kinds of writing: that of an art-historical nature (e.g. Giżycki, Kuc and Rees); writings from small independent film magazines, once the intellectual life-blood of avant-garde film activity (*Undercut*, *PIX*); polemics, as is the case with Mateusz Werner's piece; and artists' statements. It was felt that this mix of types of discourse served best our desire to present the Polish film avant-garde to the reader in its different facets and textures, and speaking in the voices of its historical times.

NOTES

1 Piotr Piotrowski's *Art and Democracy in Post-Communist Europe* (London: Reaktion Books, 2012) is excellent on the impact of the end of the Cold War in 1989.

2 On Polish art in the 1970s, see Lukasz Ronduda, *Polish Art of the 70s* (Warsaw: Centre for Contemporary Art, 2009).

3 Piotr Piotrowski's *In the Shadow of Yalta: Art and the Avant-garde in Eastern Europe, 1945–1989* (London: Reaktion Books, 2009) has been indispensable for this introduction.

4 See the *Film as Film* catalogue, edited by David Curtis (London: Hayward Gallery, 1979).

5 For a more recent account of the Film Form Workshop in context, see Ronduda, *Polish Art of the 70s*, pp. 266–274.

INTRODUCTION TO THE REVISED VERSION

A.L. Rees

This essay was originally commissioned for the first issue of *PIX* journal (winter 1993/94) by its editor Ilona Halberstadt, a Polish-born, Oxford-educated film enthusiast and former academic, whose interests cross many fields: contemporary music, social and political philosophy, world cinema, the avant-gardes. *PIX* was an extraordinary venture, or adventure, in independent film publishing. Ilona's boundless energy and tenacity somehow overcame a distinct lack of money to produce a stylish and beautifully designed journal full of unexpected artistic and intellectual conjunctions that reflected her wide and eclectic taste – for Bernardo Bertolucci and Patrick Keiller, for Viking Eggeling and Michelangelo Antonioni.

The first *PIX* featured a 60-page inner section – 'Close-Up' – wholly devoted to the films of Stefan and Franciszka Themerson. This contained original texts and documentation, a host of amazing photographs and letters from the Themerson Archive run by historians and curators Nicholas Wadley and Jasia Reichardt (Franciszka Themerson's niece), and full documentation of all their films, whether lost or surviving. My task was to put them into a wider inter-national context of experimental cinema in the 1920s to the 1940s, when the Themersons made their films, and to give some idea of what else was going on in Polish avant-garde film culture at the time.

For the historical side, I entirely relied on the few scattered secondary sources I could find in English translation, since I know no Polish, and on the evidence of the available remaining films (very few, as it turned out). But there was some guidance. David Curtis and Deke Dusinberre had champi-oned the Themersons' films in the major survey 'Film as Film' at the Hayward Gallery in 1979, and the catalogue had information on some very obscure but fascinating filmmakers, like Kazimierz Podsadecki and Mieczysław Szczuka. Dusinberre's pioneering catalogue article 'The Other Avant-Gardes' – on pre-war film experiment in Britain, Poland and the Netherlands – benefitted from conversations with the Themersons themselves in their Maida Vale flat, an archipelago of modern art as well as a working studio space.

A few years later, the programmer at the London Film Makers' Co-operative, Jo Comino, was also bitten by the Themerson bug. She got their films into LFMC distribution, fittingly enough since the Themersons had set up the first Film Co-operative in Poland in 1935, and wrote a back-page profile for the *Monthly Film Bulletin* in July 1983 of what she called their 'multi-media career'. The tradition continues: the currently available DVD of the Themersons' films is published by LUX, the LFMC's successor.

What this meant was that the Themersons lived to see a revival of interest in their films, and indeed the whole of their prodigious creative work, with major exhibitions and screenings here and abroad. Stefan Themerson's own extraordinary book on film – *The Urge to Create Visions* – bookends this era. Drafted between 1936 and 1947, it was eventually published in 1983. During this revivalist period in the mid-1980s, I showed and introduced the films on various occasions, and talked to the filmmakers several times. Polite, charming and helpful as my hosts always were, my well-meaning attempts to get details from them about the lost films, and their production, were like trying to pull teeth. They would much rather talk about their current work and ideas! At this time both were in their late seventies, and neither were in good health, but they determinedly kept working and publishing until their deaths (in 1988).

How did you make an experimental film in Poland in the 1930s? How did you get access to prints, to labs, to cameras? They made light of such problems. It wasn't that difficult, if you wanted to get things done. How did they get away with the frontal nude shot in *Europa*? Well, Stefan took the film to the censorship board, where it was viewed by the panel, some in military uniform. So what happened? Nothing, said Mr Themerson. He was too young and shy to mention it (he was twenty-two) and they were too embarrassed to comment on it, so they just passed the film, and that was that.

In fact, as revealed in a letter to his friend the film director Aleksander Ford, written from London in October 1945, and published in *PIX* 1, nothing was easy. Looking back at their early days, Stefan Themerson wrote:

When I think of our youthful years with film, I am reminded of the struggle for bits of film stock; for prediluvian cameras; for work benches cobbled together from odd sticks; for thousands of bits of paper from customs and the censor,

which one had to get, come what may, just to see the avant-garde films from
the West from which we had been isolated by a fortified wall.

Now he is 'overwhelmed by feelings of friendly envy' for the new avant-gardes
to come, who will realise their creative ideas and will 'find in their own hand
the apparatus they need for this art'. That, certainly, has come true.

By the time I wrote the essay that follows, both Themersons were dead and
I could no longer ply them with questions they didn't want to bother with,
although I am very sure that in their lifetime they were pleased that younger
filmmakers and exhibitors were so eager about these works of their own
youth. I had a motley collection of catalogues and programme notes to work
with, which contained the little I was able to glean about such exciting (and
still unknown in the UK) critics and writers of the early Polish avant-garde as
Karol Irzykowski and Stefania Zahorska, with a few translated citations from
their work. These were too fragmentary and even scrappy for me to think of
footnoting (and *PIX*, which was not an academic journal, had few footnotes
anyway).

My main sources were Mr Themerson's own writings, especially the rich
harvest of data and ideas in *The Urge to Create Visions* (Gaberbocchus/De
Harmonie, Amsterdam, 1983); the facsimile edition in English of Anatol
Stern's poem 'Europa' (1929), with information and notes about the 1932 film
(Gaberbocchus, London, 1962); the essays by Dusinberre and Jo Comino noted
above; and the catalogue *Stefan i Franciszka Themerson – Visual Researches*,
a wonderful exhibition catalogue of their films (Muzeum Sztuki, Łódź, 1982)
with essays by Urszula Czartoryska and Janusz Zagrodzki.

For background and detail about abstract art, film and Constructivism
in pre-war Poland, I used the catalogue *Constructivism in Poland 1923 to
1936*, edited by Hilary Gresty and Jeremy Lewison (Muzeum Sztuki, Łódź;
Kettle's Yard Gallery, Cambridge, 1984). Also invaluable was the catalogue
Constructivism in Poland 1923–1936: BLOK, Praesens, a.r., prepared and
edited by the Muzeum Sztuki, Łódź; the exhibition shown in 1973 at Museum
Folkwang, Essen and Rijksmuseum Kröller-Müller Otterlo. All the Muzeum
Sztuki publications noted here were introduced by its Director, Ryszard
Stanisławski, and contain contributions by Janusz Zagrodzki. I belatedly and
gratefully acknowledge these and other scholars who I pillaged while writing
my own essay. I have made a few minor changes and corrections, but otherwise it appears as published in *PIX* after Ilona tore into the first and later
drafts and – as the best of editors – showed me how to try to improve it. For
her advice, and knowledge, I am still grateful.

THE THEMERSONS AND THE POLISH AVANT-GARDE:
WARSAW – PARIS – LONDON

A.L. Rees

Polish artists between the two world wars shared a passion for the new art of cinema with such early – and diverse – modernists as Man Ray and Fernand Léger, who made films themselves, and those like Picasso, Malevich and Heartfield, who planned to do so. Among the prime movers for a Polish avant-garde cinema were members of the Constructivist movement. Like its sister groups in the Soviet Union, Holland and Germany, Polish Constructivism was both rationalistic – in its search for aesthetic purity – and socially utopian, in its faith that machine-age functionalism could build a new cultural order in the aftermath of world war. The first art movement to unambiguously embrace the mass media and the modern age, Constructivism saw art as a unified force field, in which the classic arts of painting, sculpture and architecture (purged of realism, romance and ornament) were linked with craft tradition and the new arts of photography, montage, design and cinema.

The young Polish artist Teresa Żarnower wrote as a Constructivist in 1923 that 'the artist has the broadest scope for expression in the cinema, where elements of the individual branches of art may be combined, ... enhanced by the perfection of technical methods'. As was common in this period, the dream of a new cinema came before the reality. Although Żarnower's artistic collaborator Mieczysław Szczuka began work on abstract films only two years after her statement on cinema, they were unfinished by his early death in 1927. The fulfilment of the Constructivist vision of film only came in the 1930s, just as the 'Cubist Cinema' mooted by French artists around 1912 had to wait a decade before the finance and the technology were available for such films as Léger's *Ballet mécanique*. But by the 1930s, Polish Constructivism was no longer at the forefront of art as a single voice, having split into factions. Rising militarism and fascism in Europe and dwindling prospects for utopia also battered the principle of hope embodied by the movement. Poland was itself ruled by a general, and soon had Hitler on one side of the border and Stalin on the other.

In this apparently grim climate, the young Themersons – just out of their teens – made the first Polish abstract films, and with wit and humour pursued the vision of film heralded by their older acquaintances, themselves also only in their twenties, the Constructivists Szczuka and Żarnower. In the case of the Themersons' film *Europa* (1932), these near-contemporary predecessors were honoured in letter as well as spirit, since the film partly stemmed from their own design and graphics.

In complex ways, the Constructivist legacy was passed to a new generation of experimentalists in the 1930s. Like France, where such writers as Louis Aragon, Maurice Raynal and Guillaume Apollinaire were amongst the first to support the new cinema, so too did Poland produce a number of important critics to promote non-narrative film. As early as 1913, Karol Irzykowski had attacked the failure of film drama to construct an imaginative cinema free of theatrical conventions. He continued as a voice of the avant-garde throughout the 1920s and 1930s, publishing his influential book *The Tenth Muse* in 1924, the same year as the first of Breton's Surrealist manifestos.

Despite the enthusiasm of earlier Polish Constructivists for film, the Polish avant-garde largely skipped the phase of graphic abstraction that led to the early films of Eggeling, Richter and Ruttmann in Germany, which the last two had, in any case, abandoned around 1926–27 for the first lyrical documentaries. Reviewing the situation in 1928, the critic Stefania Zahorska argued that graphic cinema should be superseded by films that abstracted the texture and light of the objective reality caught by the camera-eye, and edited by montage methods derived from musical form. She voiced a concept of photogenic filmmaking that had been eloquently promoted in France by the writings of the Polish émigré director Jean Epstein, as well as by Man Ray and Henri Chomette. Zahorska was writing in advance of the first flowering of the Polish experimental cinema, but she signalled the direction it was to take: a mixture of poetics, montage and documentary. Like Irzykowski and Jerzy Toeplitz, she supported the new filmmaking throughout the pre-war period.

The period between 1930 and 1934 was formative for the Themersons. In contrast to Constructivism, characterised by a formal bias, it was characterised, in the phrase of Karol Irzykowski, by 'the search for content', and parallel slogans were also promoted by Hans Richter in Germany as the hopeful 1920s dwindled into the harsher 1930s. Irzykowski now argued that artists and film-makers faced pressing problems of social reality and should take their subject matter from anti-fascism, anti-authoritarianism, the needs of mass audiences, the critique of visual conventions and clichés, and the growing struggle for women's rights. Artists were exhorted to mix new cinematic techniques with overtly social statements, blending poetry and polemics.

The Constructivist era and its aftermath is bridged by the prolific Mieczysław Szczuka, a pioneer filmmaker who died in 1927, in a climbing accident, aged twenty-nine. Szczuka's best-known work is in the theory of architecture – but he was protean and active in design, photomontage and graphics (coincidentally, Stefan Themerson, when making his first film, was still an architecture student). A vigorous debater in the complex stages of later Constructivism, Szczuka was a member of the group which invited Mayakovsky to visit Poland, and as a leftist radical, though not a Party member, he was also a graphic designer for Polish Communist publications, while also nevertheless designing advertisements.

Szczuka was a fierce defender of functionalist design and held that the category of art would disappear within a commitment to social practice. His essays attack purist definitions of art, the issue over which the main Constructivist group BLOK split in 1926, and which led to the exit of the painters and founders of the group Katarzyna Kobro and Władysław Strzemiński. (They had studied in the Free Studios in Moscow in 1918–1919 and worked with Malevich in Vitebsk. But even as purists they showed an interest in social activity typical of the Polish avant-garde: Malevich when visiting his homeland was criticised by his disciples for metaphysical traces in his theory of art; and in 1932 they persuaded the socialist council of the industrial city of Łódź to support one of the first museums of modern art, the still-functioning Muzeum Sztuki.) Szczuka agreed with Tatlin's Productivist group in Russia and the Bauhaus school in Germany that artists should collaborate with factories to produce strictly utilitarian objects.

But while Szczuka was arguing for a strict functionalism in design, he was also working on ideas for abstract films. In 1924, *BLOK* published his article 'Essential Elements for an Abstract Film', accompanied by a diagram of geometrical shapes and forms on a filmstrip – a graphic notation rather than anything that could be actually shot, like many outline plans of the period. Szczuka notes: 'Movement as change in place; the coming and going, but not changing, of geometrical forms, the disintegration or construction of forms'. A mini-scenario goes on to refer to colour, brightness, direction, interplay of shape, tempo, harmony and pauses.

The film was eventually drawn out on long rolls of paper, according to Stefan Themerson, who saw them in Szczuka's studio after the artist's death. The impulse for the film was probably related to the work of the ex-Dadaist Viking Eggeling, who had begun using the 'Chinese scroll' method in Zurich around 1919, later moving to Berlin, where he died in 1925 after completing his surviving project, *Diagonal Symphony*. Szczuka could have found details of Eggeling's films in the international art press (e.g. *De Stijl*), but could also have learnt of them from his friend Henryk Berlewi, recently returned from Germany, where he had belonged to the radical November Group in 1921–23. Berlewi too was experimenting with light-play as well as abstract paintings that gave the illusion of pulsating, and had reviewed his friend Eggeling's work in the journal *Albatross*.

The following year, 1925, Szczuka began the more adventurous film *He Killed, You Killed, I Killed*. The words of the title were to be shown and permutated in different typefaces and intensities, and evidently it aimed to elicit an emotive and physical response through its wordplay. Here abstraction now passes through language, the word doubling as a visual sign in the montage structure. As with the earlier abstract film, it is not known how far Szczuka got with it before his death. The only comparable semiotic film of the period is Duchamp's *Anemic Cinema* (1926), with its revolving spirals and scatological puns, or more distantly Man Ray's use of allusive titles in *L'Etoile de mer* (1928). Szczuka's second film predates the semiotic cinema of the structuralist 1970s by more than forty years.

Szczuka was to leave another legacy to the avant-garde cinema, in contrast to these lost and certainly uncompleted films, in the designs he prepared with Teresa Żarnower for the publication of the Futurist poem 'Europa', by the young socialist writer Anatol Stern. This project was to pass through many interlinked media and variations. Published in 1929, two years after Szczuka's death, the poem is a strident attack on the destructive militarism of European capitalism. In a later tribute, Stern commented on its experimental typography and collaged illustrations:

> Szczuka shows in two of his images the two faces of modern art. Chaplin bursting into sardonic laughter before the European spectacle he contemplates and Petrarch, crowned with laurels, among a thousand others, turning his back on the continent drowned in a sea of blond. Szczuka saw only the two extremes; he abhorred the debauchery of nuances.

In the words of another advocate of collage as a device in art, Walter Benjamin, the poem and its design imply that 'every document of civilization is also a document of barbarism'.

During an era rich in collaboration, it is interesting that Stern too treats the images of 'Europa' as equal in meaning to his own text. His stress on Szczuka's thought as representing 'two extremes' is in apparent contrast to the characteristic major theme of unity that runs through much Polish art of the time, and underscores Szczuka's radical politics. At almost the same time, Jean Cocteau also used the image of a laurel-wreathed muse and a bull on whose hide is traced the map of the continent (perhaps an echo of the myth of the rape of Europa). The final shots from Cocteau's *Le Sang d'un poète* (*Blood of a Poet*) offer an image of transcendence, as the poet enters eternity – while Szczuka's Petrarch turns his face from Europe 'drowned in a sea of blood', in a gesture of refusal. The two related images refer to different accounts of history, mimesis and aesthetic vision.

Cocteau's film was released in 1932, the year in which Stefan and Franciszka Themerson turned 'Europa' into a film, now sadly lost as a consequence of the wars and upheavals which it predicted and denounced. Thirty years later, the Themersons published an English facsimile of the original design, illustrating it with some surviving stills from the film, and adding another layer to the circles of history, language and place which the 'Europa' project embodied. (The film version is now recoverable only in fragments and in the descriptions given by reviews such as S. Zahorska's. In the 1980s the Themersons helped prepare a tape-slide version of the Europa material by the London Film Makers' Co-op.)

Europa exemplified a new wave of Post-Constructivist imagism. Stefan Themerson stated that the film 'took an abstract approach to reality', while Zahorska (who had argued for such an approach several years before) explained that

> the relationship between the images exists not 'realistically' but only at the level of ideology, at the threshold of symbolism. Its images [...] materially and tangibly show that Europe eats, Europe reproduces, Europe functions in the normal cycle – and continually gives birth to cannon-fodder.

The film's figurative imagery and overt social statements underline a move away from Constructivist abstract precision, while its rough, brisk expressionism and direct use of metaphor reach back to the anarchic alliances between Constructivism and Dada a decade earlier, around 1922 (at a time before hard lines had been drawn, and when the De Stijl theorist Theo van Doesburg could write Dada poems under the nonsense pseudonym of I. K. Bonset).

If the Themersons rediscovered how to fuse Constructivist form with Dadaist iconoclasm, the film also implies a link to Surrealism, whose ideas had been permeating the continent since the mid-1920s. Polish history has perhaps made its artists receptive to Surrealist irony and black humour.

Alfred Jarry, who stood high in the Surrealist canon as one of its progenitors, had set his abrasive *Ubu Roi* in an imaginary Poland, circa 1900. It was translated into Polish as *Ubu Król – czyli Polacy* (*Ubu Roi i.e. The Poles*). When Jarry wrote the play in 1894, Poland literally did not exist as a state, being totally divided up among its neighbours. *Ubu* was therefore set 'nowhere', in a dyspeptic Erewhon or Utopia. Gaberbocchus Press published the first English translation of *Ubu Roi* (1951) with illustrations by Franciszka Themerson, who went on to elaborate many versions in different media. Nick Wadley commented that 'the violent scale of Jarry's sense of the absurd was a formative influence on her development as an image-maker'.

It was possibly Surrealism that kept the Themersons, as well as others in the Polish avant-garde, from an outright descent into the growing tendency to social realism in the 1930s, which was to become institutionalised under the post-war Stalinist regime. 'The search for content' renewed the call for a radical documentary cinema in the 1930s. However, the originator of the slogan, Karol Irzykowski, had already argued a decade earlier – in his book *The Tenth Muse* (1924) – that the role of radical cinema was to 'reawaken' the image in art, blunted by convention and habit, and he continued to defend this view in the later, politicised period. Irzykowski claimed that the cinema can bring together 'the visible and the invisible': the perceived and the imagined object. Cinema has this capacity because it can manipulate and alter images, restructuring them through montage editing. His wit and his stress on unity are characteristic of the Polish avant-garde. And yet his metaphors also recall Klee (who also claimed that art must 'render the invisible visible'), just as his theorisation – 'the task of cinema [...] is to compress, to select and multiply' – affirms a semiotic of film akin to Vertov's. Irzykowski wrote:

We live in the sea of matter, ... We not only swim amid matter in large circles; we also dabble playfully at one spot, as fishes do when slightly moving their fins. The art able to show this co-existence has barely begun ... The task of the cinema, this mirror of the visible – both real and imagined, known and future – is to compress, to select and to multiply the visible, as well as to present it in growth, and this is how it earns its dignity. The visible is no longer an everyday fact but turns into something important and wonderful. The roots of the visible and the invisible may grow into unity in some metaphorical extension, just as according to Schelling the subject and the object are one.

The Themersons had links with many of the artistic groups that were formed in the late 1920s and the early 1930s, but they uniquely stayed unaffiliated to any of them. Most of the artists who promoted film did so as members of associations. In Kraków, for example, Janusz Brzeski and Kazimierz Podsadecki of the Linia Group held an exhibition of experimental photography in 1931 that included work by Man Ray, Hans Richter and Laszlo Moholy-Nagy – all of them filmmakers, incidentally – in an event that recalls the influential 'Film und Foto' show in Stuttgart in 1929. The first Avant-Garde Film conference in 1929 at La Sarraz, Switzerland (Richter, Ruttmann and Eisenstein were present), had as its topic 'the art of the cinema, its social and aesthetic purposes'. A year later in its final session in Brussels, the congress unmistakably announced a shift of purpose in its statement that the avant-garde as a purely aesthetic movement had passed its climax, and was on the way to concentrating on the social and political film, mainly in documentary form. In his unpublished book *The Struggle for the Film* (1937), Richter argued that political tensions 'made poetry no longer suitable'. The age demanded 'the documented fact', he concluded, under 'the social imperative'.

Brzeski and Podsadecki went on to form the Kraków-based 'Studio of the Polish Avant-Garde Film', screening new work that included Europa and their own films – *Sections* (1931) and *Concrete* (1933), as well as European experimental work. The two artists seem also to have wanted to combine the formal tactics of Constructivism with a freer use of images that evokes Surrealism. According to the filmmakers, the theme of *Concrete* was 'Human alienation in the technology of the city', which shows a growing distance from the urban utopianism of the earlier decade. Podsadecki's essay 'We Need the Abstract Film' echoed Zahorska's earlier defence of photogenic cinema, arguing that the camera-eye and montage editing could renew visual perception of the objective world.

Jalu Kurek, also of Linia, had been showing films since 1931, screening his own *O.R.* in 1933 – the title is an acronym for 'Rhythmic Calculations' in Polish. It was described as showing how two apparently unrelated events are 'forged into unity' by rhythm and composition – a further sign of the Unist theory widespread in the avant-garde and adopted by the Constructivist Strzemiński as the title of his aesthetic system.

Among other documented screenings, Europa was shown by the Constructivist Praesens group of artists and architects in 1933, along with work by Hans Richter and Joris Ivens, and similar shows took place in a variety of artists' groups and amateur associations in Warsaw, Łódź (The Polish Amateur Film Club), Kraków and Lwów (The Avant-Garde Film Club). Of all these early Polish filmmakers, the Themersons, the most prolific, were uniquely consistent in their intellectual perspective and visual aesthetic. The core of this approach was largely expressed in the fundamental value they gave to light.

Stefan Themerson made his first photograms when he was still at high school, by simply exposing a match flame on a photographic plate. Much later, in his book *The Urge to Create Visions*, Themerson recalled an African myth which tells of a girl throwing a handful of sparks into the sky, where they turn into the stars. Themerson playfully speculates that this is the story of the beginning of cinema; the film screen is prefigured in the 'huge dome resting upon the edges of the flat Earth on which mysterious negatives, lyrical photograms, strange and distant pictures of the sky were projected'. Suitably expanded with the aid of a home-made camera stand, and a 'great yellow coffin' of a camera made in 1910 (the year of the filmmaker's birth, as he was happy to point out), the photogram technique was adapted to animate the moving shadows of objects filmed through a translucent glass sheet covered with paper. The moving of lights during filming created the illusion of the objects in movement. In this way, abstract forms were created for the Themersons' first film, *Apteka* (*Pharmacy*, 1930), and for the more sophisticated *Europa*. Even in the live-action comic drama *Przygoda Człowieka Poczciwego* (*The Adventure of a Good Citizen*, 1937), photogrammed birds appear to fly in a mainly hand-

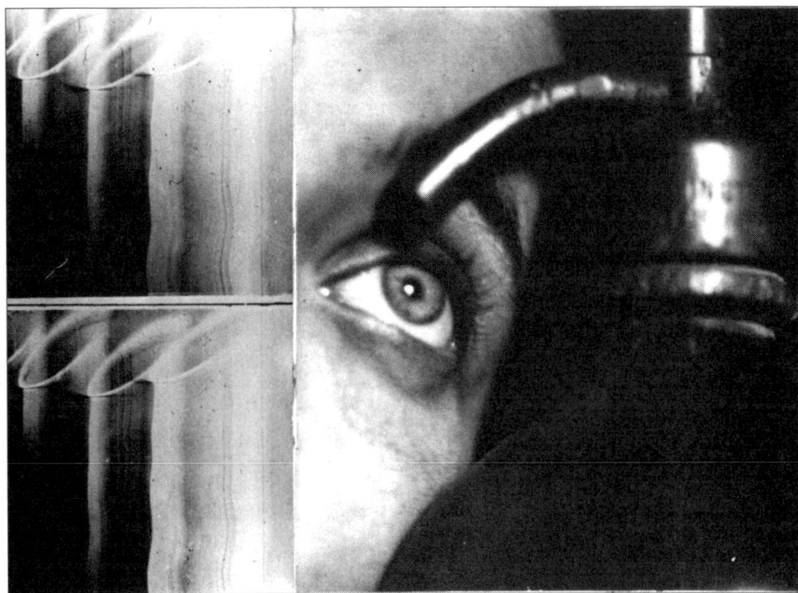

Fig. 1 *Apteka* (*Pharmacy*, 1930)

painted section. The graphic abstraction in *The Eye and the Ear* (1944/45) was especially attuned to photogram images, while in *Calling Mr. Smith* (1943) the photogram was expanded into surreal and abstract solarised colour.

The seemingly primitive photogram is thus a founding moment of the Themersons' films, and emblematic of their aim: a combination of materialist abstraction and visionary lyricism, since the photogram is both a literal record of the passage of light and a manipulated form, partly controlled and partly left to chance. The flare of a match sparked a long investigation into the tracing of light.

Stefan Themerson found many origins for the photogram: in Bushman legends, in Eskimo poems, in Indian languages that used the same word for 'shadow, soul, echo and picture', in astronomy, in mediaeval fables and in early modern art. The line he traced from the magic lantern through the camera obscura to the photogram led him, on Teresa Żarnower's recommendation, to hunt out the eccentric French poet Pol-Dives in Paris during the 1930s, where he found the elderly man giving slide-shows of his 'visual poems' in a shed, to the sound of a gramophone. In his 1937 book, Themerson prefigured the statement of another film magus, Kenneth Anger, who stated that

Fig. 2 *Przygoda Człowieka Poczciwego* (*The Adventure of a Good Citizen*, 1937)

> Centuries before photography there were talismans, which actually anticipated photographs, since the dyes they used on the cheap vellum produced patterns when they faded in the light... cunningly you printed on it a 'photograph' of the demon you wanted to capture on it.

Themerson's 'soul-trap' is more benevolent:

> Photograms are as old as the world. When the apple was still green, a little leaf got stuck to its surface. The sun shone, the apple reddened, but not under the little leaf. And when Eve took the apple, which was pleasant to the eyes, she flicked off the little leaf, but she didn't notice that a beautiful shape of the

little leaf was created there, on the peel of the apple. Neither did the serpent notice it. Nor did Adam. Nor the author of Genesis (otherwise he would have mentioned it, and he didn't).

Or perhaps he did. The Zohar comments on the opening of Genesis ('In the beginning') that

Photograms emerge in the most unexpected places, but only perhaps because one is not looking for them there. Stefan Themerson's interest in codes, typographic experiments that exchanged word and image, linguistic experiment (he published an important study of Apollinaire's *Calligrammes*), translatability and logical and formal structures, together with the Constructivist argument that the structure of art has biological roots which nonetheless should not be imitated in the work of art itself, can all be taken as a kind of inspired secular gematria. The value of his theories, and the signifying role of illumination, was expressed by Themerson in 1936 in yet another image of water to parallel Irzykowski's: 'To sing images, like a luminous fish does in the dark depths of the ocean, not with a reflected light but with one's own light.'

Modernism is sometimes seen as anti-naturalistic, because it relies so heavily on technique, concept and artifice. To some extent this is so, but the art of the Themersons is based on the connection of nature and culture rather than on antagonism between them. In this view, nature is not only a source of aesthetic experience – it is also a source of meaning and not alienated from the human mind. In the spirit of Duchamp, chance (and the intervention of nature) is welcome. Stefan Themerson often praises the conscious use of accidents. From this point of view, nature is a readymade.

The Themersons' best-known film was made in 1937. *The Adventure of a Good Citizen*, subtitled an 'irrational humoresque', shows how an unconventional gesture – in this case walking backwards – can baffle authority and challenge social norms. The good citizen of the title overhears on the telephone an instruction shouted to some workmen manhandling an awkward cupboard – 'Walk backwards, the sky won't fall if you walk backwards!' (or, in a later translation suggested by Stefan Themerson, 'Walk arse forwards'). Misunderstanding the situation, the citizen duly walks backwards through the streets and bumps into the removal men. They join forces and finally arrive in a forest, where they play with the wardrobe mirror in a lyrically photogrammed and hand-painted episode. Meanwhile, a hostile banner-waving crowd, angry at the nonconformists who choose to walk in reverse, chase after them. But the workmen and the citizen have disappeared to Parnassus in the sky, and the crowd finds that the wardrobe is an empty shell. With an imaginative leap, they too disappear. A pipe-player tells the audience that they must 'understand the metaphor'. The film ends with a shot of a naked child in a meadow.

The phrase shouted over the telephone is echoed throughout the film, in a series of transformations. In fact the skies *do* fall when the act of walking backwards incites social disapproval, just as they fall visually when 'the world turns upside down' in a sequence of photogrammed birds and hand-drawn trees. The man seen in a field celebrating his freedom by dancing half-reflected in the mirrored wardrobe door is actually inverted at this point, in a final flourish of liberty, which is almost a literal emblem of the Surrealist epoch.

Of all the Polish films of the period, this is perhaps the one closest to Surrealism in feeling. Surrealism has as many heretics as ideologues. A year before the film was made, another renegade surrealist, René Magritte, living in another small country – Belgium – beset by Europe's wars, painted *The Key to the Fields* (1936). Here again the skies have fallen: shards of broken glass lie heaped beneath a smashed window, the fragments bearing on them the images of sky and landscape, which the window still impossibly frames.

Fallen skies, imaginary birds and visionary landscape, along with images of reversal and duplication, are common to the Themersons and Magritte in these near-contemporary works, a partial meeting of minds on the far shores of Surrealism. They are linked by a shared wish to break with illusionist habit, and a taste for semantic play, literalism and paradox, while still insisting that fantasy is based on the texture of everyday life.

Unlike Borges – a writer to whom he might be compared in the intricacy of his plots and the use of emblems and logical conundrums – Stefan Themerson's fictions were always rooted in human behaviour and the strangeness of everyday reality. In his novels, he finds the extreme in the normal, while his plots are based on simple mistakes, which lead to complex situations (as in *The Adventure of a Good Citizen*). The surreal topology of his novels and writing is not chaotic but supremely orderly. Its world is balanced, but its characters – who may be humans or termites – differ from one another in their perceptions and how they describe them. From this asymmetry of individuals, disorder and misalliance can often arise. In this, Stefan Themerson never lost his early training in the sciences. Nature is always the origin, but he shares with the Polish Constructivist Karol Hiller a concept of 'rebellious matter' and with Jarry and Duchamp a belief in the laws of chance. The photogram is the emblem of this philosophy, just as anti-authoritarianism is its political ethic.

In a later radio interview (1978), Stefan Themerson recalled that the early avant-garde believed that 'a new order or disorder in art' might change the world for the better. This is the practical meaning of the film's metaphor, which the viewers are asked to understand by the pipe-player who speaks at the end of *The Adventure of a Good Citizen*. In Poland in 1937 the metaphor of the film needed little interpretation: if you conform, you may not become a fascist (the outraged crowd are a motley crew, and include a Jew in a caftan), but even so the 'forward march' of fascism will beat you. The German invasion two years later proved the point. The Themersons, who were then in Paris, were to be driven into exile to England.

The section of the film in which a mirror acts as a transition to a fantasy sequence depicted by photogram images is also a key to Themerson's imagination. Mirrors – a recurring theme in the later novels – are complementary to photograms, but seen (as it were) from the other side. While the mirror reflects the virtual image of its object, a photogram encodes directly the shadowed imprint of an object's surface. Several of the early films use two kinds of visual signification and their accompanying metaphors: the iconic image of cinematography (which works by resemblance) and the indexical photogram (in which the image is a trace of its source).

In *The Adventure of a Good Citizen*, the wardrobe mirror carried by the workmen reflects chance encounters with daily life that enter the fictional world of the narrative. Caught unawares, amused bystanders watch the antics of the filmmakers (also glimpsed in reflection) and are indiscriminately caught by the camera-eye. In the final scenes in the forest, the mirror becomes a magical object, as the citizen plays with its reflections. When the hostile crowd follow the rebels into the forest and search the wardrobe, they only find an empty frame; the mirror itself has disappeared, along with the escaped protagonists.

The mirror has become a metaphor, punning on its long history in Western art, where – as 'the reflection of reality' – it alternately stands for truth or illusion, depending on the context. Here, it stands for both. In a much later novel, *Tom Harris* (1967), the narrator experiments with a dazzling arrangement of symmetrical reflections, to work out their laws and irregularities. The theme is prefigured in the earlier film, which (as Stefan Themerson stated) can be played forwards or backwards and still retain its meaning.

Stefan Themerson argued that formal structures in logic, art and language transform reality. Like all systems, they are reflexive and lead to what he called 'thinking about thinking' – which should not stop there but go back to the consideration of human behaviour. This evokes Benjamin's argument for apperception, or audience self-awareness, in the cinema. The main visual figure for this self-reference is the mirror and its reflections. More explicitly than the other films of the period, because it is the least didactic of them, *The Adventure of a Good Citizen* also heralds a further theme in Stefan Themerson's later fiction, through its interlocking narratives in which apparently unrelated persons and events are brought together in a complex whole (rather like Kurek's work but via narrative structure rather than pure montage). The fractal symmetries of relativism receive later and equally tragic-humorous elaboration in such novels as *Tom Harris* (1967), *The Mystery of the Sardine* (1986) and *Hobson's Island* (1988), which affirm the same message as the 1936 film – that other people have the right to live too.

There is a remarkable consistency about Stefan Themerson's work as filmmaker and author, all the more striking because inconsistency is one of his major themes. He is a common-sense fantasist, for whom the most bizarre events spring from speculations based on facts. He treats ironically Kant's warning that reason should not speculate at all if it is to avoid fantasy; the dialectic of reason quickly leaps to unreasonable conclusions when left to its own laws and devices. The fantasies of reason are as self-embedded as a Themerson plot. This pessimistic view of fantasy is twisted in Themerson's later novels to yield an optimistic conclusion, just as his 'semantic poetry' (developed from the 1940s) deconstructs poetic metaphors into factual statements, paradoxically freeing their semiotic meaning. By taking logical positivism to its ironic conclusion, the essays and novels argue that the flytrap of language can be unglued and the prison-house of language given a key. As with the protagonists of *The Adventure of a Good Citizen* in their looking-glass world, the later books show that language is a mirror in which logicians can free themselves from their own labels – in this case, self-adhesive ones.

Some elements of the later films were also present in the earliest ones. The title of *Pharmacy* hints at an alchemical theme, the blend of science and lyric, which flows through its development of the home-made photogram method its makers devised: the filming of shadow-traces in negative. This three-minute work creates abstract images from items in a chemist's shop; the filmmakers were, Stefan Themerson recalled, 'indecently, unashamedly young', in their early twenties ('Franciszka was completing studies at the Academy of Art [...] I was in architecture'). He described an early screening to a film society, at a friend's invitation:

First there was an American film in which Homer (or was it Hector?) rocked in a
rocking chair. And then *Pharmacy*. Someone asked 'What are those drops doing
on the screen?' I didn't then know how to talk when I had nothing to say. Since
I had nothing to say regarding the drops on the screen I remained silent. Thus
it was concluded I must be conceited. I wasn't conceited. I was merely a young
boy from the provinces who knew what he wanted, yet thankfully was totally
unaware of the nature and immensity of the barriers set out around him. The
Himalayas, Carpathians, Alps and Pyrenees seemed to him insignificant play-
things moulded out of pailfuls of sand. We put the tin with Apteka back in my
pocket, and went out for a walk. Over the Poniatowski Bridge, to Praga and the
Wilno Station and back over the Kerbedz bridge, we walked all night and into
the morning. Such was our first meeting with the film club START – 'The Society
of Enthusiasts for Art Cinema.'

Abstracting directly from nature – by using the shadows and reflections of
real forms – the early films combined a quasi-scientific technique with highly
visionary images. Their next film, *Europa*, was far more ambitious – overtly
linked to the avant-garde of neo-Constructivist art, writing and the social
impetus of the period – and was received with greater understanding and
much enthusiasm. From the following year – 1933 – the Themersons' filmmaking underwent a subtle shift. Without losing their independent ideas,
they accepted commissions, which both allowed them to develop their range
and kept the 'social imperative' much debated during this period. This links
them not only to the work of Richter and Ivens on the continent, but also to
the similar impulse towards a radical and social cinema in the British documentary movement: within a few years they were to make contact with John
Grierson, and their later films in England ally them loosely to the kind of
cinema Grierson fought for – creative, didactic, committed.

Their first step in this direction was *Moment Musical* (1933), a three-
minute advertisement, also shown in cinemas, promoting a glassware shop,
using a Ravel soundtrack. This new phase of their work expanded with their
founding of the Film-Makers' Co-operative (S.A.F.) – the first of its kind –
which was set up to promote and fund independent production, to expand
knowledge of the film medium through screenings and – from 1937 – pub-
lish a journal, with Stefan Themerson as editor and Franciszka Themerson as
art director. Its dozen members included Witold Lutosławski, who composed
the music for the Themersons' next film, *Zwarcie* (*Short Circuit*), subtitled
'Symphony of Electricity', of 1935, funded by the Institute of Social Welfare
as a public-awareness film on safety in the home. It was given a cinema
release as a ten-minute short, and Stefania Zahorska described it in 1936

as a 'poem of objects, lines, lights – it is a drama of electricity, it is a short circuit of forms out of breath'. Stefan Themerson described later how, in one of its scenes, a figure appears on the screen and is then 'struck' by a bolt of electricity scratched on the negative. The film was constructed on the basis of its soundtrack, some of the music for which was composed in advance and some sections of which were added later, 'each note carefully synchronised with the visual elements'.

Perhaps helped by their beginning to make films at the start of the sound era, the Themersons were able to overcome one of the factors which slowed earlier avant-garde cinema to a standstill in the 1930s – the death of the silent movie and the expense of the new process. They were to use sound again in *The Adventure of a Good Citizen*, their last Polish film, in 1937, and in both their English-made films of the 1940s they extended the creative use of sound well beyond the 'musical accompaniment'.

In the meantime, however, the Themersons put their efforts into showing and publicising the avant-garde cinema, constructing a climate in which their work and that of the other S.A.F. members could be understood. Although, as it turned out, the other S.A.F. productions were not completed, its members Aleksander Ford and Wanda Jakubowska were to become influential film-makers in post-war Poland.

The magazine *f.a.* (Art Film) appeared twice, although a third issue was planned on Polish avant-garde film. The two published issues were based on visits made by the Themersons to Britain and France in order to collect film prints which could be shown in Poland.

In the UK John Grierson supplied them with *Song of Ceylon, Coalface, Night Mail* and *Colour Box* – GPO and Crown Unit films from the experimental wing of the documentary movement and mostly influenced by surrealist and abstract art. *f.a.* 1 featured articles by Len Lye, Moholy-Nagy (then living in London) and Grierson to accompany a screening of these films in May 1937.

From France they brought back mainly historic films of the 1920s, and. *f.a.* 2 carried articles on them for a second round of 1937 screenings. The films included Henri Chomette's *Five Minutes of Pure Cinema* (1926), René Clair's *Entr'acte* (1924) and Fernand Léger's *Ballet mécanique* (1924). The films were only licensed to be shown in Warsaw, frustrating the Themersons' plan to arrange a wider tour. In his notes for the films, Stefan Themerson wrote scathingly about these French films as 'museum- pieces' – but only with the aim of showing the limitations of Polish culture, for whom these older avant-garde films were still a novelty. The French collection also included Sandy's *Prétexte* (1929), Gilson's *Changements des rues* (1930) and George Lacombe's *La Zone* (1928), a study of Paris rag-pickers.

The Themersons left Poland for Paris in 1938. When World War II began a year later, Stefan joined the Polish Army and Franciszka left for London. From 1940 to 1942 Stefan stayed in France, working for the Polish Red Cross, before he too escaped to London. Here they made two further films before devoting their efforts to the Gaberbocchus Press ('Gaberbocchus' is 'Jabberwocky' in Latin) from 1948, to the Gaberbocchus Common Room, where they organised film projections, among other events, from 1957, and to their other activities in art, design and literature.

The Eye and the Ear (1944/45) was the culmination of the Themersons' ideas about film in the previous decade. During the 1930s, they had conceived an experimental cinema devoted to research and applied art, albeit with an imaginative core. Stefan Themerson proposed a kind of cinema which would include educational films, documentaries and advertisements, and cross realism with abstraction. The final two films in fact took up these ideas, constructing a cultural politics for the new cinema.

The Eye and the Ear embodies this urge towards didactic and experimental ideas, and was made as an artistic collaboration between music, graphic art, cinematography, image and sound. The film is constructed in four sections based on songs by the Polish modern composer Karol Szymanowski. Each song is used to explore different ways of showing pictorial equivalents to the musical ideas. 'Green Words' uses 'intentionally naive images' (Stefan Themerson) as illustrations of the music. 'St. Francis' shows a formal analysis

Fig. 3 *The Eye and the Ear* (1944/45)

Fig. 4 *The Eye and the Ear* (1944/45)

of musical shape, which 'Rowan Towers' takes further through mapping the song in geometry and arithmetic. The final section, 'Wanda', uses abstract images taken from nature – shots of water – with photograms based on the human hand. It has, overall, the shape and development of a spiral.

The film's aim and many of its processes reach back to the earlier period of the Themersons' work and develop further their cinematic approach. Szczuka's graphic cinema, for example, is here elaborated in the detailed analytical musical and visual score made to synchronise the film. Sound and vision are treated on equal terms: a modernist impulse towards the conceptual separation of parts within a constructed whole, and an implicit critique of the romantic synesthetic 'fusion of the senses' announced in Wagner's programme for the totalising work of art. The film perfected the results of years of research into these issues. The collapse of its funding agency (The Polish Film Unit) limited the film's distribution.

At almost the same time they worked on their only colour film – *Calling Mr Smith* (1943), a ten-minute propaganda piece denouncing the destruction of Polish national culture under the Nazi regime (and hence ironically echoing some of the themes of *Europa* a decade earlier). The slightly awkward text and the overripe voice of Mr Smith, the English 'Good Citizen', are less important than the extraordinary visual and audio construction of the film.

The film exploits the primitive Dufay colour process by heightening its rough non-realist contrasts (it was mainly used for animation, as in Lye's *Colour Box*) through solarisation, negative stock and printing through filters. Produced for the Film Unit of the exiled Polish Government, the first part illustrates the vandalism and anti-Semitism of Nazi cultural policies, and then attacks German political brutalities (a shot of a girl hanging from a gallows was censored in Britain, its shock effect evidently working too well). The soundtrack is also manipulated, as when the Horst Wessel Nazi marching song is slowed and speeded to parallel the deconstructed montage of documentary footage which it accompanies. Here too, the researches into sound and non-naturalism of the preceding period come to fruition, in a film that exemplifies the abstract approach to reality which formed the Themersons' cultural programme of the 1930s.

The films of the Themersons are intimately tied to the period in which they were made, although they kept a distance from all of the formal groups of the period; in this sense they were part of an epoch and also eccentric to it. In other respects, their independence allowed them to create a unique vision of the modern media far in advance of the period. Stefan Themerson's 1928 essay on radio, for example, looks ahead to an audio-visual culture which is more attuned to the electronic present, envisaging stereo, 3D and multiple selection of programmes.

Similarly, their willingness to accept commercial and state commissions was related to the period in which they worked (exemplified by Grierson's methods of promoting a new cinema through similar methods), but it is also remindful of the shifting during the climate of the 1980s of younger avant-garde film and video makers towards commercial and promotional art. The Themersons themselves stopped filmmaking in the mid-1940s, partly because the future of commissioned work seemed to threaten unwelcome compromises.

In his radio interview (1978), Stefan points to the ironies and cynicism inherent in the contemporary interpretation of the old avant-garde:

The zeal, the ardour, the need to explore new possibilities – in the cinema, for example – the urge to create visions, a certain confidence that one can change the world for the better, that a new order or disorder – in art, a new logic, a new science, having new economic necessities, will impose the peaceful state of justice ... it is very bizarre that the works of art, created in that spirit, this way of thinking, should today have a purely aesthetic or even commercial value.

It is not surprising that, as two artists who placed such a high value on creative freedom – for both maker and viewer – they founded their own press in 1948, allowing them the space to explore 'the urge to create visions' as they saw fit. In this way they ended a period in which, as Stefan Themerson wrote, they had been devoted to 'conquest and control of the film material, and passion-ate experimentation'. Like the Good Citizen, their heads may have been in the clouds, but their feet were firmly on the ground.

Originally published in PIX, no. 1, winter 1993/94. Reprinted here in a slightly modified version.

CHAPTER TWO

'THE INEXPRESSIBLE UNEARTHLY BEAUTY OF THE CINEMATOGRAPH':
THE IMPACT OF POLISH FUTURISM ON THE FIRST POLISH AVANT-GARDE FILMS

Kamila Kuc

The apparatus itself is… in a way always theoretical – a concept as much as a form, a machination as much as a machine.[1]

The films of Franciszka and Stefan Themerson are often recognised internationally as the only Polish avant-garde films of the 1930s, while the period preceding them remains a distinctly under-researched field, particularly in the English-speaking world. To claim, however, that other avant-garde films existed before and were made simultaneously with the Themersons' work in Poland seems somehow controversial, since most of this material did not survive. For example, as early as 1916, Feliks Kuczkowski made his first animated piece, *Flirt krzesełek* (*Flirting Chairs*), according to his principle of 'synthetic-visionary' film.[2] If they had survived, his creations would have been the first examples of avant-garde/artists' film made by a Pole in the Polish territories.[3] Unfortunately, Kuczkowski's experimental work no longer exists, thus its status in the history of Polish avant-garde film cannot be fully assessed. Jalu Kurek's film *OR: Obliczenia rytmiczne* (*Rhythmical Calculations*, 1934), as well as the first three films by the Themersons, share the same fate and now exist only in the form of reconstructions.[4]

Nonetheless, as a contemporary researcher of Polish avant-garde film, I find myself in a privileged position of having access to a wide array of materials that have been previously unavailable.[5] This makes it possible to claim that in order to fully assess the nature of Polish avant-garde film, we need to go back to its relationship with avant-garde movements that emerged in the 1920s. In this essay I look at the impact of Polish Futurism (1919–1922) on the first Polish avant-garde films made in the 1930s. The focus here will be particularly on Kurek's *Rhythmical Calculations*, and despite the fact that much has been written on the work of the Themersons, aspects of *Europa* (*Europe*, 1932) and *Calling Mr Smith* (1943, UK) will be revisited here in relation to Polish Futurism. Although these films have been present in theoretical discourse, it is my contention that the impact of Polish Futurism on them has been understated.[6] Tadeusz Miczka's article 'Cinema as Optic Poetry: On Attempts to Futurise the Cinematograph in Poland of the 1920s and 1930s' (1998) remains the most comprehensive account of the relationship between Polish Futurism and avant-garde film, and it serves as a starting point in my enquiry.[7]

The general absence of critical discourse regarding Polish Futurism's involvement with film is striking. This is related to the fact that Polish Futurism was primarily a literary movement, and thus lacking a significant body of work in the field of visual arts. For this reason, numerous film historians see the Polish Futurists' involvement with film as limited. In this chapter I hope to offer an alternative view. My main aim is to investigate the grounds for what became an avant-garde film discourse in the 1930s. Despite the fact that no Futurist films were made in Poland per se, Polish Futurists' film scripts, cine-novels and cine-poems, as well as their critical writings on film (particularly by Anatol Stern, Jalu Kurek and Bruno Jasieński), contributed to the flourishing film discourse that took place in Poland in the 1920s and which should not go unnoticed when evaluating the achievements of the Polish avant-garde film in the 1930s.[8] A larger argument here is that the theoretical discourses were as important in the process of formulating the avant-garde film culture in Poland as the films themselves. Thus projects that were written by the artists, filmmakers and critics but never turned into films also deserve their recognition, as they contributed to the contemporary cultural climate. As Miczka points out:

> historians of the tenth Muse cannot ignore this area in which 'cinema exists without film' since it appears that the art of moving pictures also benefited from the relationship with futurism.[9]

Similarly, Tom Gunning believes that the achievements and attempts of early cinema – and I would argue the same could be said about avant-garde film – should not be judged 'in terms of their realization (or the lack of it), but rather as expressions of broad desires which radiate from the discovery of new horizons of experience'.[10] These 'unrealised aspirations harbor the continued promise of forgotten utopias, as asymptotic vision of artistic, social and perceptual possibilities'.[11] Most recently, Pavle Levi in his book *Cinema by Other Means* (2012) proposes that a history of avant-garde film 'is a tale of the multiple states or conditions of cinema, of a range of extraordinary, radical experiments not only with but also "around" and even without film'.[12]

While investigating the separation between film and cinema, Levi argues that of importance are cinematic and non-cinematic interventions – 'cinema by other means' – which involve a number of film-related activities (photo-collages, drawings, paintings, cine-poems), as well as theoretical writings. Levi also discusses the concept of 'written cinema', which was practised in the 1920s and 1930s within the key avant-garde movements: Dada, Futurism, Constructivism and Surrealism. As he aptly puts it, at stake was the production of the theoretical discourse and the scripts prior to the making of the actual films.[13] Levi proposes that the dialectical interplay 'between film and cinema' can be understood 'only if we fully endorse the principle of inseparability of theory and practice'.[14] In a similar vein, Jonathan Walley proposes in his concept of 'paracinematic' practices that many early film-related activities were 'cinematic' in nature, yet they were not 'embodied in the materials of film as traditionally defined'.[15] The art of film, Walley argues, does not need to be defined by the specific medium of film, and instead, cinema's essence is elsewhere.[16] This reflects Levi's belief that cinematic imagination reaches beyond the films themselves, as will be demonstrated here in relation to Polish Futurists' experiments with film.[17]

Around 1912 many painters began to see film as an inspiration for representing movement, the most famous example being Pablo Picasso, who was an avid movie-goer. Another Cubist painter, Leopold Survage, created a series of drawings for his film *Le Rhythme Coloré* (1914), which was never completed because of the outbreak of the war. The twentieth-century avant-gardes officially began their adventure with the moving image with the Russian Futurist film *Drama in the Futurist Cabaret No. 13* (Victor Kasyanov, 1914).[18] Italian Futurist films soon followed, such as *Amor pedestre* (Marcel Fabre, 1914), *Vita Futurista* (Arnaldo Gina, 1916) and *Il Perfido Incanto* (Anton Giulio Bragaglia, 1918). There was also Aldo Modinari's *Mondo Baldina* (1914), disliked by the leader of Italian Futurism, Filippo Thomaso Marinetti.[19] Many artists saw film's potential as a 'magic force – a means of creating a world of fantasy', as was the case with Vassily Kandinsky and Arnold Schönberg's ideas for filmic compositions, *Der gelbe Klang* (*The Yellow Sound*, 1911) and *Die glückliche Hand* (*The Hand of Faith*, 1913).[20] The latter project was not filmed at the time but was eventually presented as a theatrical production between 1928 and 1930. The most successful attempt of this kind was Hans Richter and Viking Eggeling's 1919 film, an animation composed of their two drawings, *Preludium* and *Horizontal-Vertical Mass* (both from 1919).[21] Many leading avant-garde artists, poets and critics were interested in making films, yet never managed to realise any of their scripts. Alongside their attempts, they often published critical pieces concerning film. For instance, Kasimir Malevich wrote extensively about cinema, but his scenario for an abstract film was never turned into one.[22] Similarly, Anatol Stern's desire to make an avant-garde film never came to fruition, although he wrote articles on film and scripts that were turned into commercially successful films.[23] Vladimir Mayakowski was less fortunate in this area, as his scenarios were rejected and eventually became adapted stage plays.[24]

As already mentioned, Poland would have had its first avant-garde film made in 1916, if only Kuczkowski's animated experimental film had survived. But his films are now lost, and among the most commonly discussed Polish avant-garde films is Franciszka and Stefan Themerson's *Europe* (*Europa*), made in 1932. Before I discuss it in relation to Polish Futurism, it is important to point out that the fact that no Futurist films were made in Poland is not surprising, or unusual, especially when considering that Marinetti himself did not formulate his ideas about film until 1916 (the year when Kuczkowski made his first animated film, *Flirting Chairs*). In his article, Miczka states, somehow ironically, that 'Polish avant-garde cinematography can [...] boast only two fine works of undoubtedly futuristic origin' (referring to *Europe* and *Rhythmical Calculations*),[25] but it is important to remember that on the whole, only a handful of avant-garde films were made internationally in the early 1920s.[26] There were several reasons for this. The primary reason was the limited experience of painters and poets with the new medium of film and the lack of appropriate equipment: only 35mm cameras were available, and these were usually too expensive to experiment with, and were used mainly on large productions. Film was more costly and complicated to produce than painting.[27] Unlike Eggeling and Richter, and the Russian and Italian Futurists, Polish Futurists did not manage to complete any films. Taking into consideration the fact that at that time German and Russian film industries, for example, were well developed in comparison with that of Poland, which until 1918 was still under occupation, it is hardly surprising that there was little scope for experimentation in the area of film. This wider perspective seems to be lacking in Miczka's otherwise informative article.

Given this climate, it is perhaps also not surprising that the first widely acclaimed Polish avant-garde film, *Europe*, owes its roots to Futurism – the first internationally recognised Polish avant-garde movement. *Europe* is based on a Futurist poem-script of the same title by Anatol Stern, one of the key poets of Polish Futurism.[28] Stern's 'Europe' is a Dada-like apocalyptic vision of the world. Although the poem was written in 1925, thus some years after the decline of Futurism in Poland,[29] the piece is filled with rage against politicians and the socio-political situation in Europe, much in the style of Futurism:

> Abecedary of slaughter
> of dirt lice fires
> and mercy
> united states
> and argentine brazil chile
> states at war
> phenomena and noumena
> eternity and nothingness – two fattened boxers
> who will always win
> we
> who wolf meat
> once a month
> we
> who breathe sulphur
> expensive sulphur
> like air –
> we who drag along the streets
> our queue of sunken bellies
> our powerless feasts
> stuffing our pockets
> we shall
> lose
> lose
> lose
> as always!!![30]

Stern's piece was initially illustrated with photo-collages by the Constructivist artist Teresa Żarnowerówna, and then by Mieczysław Szczuka's designs (both from 1929). Szczuka's 'poesio-graphic' composite photographs betrayed the legacy of Futurism in his fascination with dynamic elements. His illustrations contain

Fig. 5 'Europa' (1929), photomontage design for Anatol Stern's poem by Teresa Żarnowerówna

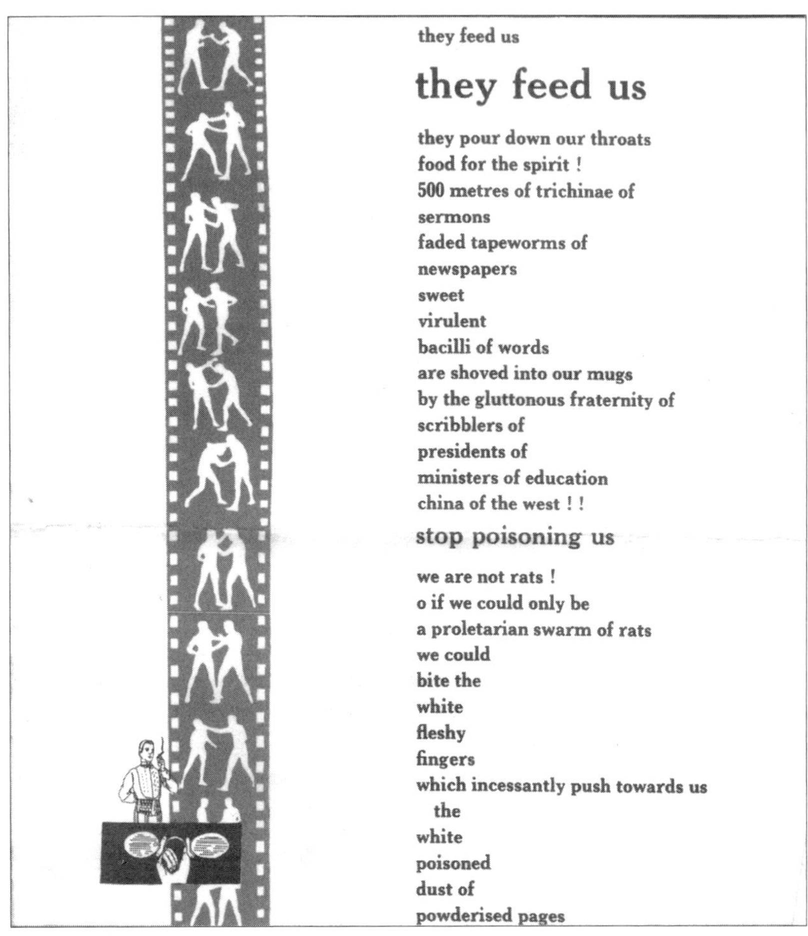

Fig. 6 'Europa' (1929), a design for Anatol Stern's poem by Mieczysław Szczuka

numerous references to cinema: the image of Charlie Chaplin and a drawing of a red film strip with two male figures wrestling and a well-dressed man smoking a cigarette is drawn in a fashion that resembles a scene from a film. But this aggressive mood of the poem and its overall energy was perhaps best captured in Stefan Themerson's Dada-like militant depiction of a woman placing her hand inside the mouth of a crying baby in his photomontage titled *Scream* (1930/31).

An anarchic prediction and denouncement of wars and socio-political upheavals, *Europe* was lost during World War II. What remains of the film are just a few stills and the Themersons' own recollection of the original script. In a letter to Piotr Zarębski, who in 1988 remade the Themersons' *Europe* from the remaining frames, Stefan Themerson stated that 'Stern's poem was not

                                                    THE STRUGGLE FOR FORM

the "inspiration" for the script'; it 'was the script, because it was written in the style of a script'.[31] According to Polish art historian Janusz Zagrodzki,

The film faithfully passed on the motif of Stern's poem; a vision of Europe gone mad, blindly racing towards its own destruction. Changes in the tempo of narration and astonishing contrasts were introduced by using the single frame technique, eliminating certain phases of motion, intensive editing, condensed cuts, multiple images and repetition.[32]

There was no sound in the ten-minute long *Europe*, thus the images functioned on an autonomous level.[33] The film aesthetic, it seems, was also reminiscent of Dada. Although as a unified art movement Dada did not exist in Poland, much of its attitude was present in Polish Futurism.[34] A leading member of Polish Futurism, Aleksander Wat, writing in retrospect, stated that he believed that Polish Futurism had its greatest roots in Dada (and Russian Futurism), more than in Italian Futurism.[35] According to Polish art historian Andrzej Turowski, Polish Futurists, like Dada artists from Zurich, were rebelling against art and believed themselves to be social revolutionaries.[36] This political activism and critique is visible in Stern's poem and honoured in the Themersons' film.

In the preserved scenario for *Europe*, which Stefan Themerson described to the leader of the Polish 1970s film avant-garde Józef Robakowski in 1973, there was a description of the following scene: 'drawing by George Grosz -/ in place of a heart: a motor animated frame by frame'.[37] This suggests the presence of both Dada (Grosz) and Futurist (a motor) aesthetics. This Dada-like energy is also visible in another part of the scenario: 'a shot of a helmeted soldier in a trench throwing a grenade, the third intersection was barbed wire [...] open hand on a cross, nail'.[38] In this context, *Europe*, as an anti-war statement, can also be seen as a reflection of the Polish Futurists' refusal to glorify the machine aesthetic because of its links to war. Polish Futurists did not share the same enthusiasm for the war as their Italian colleagues, and in this aspect they resembled the Dada artists.[39] In Poland, Futurism emerged in 1919,[40] almost a decade after its appearance in Italy (1909) and Russia (1910),[41] in a moment when the country needed fresh national ideology to affirm the new, independent state.[42] This new ideology had to be different from that of the nineteenth century, since the idea of a struggling Romantic artist now seemed anachronistic.[43] The new socio-political situation called for an adjustment of spiritual values, first of all among the intelligentsia, who were the greatest supporters of tradition and artistic canons such as Romanticism. The emergence of Futurism in Poland was a reaction to this new and rapidly changing reality of independent Poland. As I already stated, because of the recent memory of the Great War, Polish Futurists, more like the Dada artists, refused to glorify the machine and accept its uses in the war. Stern remarked:

Polish Futurism's political inclinations were much more to the left, and the Italian Futurists' political extremism did not pass without critique from both Polish and Russian sides, especially when many Italian Futurists joined the fascist movement.[45] Unlike their Italian colleagues, Polish Futurists saw both tradition and a new technological civilisation, with the machine as its main product, as garbage: 'we destroy the city. All mechanism-airplanes, tramways, inventions, the telephone. In place of them, primitive means of communication.'[46] They ridiculed Marinetti's cult of the machine and ironically proposed loving and marrying 'electrical machines' in order to produce 'dynamo-children'.[47] This scepticism of Polish Futurists towards the machine and modern technological developments would later be reflected in the work of some Constructivist artists and filmmakers, for instance Janusz Maria Brzeski, whose series of photomontages, *Narodziny Robota* (*The Birth of a Robot*, 1933), depicted the world destroyed by technology. In his photomontages and films, Brzeski created an apocalyptic version of civilisation and culture destroyed by the improvements of technology.[48] This catastrophic view of the declining Europe is present in both Stern's poem and the Themersons' adaptation of it. A. L. Rees proposes that *Europe* illustrated 'a new wave of post-Constructivist imagism'.[49] According to him, the Themersons fused 'Constructivist form with Dadaist iconoclasm'.[50]

But in many descriptions of *Europe*, the significance of one detail seems to have been overlooked: the very fact that the Themersons chose the Futurist poem for the main subject of their film. Despite possessing a wide knowledge of the European literature, the Themersons remained faithful to their Polish heritage. Miczka believes that *Europe* 'owes its artistic shape primarily to the futurist poetic "script"'.[51] This suggests not only that Futurist poems could be easily adapted into scripts, but that the Themersons possibly wanted to bring the achievements of Polish Futurism to wider attention. In this way the legacy of Polish Futurism was acknowledged by the leading figures of Polish avant-garde film. This indicates the need for a more detailed investigation of the impact of the Polish avant-garde on the Themersons' work in general. On the whole, *Europe*, both as a film and as a poem, constitutes a convincing example of the 'two-way traffic' that characterised Polish Futurism, where poetry supported cinema and vice versa, as will be explored throughout this chapter.

It is worth mentioning here that, although not based on any Futurist literary source, the Themersons' *Calling Mr Smith* (1943) can be seen as being characterised by the same Futurist and Dada-like rebellious attitude towards Western civilisation. Made in London a decade later, like *Europe*, the film constituted an anti-Nazi statement.[52] This surviving poetic documentary uses a fusion of cartoon animated images with photomontages, photograms and double exposure, as well as saturated and solarised imagery, to convey the filmmakers' moral and philosophical stance towards the Nazi atrocities.[53] More importantly, *Calling Mr Smith* marks the Themersons' identity as Poles and political filmmakers who believed that film could be used as a weapon against social injustice, as remarked in Stern's already quoted statement. The film poses a question: how can Germans, who in the past produced such cultured people, be so barbaric now? Bach's music is played interchangeably with the Nazi hymn 'Horst Wessel Lied', which is acoustically distorted to add a sense of irony. The majority of slides used in the film were hand-made and filmed through colour filters and newsreel footage, mixed with still images. Shot in Dufay colour, the film is based on powerful contrasts.[54] Images of beauty, such as iconic cultural artefacts (ancient architecture and sculpture, a face and body of Christ featured as a medieval sculpture, a pastel of a child's face, *Helenka* (1900), by the leading Polish Romantic artist Stanisław Wyspiański) are juxtaposed with images of ferocity (the sign of the swastika is depicted shortly before we see documentary footage of starving mothers and dying children and the controversial image of the hanging woman).[55] *Calling Mr Smith* alludes to Poland's martyrological tradition, implying that the Christ on the cross is a tortured Europe (i.e. Poland). In its aesthetics and the use of photo-collages, photomontages and animated sequences, the film to some degree resembles Norman McLaren's *Hell Unltd* (1936).[56] Like McLaren's film, *Calling Mr Smith* mixes archival footage, animation and live action, all rapidly edited. These films are structured not as a narrative but as a sequence of images with political themes, which are announced in the titles. Both *Europe* and *Calling Mr Smith* demonstrate the impact of Nazi politics on the Themersons' work and their possible affinity with Futurist and Dada tactics, which reflects Rees's belief that Polish modernism was unique in merging 'Constructivism with Dada-surrealism, a vivid internationalising blend for the beleaguered inter-war years'.[57]

But to further investigate the connection between Polish Futurists and the Themersons, let us return to Stern one more time. Of all the Futurist poets, Stern was the most widely published in the area of film criticism. He was a fierce defender of film's autonomy from other arts, particularly literature and theatre. He believed that a literary form no longer constituted an appropriate representation of reality and that film should take its place as a new art of contemporaneity.[58] Stern thought that painting and poetry owed to cinema a return to the abstraction of forms, which he believed was also the essence of film: 'Sensual abstraction is the kingdom of cinema.'[59] In its form and structure, the Themersons' *Europe* reflects Stern's belief in the links between cinema and poetry, as the film constitutes an attempt to find film's unique language through experimentation. This is seen, as in Futurist poetry, in the simplicity and economy of the use of filmic material. Stern's preoccupation with rhythm in poetry and film is also visible in the Themersons' employment of montage. Conversely, as an example of this two-way traffic, Stern also discussed new ways of writing poems that recalled film editing, stressing simultaneity and the use of short sentences, as in 'Europe'. He considered Jerzy Jankowski a precursor of such a style of writing, as seen particularly in Jankowski's telegraphic messages:

The inexpressible unearthly beauty...

of the cinematograph

having seen it once it is worth suffering death.[60]

Like the Themersons, Stern valued the achievements of the French Impressionists, embodied in their concept of *photogénie*. He particularly appreciated the films of René Clair, Man Ray and Luis Buñuel[61] for their illogical structures, also favoured by Jalu Kurek. Stern was of the opinion that all the 'principles of composition as understood till now' needed to be abolished in order for film to free itself from the conventions of popular cinema.[62] Both Stern and Kurek were in favour of non-realist cinema. For Kurek cinema was not 'an illustrator of everyday life, or an optical chronicle of life [...] cinema is optic poetry'.[63] Recalling the French director Abel Gance, Kurek believed that the modern epoch 'belonged to images', and for him the main link between film and poetry lay in the condensation of words and images, as well as in the creation of non-narrative structures that evaded coherent interpretations.[64] Kurek's *Rhythmical Calculations* (1934) thus possesses many elements of Polish Futurism. This now lost film was a mixture of figurative and non-figurative elements and can now be viewed in the form of a reconstruction by Ignacy Szczepański (1985), from a scenario by Marcin Giżycki (based on Kurek's notes).[65] *Rhythmical Calculations* opened with a sequence showing a

rotating globe, a schema of a solar system in movement and the rhythm of a
heartbeat, intercut with shots of a clock and an aeroplane about to take off.[66]
This was followed by a more lyrical section – shots of legs juxtaposed with
depictions of cityscapes, with skyscrapers and trees.[67] All of these scenes work
on the basis of association rather than cause-and-effect-based logical narrative structure. The text appearing on the screen reads: 'direction, tension'
(upper part) and 'the life of a man is the beating of his heart, which meas-
ures the working patterns of blood' (lower part). Kurek's text brings to mind
Czyżewski's poem 'Hymn do maszyny mego ciała' ('Hymn to the Machine of
My Body', 1922):

> blood
> stomach
> they pulsate
> coils
>
> pepsin
> heart
> the beat
> of my
> brain
>
> blood
> blood
> strained
> intestine
>
> cables to my veins
> twisted wire conductor
> to my heart
> battery
> have pity on me
> my heart
> dynamo-heart
> electric lungs
> magnetic diaphragm
> of the belly
>
> one one one
> my heart beats come

electric heart one

transmission belt
of my intestines
two two two

have pity on me
one two

the telephone of my brain
dynamo-brain
three three three
one two three
the machine of my body
function turn
live.[68]

Czyżewski's lines 'blood / stomach / they / pulsate / coils [...] the beat / of my brain / blood / blood / strained / intestine / cables to my veins [...] my heart / dynamo-heart / electric lungs' further resemble Kurek's *Rhythmical Calculations*: 'human life', 'blood', 'rhythm of a heart'. Czyżewski talks about 'electric lungs' and compares veins to cables. The rhythm of a heart is the rhythm of a working machine, and Kurek's film also alludes to this in the images and sounds of a pulsating heart, a plane's quickly moving propeller and a ticking clock. Both the poem and the film treat the human body as if it were a machine. This perfectly working machine – machine-heart, telephone-brain – then sends electrical impulses to the rest of the body. The emphasis is on anatomy and human physicality. The literal shape of Czyżewski's poem is that of a human body, which brings to mind the Polish Futurists' treatment of the machine as an organic part of the human body.

It was Jasieński who believed that Italian Futurism saw the machine as an ideal pattern and organism, superior to the human; that Russian Futurism treated it as a slave to the proletariat, with a purely economic function; and that Polish Futurism, meanwhile, saw the human itself as a material machine, as an extension of human biological machinery.[69] In his preference for the abstracted vision of reality and the employment of shots of body parts rather than the framing of whole bodies, or faces, Kurek might have been paying homage to the Italian Futurist film *Amor pedestre* (1914), in which a love story is depicted through close-ups of the protagonists' feet.[70] In Kurek's film we see the crossed legs of men and women, and finally a man and a woman sitting on a bench. As also exemplified in Fabre's film, *Rhythmical Calculations* is an expression of Kurek's belief in the redundancy of actors in film. He thought that film should use objects and abstract impressions rather than actors. Kurek's belief also resembles the key concerns of the leading figure of the French Impressionism and another Pole, Jean Epstein. In his theory of animism, Epstein proposed dramatising objects, making them appear cinematic and giving them new meanings.[71] In a similar fashion, Kurek believed that cinema's unique features could be best explored when actors are eliminated.[72] It is not certain that he would have seen Fabre's films, but out of all the Polish Futurists, he enjoyed the closest links to Italian Futurism. From 1922 he was in close correspondence with Marinetti, and in 1924 he studied in Naples, where he met Marinetti and his wife, the painter

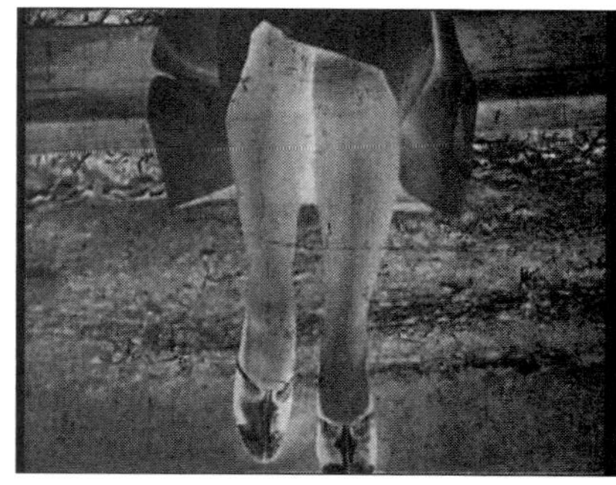

Fig. 7 Jalu Kurek, *Rhythmical Calculations* (1934)

Benedetta Cappa. From that time on Kurek translated much of the Italian Futurist poetry, eventually publishing an anthology *Chora fontanna: Wiersze futurystów włoskich* (*Sick Fountain: The Poems of Italian Futurists*, 1971).[73]

Kurek's and the Themersons' approach to experimental filmmaking reflects a Futurist belief in the connection between film and poetry. The Polish Futurists were fascinated by the fluid nature of the cinematograph, which constituted an important component of their poems, many of which remain untranslated.[74] The Polish Futurists' attitude to poetry is important here, because to a great extent it defines their approach to film. They were against the mediocre qualities of Polish film scripts, hence their appreciation of Mayakovsky's views expressed in his poem 'Cinema and Cinema' (1922), in which he took aim at the mass production of melodramas and proclaimed cinema as 'a view of the world', 'innovator of literature', 'destroyer of aesthetics' and 'distributor of ideas'.[5] But it was the innovative poetry of Apollinaire that particularly fascinated Polish Futurists. Stern believed that Apollinaire's way of writing poems (as well as the work of Auden, Cendrars, Jacob and Neruda) could influence 'new poetic aesthetics in film'.[76] He translated Apollinaire's poetry and wrote a monograph on Apollinaire, paying particular attention to the poet's Polish origins.[77] Polish Futurists believed that poetry and film should be surprising, echoing Apollinaire's ideas in 'The New Spirit and the Poets' (1917): 'the new spirit fills the universe with life and will manifest itself formidably in literature, in the arts, and in everything that is known'.[78] Apollinaire had a particular influence on Polish Futurism in his employment of free verse and the idea of simultaneity as the main rule by which new poetry should be created. For the Polish Futurists this meant that cinema should cease to follow any logical structure and instead, as Stern proposed, resemble the more arbitrary and impulsive nature of poetry. For Apollinaire poetry should be visual, as he insisted on its particular shape on the page and sound effects created by the reading of it: 'a perception of dark/light figures arranged on a light/dark surface'.[79] This was an attractive proposal to the Polish Futurists, since it resembled ways in which one perceives film. Apollinaire's own poems, such as 'Coeur et Miroir' ('Heart and Mirror', 1914) and 'Il Pleut' ('It's Raining', 1916), have visually striking forms, with words running up and down the page, often being broken into separate syllables and letters, with different font sizes. This can be seen in Czyżewski's already mentioned poem 'Hymn to the Machine of My Body', which was portrayed on the page in the shape of a human body, bringing to mind Apollinaire's *Calligrammes* (1913–1916).[80]

Most importantly here, in their poetry, Polish Futurists referred to the cinema, as well as the experience of watching films. Czyżewski's short poem 'Sensacja w Kinie' ('Crime in the Cinema', 1921) describes the experience of watching a crime film in a Cinema Palace in Bombay. The poet makes an obvious reference to contemporary cinema by alluding to the names of famous actors, Olaf Fönss (in Czyżewski's poem there is an Ola Föns; 'Ola' in the Polish language is a female name) and Mia Mai.[81] When writing about Czyżewski's poems, Polish literary critic Jan Józef Lipski describes them as being written like a 'suggestion for a film director' and 'poems-scripts', using 'a technique of a miniature film scenario'. Lipski mentions a 'transfer of filmic elements into poetry' as the key component of many of the Polish Futurist poems.[82] The use of cinematic elements in Czyżewski's poems relates largely to cinema's ability to create a captivating illusion of reality and the laws that govern it. 'Crime in Cinema' intentionally confuses the distinction between fact and fiction: the reader is not certain whether the events portrayed are happening in real life or whether the author is describing a film.

Jasieński's poem 'Miasto. Synteza' ('City. Synthesis', around 1921) is a good example of Apollinaire-like simultaneity in its depiction of small dramatic scenes set in a variety of scenarios. We read erratic records of people's conversations, placed in a panoramic, synthetic picture of a city's night life, referred to as 'a factory of people'.[83] In the intensity of experiences described, the poem resembles types of cinematic narration:

> A steady rain pelts down.
> It spits water against the window panes.
> A policeman walks, walks to a corner,

Every time he stops – he listens...
Nothing.
The windows have lowered their shades.
There, in the hotel,
A light is burning all night.
Someone is sick.
They have sent for a doctor.
Through the window you can sometimes see a slim brown-haired woman.
The whole first floor is dark, dead silent . . .
On the third floor a small light –
An older man has lured there a seven-year-old girl
and rapes her on a chair.
The child has wide-opened eyes...

The policeman is walking on the corner
Back and forth. Back and forth.
And looks in the black windows.
From behind a corner a thief spies on him.
It is raining.
They are getting wet.[84]

Jasieński's fascination with the criminal and morbid brings to mind a film thriller, set in a city at night. The poet uses unrestricted narration, so that the reader (the viewer) knows more than the policeman, who is thus unable to intervene. In Jasieński's most cited Futurist poem, 'Przejechali. Kinematograf' ('They Drove Past. The Cinematograph', 1921), the story is told from the point of view of a reporter hiding behind a camera lens. The poet describes watching a film, in which he sees:

A female freckled servant in a polka-dotted white blouse
Someone slender, with heron's feather
– 'Will you come?...' '– I can't...'
Juuump!
Cars. Platforms. Droshky.
The Cinematograph bicycle spoke
with wheels crushed on a dried asphalt.
– 'Wait...' – 'No, no, don't ask, because I could surrender...'
Ding! Dong!!
A red tram rolled from the alleys.
One. Two.

They passed each other briefly, cutting the way
The ominous singing of the grinding tracks...
A small man in a brownish grey overcoat...
Crack!!!
Stoppp!!
Brake!
Aaaaaaaaaa!
They drove past!! They drove past!![85]

Here the influence of film and Apollinaire's concept of simultaneity in the way Jasieński 'creates' sound is particularly visible: 'Ding! Dong!!', 'Crack!!!', 'Stoppp!!'[86] Like Stern, Jasieński published many pieces on contemporary film. He saw film as having the potential to achieve something new that had not been done in any other arts.[87] But this potential, Jasieński thought, was wasted by the growing commercialisation of the film industry and its unambitious productions and could only be saved by experimental films.[88]

When talking about the influence of film on Futurist poems, Jerzy Jankowski's 'Pszeczucie' ('Premonition', 1921; the Polish title is deliberately misspelled to subvert the grammatical rules) cannot be omitted. Here the spectre of death is framed as in a series of filmic close-ups, and is superimposed on the face of a dying woman.[89] The reader's attention is riveted to a 'beholding and seeing' omniscient narrator, as in a film. 'Premonition' brings to mind a scene from Fritz Lang's *Destiny* (1921), in which a young woman (Lil Dagover) meets Death (Bernhard Goetzke) in a room filled with life-sized candles. He explains to her the significance of burning candles, which symbolise dead people. As Death parts his hands, he raises a flame off a candle. This image dissolves into a body of a toddler, which quickly vanishes, indicating that the child had died. A series of close-ups on the woman's face, like in Jankowski's poem, shows her despair at the presented image.

All of the above poems could be described as using script-writing methods, embodied in the short sentences, which are often abruptly cut to resemble film editing techniques. Many of them have no particular plot, use de-dramatised action and blur the characters' psychological contours.[90] In the above pieces Polish Futurists proposed subjective storytelling as seen in cinema, which was considered by Marinetti the ultimate expression of the Futurist poly-vision. He believed cinema to be an autonomous art that should never copy but rather distance itself from reality:

ONE MUST FREE THE CINEMA AS AN EXPRESSIVE MEDIUM in order to make it the ideal instrument of a new art, immensely vaster and lighter than all the existing arts [...] only in this way can one reach that polyexpressiveness towards which all the most modern artistic researches are moving.[91]

Polish Futurists' poems and cine-poems testify to their belief in the freedom of language, created outside of any logic, which was manifested in the deformation of words, the destruction of punctuation and the use of different typographies and inserts of illustrations. As Polish film historian Tadeusz Miczka suggests, the Polish Futurists' fascination with cinematographic techniques expanded the sphere of literary expression and encouraged 'the futurization of the cinematograph', which began 'on the pre-filmic level' together with 'attempts to modernize script-writing'.[92]

It is worth noting that the cinema seems to have influenced Polish Futurist poetry more than prose, with the exception of Kurek, who wrote numerous film novels and novellas. His *S.O.S. Zbaw Nasze Dusze* (*S.O.S.: Save Our Souls*, 1927) includes numerous montage-like sequences, collages of seemingly unrelated events, kaleidoscopic changes of action, sensitivity to colour and light, and voyeuristic characters who often go to the movies or look through camera lenses. In this particular novel, the cause-and-effect rule disappears and the chronology of events as well as all grammatical codes are subverted. Images of various events are juxtaposed with on-screen-like text printed in bold, as if to suggest inter-titles in cinema.[93] Kurek wanted readers to feel as if they were watching a silent movie. His other film novella, *Kim był Andrzej Panik? Andrzej Panik Zabił Amundsena* (*Who Was Andrzej Panik? Andrzej Panik Killed Amundsen*, 1926), was written like a script.[94] In this apparently autobiographical piece the main hero is a journalist named Jalu Kurek. Most of the novel's action takes place in the cinema, and the sequence of literary events, according to Miczka, was modelled on the film editing process.[95] It is the story of a man who confused his life with a film, and its moral is that we should remember that what we see on the screen has little to do with reality, as the hero finally declares his belief in life rather than events on screen.[96] The above examples of Polish Futurist poetry and prose in relation to the Themerson and Kurek pieces constitute a perfect example of this two-way traffic, where poetry influenced film and where literature was 'rejuvenated by cinema'.[97]

In summary, although Polish Futurists did not make any films, their admiration for the art of film manifested itself in the production of cinematic poems, cine-scripts, film novels and critical responses to contemporary productions. According to Miczka, Polish Futurism revolutionised script writing and, as seen in the example of Stern's 'Europa', many of the Futurist writings were treated as script projects. Aside from their cine-novels, poems and scripts, Polish Futurists' critical writings on cinema require a closer exploration and evaluation, as many of their texts attempted a dialogue with the developments of avant-garde films in other countries. This was evident in the case of Stern's and Kurek's interest in the notion of *photogénie* in the late 1920s. In this concept they saw an expression of cinema's ultimate autonomy from other arts, as well as a certain artistic freedom for which these artists fought within the realm of Futurism.

In this chapter I have managed to discuss only a handful of the Futurist cine-poems, novellas and critical pieces on film, but there is no doubt that they constituted an important step in the development of experimental film and provided further inspiration for the future attempts at creating alternatives to popular film throughout the late 1920s and 1930s. In order to evaluate the impact of Polish Futurism on the later avant-garde films appropriately, it is important to understand at least some of the reasons why the Futurists did not manage to create any films. Although in his article Miczka offers numerous possible reasons, among them the lack of theoretical programme and a cinematic manifesto, he fails to offer a more coherent perspective. I have looked at Polish Futurism and film in relation to the achievements of the contemporary international avant-garde filmmakers and suggested that the lack of Polish Futurist films in Poland was not unusual at the time, particularly given the general context of avant-garde film (how very few films were made at the time), as well as the poor state of the Polish film industry in the 1920s. I have thus proposed that the Polish Futurists provided a rather significant input to the development of later avant-garde films and discourses. As Miczka writes:

> despite the mere handful of futuristic ideas concerning film, the trend was, nevertheless, an important step in the development of cinema, providing inspiration for the future.[98]

Polish Futurism is therefore significant to the Polish avant-garde film, not because of its achievements but because of the influence it had on its later developments in the 1930s, which should not be understated.

NOTES

1 Philippe Dubois, 'Photography Mise-en-Film: Autobiographical (Hi)stories and Psychic Apparatuses', Patrice Petro, ed., *Fugitive Images: From Photography to Video* (Bloomington: Indiana University Press, 1995), p. 28.

2 For details on Feliks Kuczkowski (1884–1970) see for example Giżycki, 'Irzykowski, Kuczkowski and the Tradition of "Visionary Film" in Poland', *Afterimage*, no. 13, autumn, 1987; and Kuczkowski, 'Wspomnienie o filmie przyszłości', typescript in the collection of the Archive of Polish National Cinematheque, Syg.A.129, Warsaw [1955].

3 See for example Giżycki, 1987.

4 The reconstruction of Rhythmical Calculations can be seen on the *Filmoteka Museum* website: http://filmoteka.artmuseum.pl/?l=0&id=393. Excerpts from the film can also be seen in Szczepański's documentary, *Jalu Kurek* (1985). In 2001 the American experimental filmmaker Bruce Checefsky reconstructed the Themersons' first film, *Apteka* (*Pharmacy*, 1930), also available on the *Filmoteka Museum* website (http://filmoteka. artmuseum.pl/?l=1&id=762), and in 2006, *Drobiazg melodyjny* (*Moment Musical*, 1933), available on *Vimeo*: http://vimeo.com/25712651. Piotr Zarębski's reconstruction of *Europe, Europa II* (1988), can also be seen on the *Filmoteka Museum* website: http:// filmoteka.artmuseum.pl/?l=1&id=1296.

5 Here I ought to acknowledge the pioneering research of Marcin Giżycki and Ryszard Kluszczyński, the key theorists of avant-garde film in Poland. But it is Giżycki in particular who in his publications resurrected a number of obscured figures of the Polish avant-garde film, namely Kuczkowski. A. L. Rees's essay, which opens this collection, remains a classic piece on the Polish avant-garde film in the English-speaking world.

6 See for example Giżycki, *Awangarda wobec kina: Film w kręgu polskiej awangardy artystycznej dwudziestolecia międzywojennego* (Poznań: Wydawnictwo Małe, 1996); Ryszard Kluszczyński, ed., *Film awangardowy w Polsce i na świecie* (Łódź: Łódzki Dom Kultury, 1989) and *Film – sztuka Wielkiej Awangardy* (Warszawa, Łódź: Państwowe Wydawnictwo Naukowe, 1990); and Jadwiga Bocheńska, *Polska Myśl Filmowa do roku 1939* (Wroclaw, Warszawa, Kraków, Gdańsk: Zakład Naukowy im.Ossolińskich, Wydawnictwo Polskiej Akademii Nauk, 1977). Most of these key sources underplay the impact of Polish Futurism on the development of avant-garde film in Poland in the 1930s.

7 See Tadeusz Miczka, 'Cinema as Optic Poetry: On Attempts to Futurise the Cinematograph in Poland of the 1920s and 1930s', *Canadian Slavonic Papers*, no. 40, March–June, 1998; and 'Kino jako poezja optyczna. Próby futuryzacji kinematografu w Polsce w latach 1918–1939', Jan Trzynandkowski, ed., *Kino-film: poezja optyczna?* (Wrocław: Uniwersytet Wrocławski, 1995).

8 For a collection of some of the Futurists' critical writings on film, mainly those of Anatol Stern and Jalu Kurek, see Giżycki, ed., *Walka o film artystyczny w międzywojennej Polsce* (Warszawa: Państwowe Wydawnictwo Naukowe, 1989); and Anatol Stern, *Wspomnienia z Atlantydy* (Warszawa: Wydawnictwa Artystyczne i Filmowe, 1959).

9 Miczka, 1998, p. 4.

10 Tom Gunning, 'Loie Fuller and the Art of Motion', *La decima musa: Il cinema e le altre arti. The Tenth Muse: Cinema and Other Arts. Proceedings of the VI Domitor Conference / VII International Film Studies Conference* (Udine: Arti Grafiche Fruilane, 2001), p. 25.

For a similar approach, see Ian Christie, 'Before the Avant-Gardes: Artists and Cinema, 1910–14', in the same volume; and Jan-Christopher Horak, *Lovers of Cinema: The First American Film Avant-Garde 1919–1945* (Wisconsin: University of Wisconsin Press, 1995).

11 Gunning, 2001, p. 25.

12 Pavle Levi, *Cinema by Other Means* (Oxford: Oxford University Press, 2012), p. xiii. I am indebted to Greg DeCuir for his recommendation of Levi's book. The phrase 'around film' was borrowed by Levi from the filmmaker Slobodan Šijan. See Levi, 2012, p. 161.

13 Levi, 2012, p. xiii.

14 Levi, 2012, p. xvi.

15 Jonathan Walley, 'The Material of Film and the Idea of Cinema: Contrasting Practices in the Sixties and Seventies Avant-Garde Film', *October*, no. 103, winter 2003, p. 18.

16 Ibid.

17 Levi, 2012, p. 46. Here Levi gives an example of Monny de Boully's scenario 'Doctor Hypnison, or the Technique of Living' (1923), which was always referred to as a 'paper movie'.

18 See Christie, 2001 and 'The Avant-Gardes and European Cinema Before the 1930s', John Hill and Pamela Church Gibson, eds., *World Cinema: Critical Approaches* (Oxford; New York: Oxford University Press, 2000), 'Film as a Modernist Art', Christopher Wilk, ed., *Modernism: Designing a New World (1914–1939)* (London: V&A Publications, 2006) and 'From Bauhaus to Arthouse', *Sight and Sound*, vol. 22, no. 6, June, 2012. See also A. L. Rees, 'Movements in Film 1912–40', Stuart Comer, ed., *Film and Video Art* (London: Tate Publishing, 2009).

19 For some literature on the earliest Italian experiments with film, see Bruno Corra, 'Abstract Cinema – Chromatic Music', Umbro Apollonio, ed., *Futurist Manifestos* (London: Thames and Hudson, 1973) [1912] and Birgit Hein, 'The Futurist Film', David Curtis, ed., *Film as Film: Formal Experiment in Film 1910–1975* (London: Hayward Gallery, 1979).

20 See for example Standish D. Lawder, 'Film as Modern Art: Picasso, Survage, Kandinsky, Schönberg', *The Cubist Cinema* (New York: New York University Press, 1975).

21 See Rees, 'The Absolute Film', *A History of Experimental Film and Video* (London: British Film Institute, 1999), Michael O'Pray, 'The 1920s: The European Avant-Gardes', *Avant-Garde Film: Forms, Themes and Passions* (London and New York: Wallflower Press, 2003) and R. Bruce Elder, 'Modernism and Absolute Film', *Harmony and Dissent: Film and Avant-Garde Movements in the Early Twentieth Century* (Ontario: Wilfrid Laurier University Press, 2008).

22 Kasimir Malevich, 'Art and the Problems of Architecture: The Emergence of a New Plastic System of Architecture: Script for an Artistic-Scientific Film', Oksana Bulgakova, ed., *Kazimir Malevich: The White Rectangle: Writings on Film* (Berlin; San Francisco: PotemkinPress, 2002) [1927].

23 See Jolanta Lemann, 'Poglądy filmowe Anatola Sterna w dwudziestoleciu międzywojennym (na przykładzie publikacji i działalności społecznej)', Alicja Helman and Alina Madej, eds., *Film polski wobec innych sztuk* (Katowice: Uniwersytet Śląski, 1979), p. 134. See Miczka, 1998, p. 10 for the list of films based on Stern's scripts.

24 As Vertov points out, Mayakovsky 'could not overcome cinema's bureaucratic officialdom.

His scripts were either rejected or included in the thematic plan but never made. Or they were so disfigured in the process of production that he was "quite ashamed" of them.' See Dziga Vertov, 'More on Mayakovsky', Richard Taylor, eds., *Inside the Film Factory: New Approaches to Russian and Soviet Cinema* (London: Routledge, 1994) [1934–1935], p. 340.

25 Miczka, 1998, p. 11.

26 Although linked closely to the Constructivist principles, Janusz Maria Brzeski's *Przekroje* (*Sections*, 1931) and *Beton* (*Concrete*, 1933) also betray an interest in the city and the machine, much in the Futurist fashion. See Janusz Zagrodzki, *Janusz Maria Brzeski, Kazimierz Podsadecki 1923–1936. Z pogranicza plastyki i filmu* (Łódź: Muzeum Sztuki, 1981).

27 For more details, see Lawder, 1975, pp. 46–47.

28 There exists an extensive literature on the Themersons. For the most recent catalogue, see Paweł Polit, ed., *The Themersons and the Avant-Garde* (Łódź: Muzeum Sztuki w Łodzi, 2013). For documentary films on the Themersons, see *Franciszka i Stefan* (Tomasz Pobóg-Malinowski, 1975) and most recently *Themerson&Themerson* (Wiktoria Szymańska, 2010).

29 On the decline of Polish Futurism, see Richard Lourie, ed., *Aleksander Wat. My Century: The Odyssey of a Polish Intellectual* (Berkley: University of California Press, 1988) and Stern, *Bruno Jasieński* (Warszawa: Wiedza Powszechna, 1969).

30 Stern, 'Europa (Fragment)', *Iluzjon*, no. 3, 1989. The translation of the poem used here comes from a display of the exhibition *Breaking the Rules: The Printed Face of the European Avant Garde 1900–1937*, British Library, 9 November 2007 to 30 March 2008.

31 Stefan Themerson, 'Europa: A Letter to Piotr Zarębski', 14 April 1988, Benjamin Cook and Łukasz Ronduda, eds., *The Films of Franciszka and Stefan Themerson*, a booklet accompanying a DVD with Themersons' surviving films (London: LUX, 2007), p. 35.

32 Zagrodzki, 1981, p. 33.

33 For some examples of the contemporary reception of *Europe*, see Jerzy Toeplitz, 'Europa', *Kurier Polski*, 1933; Stefania Zahorska, 'Polski film Dobry!', *Wiadomości Literackie*, no. 52, 1932; and Anonymous, 'Europa, czyli grube nieporozumienie z filmem eksperymentalnym', *Ekspress Poranny*, 31 January 1933.

34 See the publication of Kurt Schwitters' non-Dadaist texts, 'Dadaism', in the Constructivist magazine *Blok*, no. 1, 1924. Stanisław Ignacy Witkiewicz's (aka Witkacy) *Papierek lakmusowy* (1921) is a pastiche of a Dada manifesto. On the connection between Polish Futurism and Dada, see for example Marek Bartelik, *Early Polish Modern Art: Unity in Multiplicity* (Manchester and New York: Manchester University Press, 2005), pp. 171 and 174, and Andrzej Turowski, 'Dadaistyczne konteksty', *Awangardowe Marginesy* (Warszawa: Instytut Kultury, 1998).

35 Wat, 1977, p. 25.

36 Turowski, 1998, p. 53.

37 Stefan Themerson, 'Europa: A Scenario', a letter to Józef Robakowski, Cook and Ronduda, 2007 [1973], p. 28.

38 Ibid.

39 In their final joint publication, 'Nóż w Bżuhu' ('Nife in the Beli', 1921), the Polish Futurists seemed to have been indebted to the 1916 Dada manifesto in their nihilism and

pessimistic attitude towards Poland's political future. The title refers to Marinetti's original manifesto, and the correct Polish spelling would have been 'Nóż w brzuchu' ('Knife in the Stomach'), but Polish Futurists deliberately modified the spelling to challenge the grammatical rules. See Zbigniew Jarosiński and Helena Zaworska, eds., *Antologia polskiego futuryzmu i Nowej Sztuki* (Wrocław, Kraków: Zakład im.Ossolineum, 1978), p. 29.

40 For more details on Polish Futurism, see Bogdana Carpenter, *The Poetic Avant-Garde in Poland, 1918–1939* (Seattle and London: University of Washington Press, 1983) and Wat, 'Wspomnienia o futuryzmie', *Miesięcznik Literacki*, no. 2, 1930.

41 On Italian Futurism, see Umbro Apollonio, *Futurist Manifestos* (London: Thames and Hudson, 1973). On Russian Futurism, see Anna Lawton, ed., *Russian Futurism Through Its Manifestoes, 1912–1928* (New York and London: Cornell University Press, 1988).

42 Although Polish Futurism emerged in 1919, the news about Marinetti's 1909 manifesto reached Poland the very same year. Carpenter suggests that Polish Futurism might have started in 1914, with Jerzy Jankowski's (1887–1941) poems, which employed phonetic orthography and were written in the spirit of Italian Futurism. See Carpenter, 1983, p. 3. See also Ignacy Grabowski, 'Najnowsze prądy w literaturze najnowszej. Futuryzm', *Świat*, no. 40, 1909.

43 Carpenter, 1983, p. xiii. In addition, see Piotr Piotrowski, 'Modernity and Nationalism: Avant-Garde Art and Polish Independence, 1912–1922', Timothy O. Benson, ed., *Central European Avant-Gardes: Exchange and Transformation 1910–1930* (Cambridge: Massachusetts Institute of Technology Press, 2002), p. 315.

44 Stern, *Bruno Jasieński* (Warszawa: Wiedza Powszechna, 1969), p. 27.

45 For more details, see Stern, 1969, p. 61. Mussolini's victory in the 1922 elections was greeted with some interest in Poland. An unsigned article praised the Italians for a 'healthy instinct' in supporting the fascists, thus preventing the socialists from ruling the country. Anonymous, 'Zwycięstwo faszystów', *Tygodnik Ilustrowany*, no. 46, 11 November 1922, p. 7.

46 An excerpt from *Gga*, quoted in Carpenter, 1983 [1919], p. 7.

47 Carpenter, 1983, p. 7. See also Jarosiński and Zaworska, 1978, p. 52, footnote 4.

48 For more details see Jerzy Malinowski, 'Janusz Maria Brzeski i Studio Polskiej Awangardy Filmowej. Program kin studyjnych', Kraków, May, 1975 and Zbigniew Wyszyński, 'Krakowska awangarda filmowa lat trzydziestych', *Kino*, no. 12, 1975.

49 Rees, 1993, p. 90.

50 Ibid., p. 91.

51 Miczka, 1998, p. 11.

52 For more details see Stefan Themerson, *The Urge to Create Visions* (Amsterdam: Gaberbocchus/De Harmonie, 1983) [1937].

53 Three of the Themersons' surviving films, *Przygoda człowieka poczciwego*, (*The Adventures of a Good Citizen*, 1937), *Calling Mr Smith* (1943) and *The Eye and the Ear* (1944/1945), are available on a DVD compilation: *The Films of Franciszka and Stefan Themerson* (London: LUX, 2007).

54 Dufay colour was previously used by Len Lye in his animated film *Colour Box* (1935, UK).

55 The British censors considered *Calling Mr Smith* too brutal and requested its removal. The Themersons refused to do so, and the film was only shown privately in October

1943 at the Polish Film Unit and the Edinburgh Film Guild. See Stefan Themerson, 1937, p. 45.

56 See for example Terence Dobson, *The Film Work of Norman McLaren* (Sydney: John Libbey & Co Ltd, 2007) and Jamie Sexton, 'Hell Unltd', *Screenonline*, http://www. screenonline.org.uk/film/id/440480/index.html (accessed 26 September 2012).

57 Rees, 1999, p. 54. See also Deke Dusienberre, 'The Other Avant-Gardes', Curtis, 1979.

58 Stern wrote about film obsessively and was an editor of numerous film columns in major magazines and journals. See Stern, 'Kino', *Skamander*, no. 28, 1922; 'Przeróbki literackie na ekranie', *Kinema*, no. 17, 1922; 'Malarstwo a kino', *Skamander*, nos. 29–30, 1923; and 'Uwagi o teatrze i kinie', *Reflektor*, no. 1, 1924. See Stern, 1959 and Giżycki, 1989.

59 Stern, 'Uwagi o teatrze i kinie', *Reflektor*, no. 1, 1924, p. 7. See also Giżycki, 1989, p. 82 and Alfred Kowalski, 'U tworców polskiego filmu. Rozmowa z Anatolem Sternem', *Świat Filmu*, no. 2, 1937.

60 Jankowski, quoted in Sergiusz Sterno-Wachowiak, *Miąższ zakazanych owoców: Jankowski, Jasieński, Grodziński* (Bydgoszcz: Wydawnictwo Małe, 1985), p. 44, translated in Miczka, 1998 [c. 1920], p. 5.

61 For Stern's recollection of his first meeting with the Themersons, see Stern, 'Europa. Polski film awangardowy', 1959 [1933], pp. 168–169. For the connections between French Impressionism and Surrealism, see for example Ian Aitken, 'Into the Realm of the Wondrous: French Cinematic Impressionism', *European Film Theory and Cinema: A Critical Introduction* (Edinburgh: Edinburgh University Press, 2001).

62 Stern, 'Kilka uwag o przyszłej sztuce ekranu', 1959 [1924].

63 Kurek, 'O nowe drogi w kinematografii. Jeszcze o filmie artystycznym', *Kino dla Wszystkich*, no. 6, 1927, p. 3.

64 See Jalu Kurek, 'Kino – zwycięstwo naszych oczu', *Głos Narodu*, 2 March 1926. For Kurek's other writings on cinema, see 'O nowe drogi w kinematografii. Jeszcze o filmie artystycznym', *Kino dla Wszystkich*, no. 6, 1927; 'O filmie "artystycznym" i "stosowanym"', *Kino dla Wszystkich*, no. 56, 1928; 'Uwagi o filmie', *Linia*, no. 3, 1931; and 'Nogi dziewczęce. Polska awangarda filmowa', *Światowid*, no. 26, 1933. See also Giżycki, 1989 for a selection of Kurek's writings.

65 For more details, see Giżycki's reconstruction of the scenario, 'Aneks: Hipotetyczna rekonstrukcja filmu "Or" Jalu Kurka', Giżycki, 1989. See also Kurek, 'Objaśniam OR', *Linia*, no. 5, 1933.

66 Giżycki, 1996, p. 104.

67 For more details see Moassi, 'Awangarda filmowa w Krakowie. "Or" Jalu Kurka i "Europa" Franciszki i Stefana Themersonów', *Nowy Dziennik*, 12 June 1933; Kurek, 'Wspomnienia ze "Straży Przedniej" (Z dziejów filmowej awangardy krakowskiej)', *Kwartalnik Filmowy*, no. 3, 1961; and Zbigniew Wyszyński, 'Krakowska awangarda filmowa lat trzydziestych', *Kino*, no. 12, 1975, p. 64.

68 Czyżewski, 'Hymn do maszyny mego ciała', translated in Carpenter, 1983 [1922], p. 27.

69 See Bruno Jasieński, 'The Polish Nation: A Manifesto Concerning the Immediate Futurisation of Life' and 'Manifesto Concerning Futurist Poetry', Benson, 2002 [both 1921].

70 Miczka, 1998, p. 11.

71 See Jean Epstein, 'On Certain Characteristics of Photogénie', Richard Abel, ed., *French*

Film Theory and Criticism, Vol. 1: 1907–1929 (Princeton, New Jersey: Princeton University Press, 1988) [1924], p. 317. See also Zbigniew Czeczot-Gawrak, *Jan Epstein. Studium natury w sztuce filmowej* (Warszawa: Wydawnictwa Artystyczne i Filmowe, 1962), pp. 23–24.

72 Kurek, 1928, p. 8. One of the first Polish avant-garde filmmakers who made films without actors and made this central claim in his writings on film was Kuczkowski. In the 1920s, similar views were shared by a number of art and film critics, namely Stefania Zahorska. See Zahorska, 'Film abstrakcyjny', *Wiek XX*, no. 8, 1928, p. 15. See also Whoopee, 'Bez aktorów. Wizja przyszłości', *ABC*, 16 August 1932, and 'O prawdziwe kino. Co widzimy na ekranie, a co jest istotą sztuki filmowej', *ABC*, 16 March 1930.

73 Kurek was often referred to as 'the disciple of Marinetti', although he objected to this label. He claimed that Polish poetry was in no way influenced by Marinetti: 'I was not a pure futurist [...] I was an heir and student of Marinetti but I was in the senior class.' Kurek, *Chora fontanna* (Kraków: Wydawnictwo Literackie, 1971), p. 7. See also Elżbieta Cichla-Czarniawska, *"Heretyk awangardy" Jalu Kurek* (Lublin: Wydawnictwo Lubelskie, 1987), pp. 14–36.

74 For details see Ewa and Marek Pytasz, 'Poetycka podróż w świat kinematografu, czyli kino w poezji polskiej lat 1914–1925', Helman and Miczka, eds., *Szkice z teorii filmu* (Katowice: Katolicki Uniwersytet Lubelski, 1978), and Jan Kucharczyk, 'Pierwiastki filmowe w twórczości literackiej Tadeusza Peipera i Jalu Kurka', *Kwartalnik Fimowy*, no. 1, 1965.

75 Mayakovsky, 'Cinema and Cinema', Christie and Taylor, 1994 [1922], p. 39. For some examples of the Polish critics' disappointment with the state of Polish cinema, see Antoni Słonimski, 'Bezczelność producentów tandety', *Wiadomości Literackie*, no. 44, 1928; Seweryn Romin, 'Śmierć sztuce', *Kino-Teatr*, no. 11, 1929; Barbara Armatys, 'Dorobek publicystyczny i dzialalność społeczna "STARTU" (1930–1935)', *Kwartalnik Filmowy*, no. 1, 1961; and Leszek Armatys, 'Myśl filmowa i dzialalność artystyczna "STARTU" (1930–1935)', *Kwartalnik Filmowy*, no. 1, 1961.

76 See Lemann, 1979, p. 142.

77 Translations of some of Apollinaire's works appeared in the Polish press in fragments. *Alcools* (1913) was published in the early 1920s. Stern's book, *Dom Apollinaire'a* (1973), with a cover designed by the Constructivist artist Henryk Berlewi, is devoted solely to the author's investigation of Apollinaire's Polish origin, and it testifies to the Futurists' fascination with the figure of the poet. For a selection of Polish sources on Apollinaire, see for example Julia Hartwig, *Apollinaire* (Warszawa: Państwowy Instytut Wydawniczy, 1961), and ed., *Guillaume Apollinaire. Listy do Madeleine* (Kraków: Wydawnictwo Literackie, 1976); and Adam Ważyk, 'Guillaume Apollinaire', *Wiadomości Literackie*, no. 1, 1928.

78 Apollinaire, 'L'Espirit nouveau les poètes', Roger Shattuck, ed., *Selected Writings of Guillaume Apollinaire* (New York: A New Directions Book, 1971) [1917], p. 237. See also Francis Steegmuller, *Apollinaire, Poet Among the Painters* (London: Penguin Books, 1963).

79 See Shattuck, 1971, p. 19.

80 Czyżewski's poem 'Ogród mechaniczny' (1922) also resembles Apollinaire's visual poems. See Carpenter, pp. 28–29.

81 See also Miczka, 1998, p. 5. Olaf Fönss (1882–1949) was a Dutch actor who often played in crime and period films. Mia May (1884–1980) was an Austrian actress, one of the first divas of the German cinema, who starred in many UFA productions.

82 Jan Józef Lipski, 'Tytus Czyżewski', Irena Maciejewska, Jacek Trznadel, Maria Pokrasenowa, eds., *Literatura polska w okresie międzywojennym*, vol. 3 (Kraków: Wydawnictwo Literackie, 1993), pp. 15–17.

83 For an in-depth discussion of Polish Futurist poems, see Carpenter, 1983, pp. 21–64. For materials on individual Polish Futurists, see for example Edward Balcerzan, *Bruno Jasieński. Utwory poetyckie, manifesty, szkice* (Kraków: Polska Akademia Nauk, 1972); Nina Kolesnikoff, *Bruno Jasienski. His Evolution from Futurism to Socialist Realism* (Waterloo, Ontario: Wilfrid Laurir University Press, 1982); Alicja Balcuch, *Tytus Czyżewski. Poezje i próby dramatyczne* (Wrocław, Warszawa, Kraków: Zakład im. Ossolińskich, 1992); Sergiusz Sterno-Wachowiak, *Miąższ zakazanych owoców: Jankowski, Jasieński, Grodziński* (Bydgoszcz: Wydawnictwo Małe, 1985); Andrzej K. Waśkiewicz, ed., *Anatol Stern. Wiersze Zebrane*, vols. 1 and 2 (Kraków: Wydawnictwo Literackie, 1986).

84 Jasieński, 'Miasto. Synteza', translated in Carpenter, 1983 [c. 1921], p. 36.

85 Jasieński, 'Przejechali, Kinematograf', Lentas and Ogonowska, 2008 [1921], p. 40. My translation.

86 For a discussion on the sound aspects of Polish Futurist poems, see Beata Śniecikowska, *"Nuż w Uhu?" Koncepcje dźwięku w poezji polskiego futuryzmu* (Wrocław: Universytet Wrocławski, 2008).

87 Here one could also add the critical writings of Tadeusz Peiper, who can be seen as a bridge between Futurism and Constructivism. He argued that 'the most essential and important element of every art is what other art cannot bring out'. Peiper, 'Ku specyficzności kina', *Zwrotnica*, no. 3, 1923, p. 11, and 'Futuryzm (Analiza i krytyka)', *Zwrotnica*, no. 6, 1922.

88 Jasieński, 'Kina krakowskie', *Zwrotnica*, no. 3, 1922. See also Czyżewski, 'Krajobraz w kinie', *ABC*, 3 October 1932, 'Film abstrakcyjny', *ABC*, 19 July 1932, and 'Film konwencjonalny', *ABC*, no. 290, 1932.

89 Miczka, 1998, p. 5.

90 See Miczka, 'Literatura odnowiona kinem', *Film na Świecie*, nos .325–326, 1986, p. 45.

91 See Filippo Tommaso Marinetti, with Bruno Corra, Emilio Settimelli, Arnaldo Ginna, Giacomo Balla, Remo Chiti, 'The Futurist Cinema', Apollonio, 1973 [1916], p. 208. See also Marinetti, 'The Founding and Manifesto of Futurism' [1909], 'Destruction of Syntax – Imagination Without Strings – Words-in-Freedom' [1913], as well as Marinetti's letter to the readers of *Zwrotnica*, 'List', *Zwrotnica*, no. 6, October 1922.

92 Miczka, 1998, p. 9.

93 For an overview of the influence of the cinematograph on literature, from the Young Poland to the 1930s, see Katarzyna Taras, *Witkacy i film* (Warszawa: Oficyna Wydawnicza Errata, 2005). See also Sterno-Wachowiak, 1985, and Edward Balcerzan, 'Wstęp', *Bruno Jasieński. Utwory poetyckie, manifesty, szkice* (Kraków: Polska Akademia Nauk, 1972).

94 See Kurek, 1961, p. 58.

95 Miczka, 1998, p. 6. For more details on Kurek's novels, see Cichla-Czarniawska, 1987, pp. 46–56, and Taras, 2005, pp. 50–56.

96 See also Bolesław Prus's story 'Widziadła', *Pion*, no. 15, 1936, pp. 6–7, and Irzykowski's play *Człowiek przed soczewką. Czyli sprzedane samobójstwo* (*The Man Behind the Lens or a Suicide for Sale*, 1908, first published in 1938), which can be compared with Apollinaire's short story 'A Fine Film' (1904), part of 'The False Messiah, Amphion or The Stories and Adventures of the Baron of Ormesan (1907). See Christie, *The Last Machine: Early Cinema and the Birth of the Modern World* (London: British Film Institute, 1994), pp. 48–49, and Levi, 2012, p. 72.

97 Miczka, 1998, p. 4.

98 Ibid., p. 2.

EXCERPTS FROM THE 'ARCHIVES' OF THE POLISH AVANT-GARDE

Kamila Kuc

Because it is the nature of the avant-garde to pose a challenge to traditional modes of expression, its artists had to rely on alternative routes of communication. Many key activities that formed the art of the avant-gardes found their reflection in a variety of publications, be they artists' books or small art magazines. Poland was no exception.

This short presentation of examples from the printed press can only give a taste of the rich array of materials that were circulating among the main avant-garde centres of Poland – Warsaw, Cracow, Poznań and Łódź – and were often distributed abroad (Berlin, Vienna, Paris). Among the examples presented here are six types: graphic poems (Czyżewski, Stern), manifestos (the Futurist 'Nuż w Bżuhu'), photomontages (Szczuka, Janusz Maria Brzeski) and book covers (*Earth to the Left*, *Apollinaire's House*) and magazine covers (*f.a.* and *BLOK*, to name just two).

Much has been written about the significance of small magazines to the avant-garde formations. Often named after avant-garde movements (*Praesens*), they were not for wide circulation and were mostly short lived. Nonetheless, they played a major part in the lives of artists. These magazines formed a platform for a debate among local artists. They also ensured an interchange of international texts and art works; much of *BLOK* was devoted to the work of Malevich; *Zwrotnica* published the works of Marinetti, Le Corbusier,

Malevich and Léger on a regular basis). They also printed artistic programmes and manifestos (*BLOK* and the Constructivist editorial-manifesto). Often created by ephemeral groups of artists (Czyżewski was first associated with the Formists, before joining Futurism), they reflected the collaborative nature of the avant-garde. Above all, small magazines demonstrated the interdisciplinary (painting, fashion, typography, architecture, theatre, film, dance) and international (as opposed to national) nature of the avant-gardes. They also blurred boundaries between high and low art through their associations of art with technology (*Zwrotnica, BLOK*).

Included in this context is also one of the most popular magazines devoted solely to film, *Film Polski*. Although publishing articles mainly about large Polish productions, the magazine often printed articles by the newly emerging film critics (Stern, Irzykowski, Leon Brun). Most importantly, from the mid-1920s, much of the content in *Film Polski* began reflecting the general dissatisfaction of the critics with the poor artistic standard of Polish films. This would continue until the 1930s, when the first avant-garde film organisations, such as START (The Society of the Lovers of Artistic Film), SAF (The Society of Film Auteurs) and Klub Filmowy Awangarda (Film Club Avant-Garde), were created to encourage the production and discussion of artistic films.

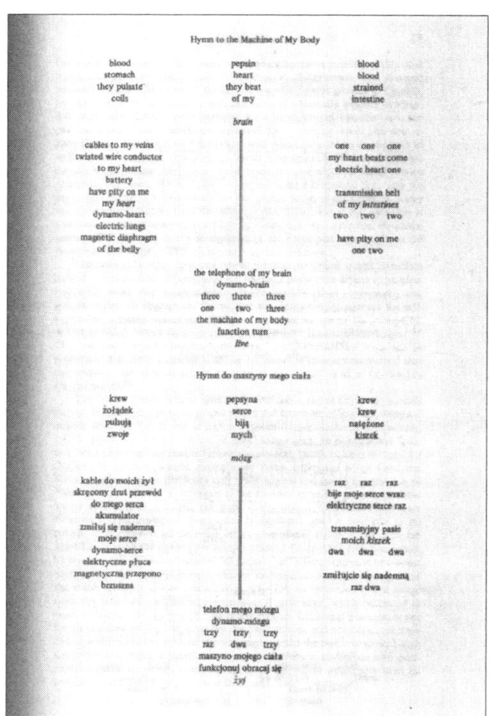

1. Tytus Czyżewski's Futurist poem 'Hymn to the Machine of My Body' (1922)

2. 'Nife in the Beli', Futurist manifesto, *Jednodńiuwka futurystuw*, no.2, November 1921

3. *Earth to the Left*, a volume of poetry by Anatol Stern and Bruno Jasieński, cover design by Mieczysław Szczuka (1924)

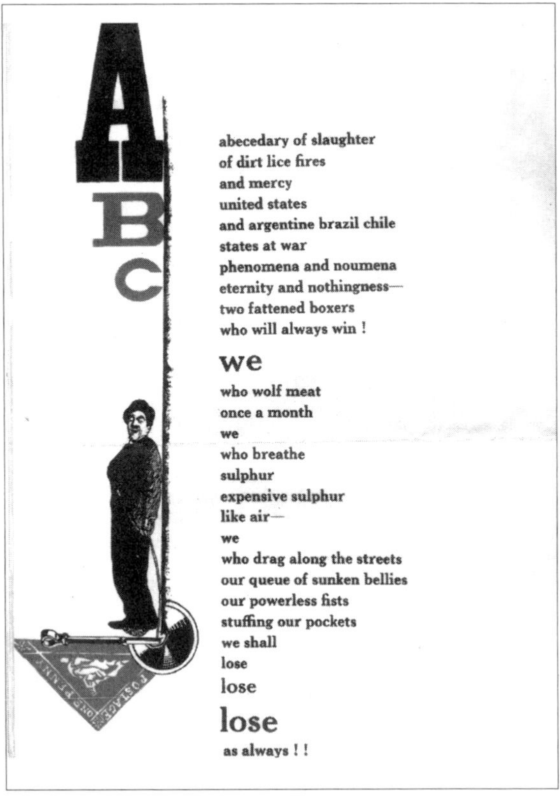

4. 'Europa' (1929), a design for Anatol Stern's poem by Mieczysław Szczuka

5. The Constructivist journal *BLOK*, nos. 8–9, November/December 1924

6. The Constructivist journal *BLOK*, 8 March 1924

7. The Constructivist magazine *Zwrotnica*, no. 3, 1922

8. *Dźwignia* magazine, no. 1, March 1927

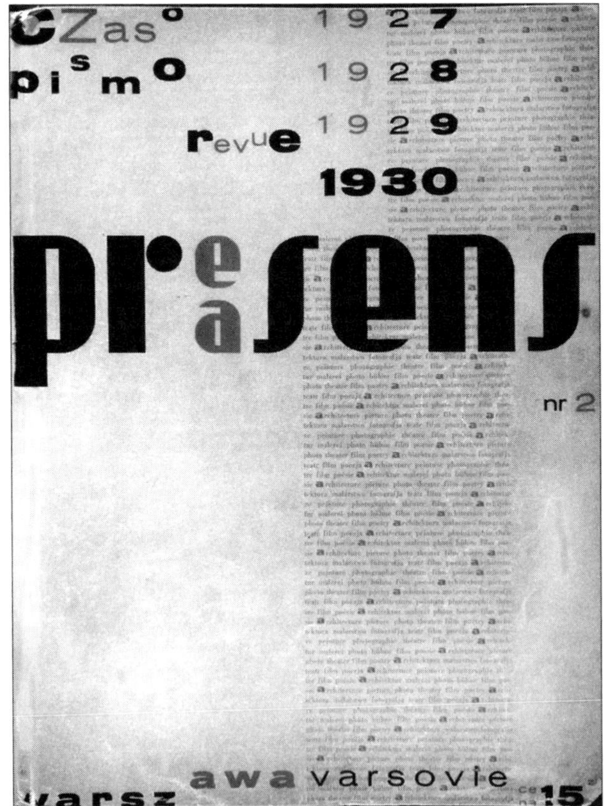

9. *Praesens*, no. 2, 1930

10. Mieczysław Szczuka's design for Anatol Stern's book *Apollinaire's House* (1973)

11. *The 20th Century Idyll*, a photomontage from *The Birth of a Robot* series (Janusz Maria Brzeski, 1933)

12. *Dwie cywilizacje*, a photomontage from *The Birth of a Robot* series (Janusz Maria Brzeski, 1933)

THE SEARCH FOR A 'MORE SPACIOUS FORM': EXPERIMENTAL TRENDS IN POLISH DOCUMENTARY (1945–1989)

Mikołaj Jazdon

I have always aspired to a more spacious form that would be free from the claims of poetry or prose and would let us understand each other without exposing the author or reader to sublime agonies.

Czesław Miłosz, Ars Poetica?

The term 'avant-garde' has been rarely used with reference to Polish post-war documentary film.[1] This does not mean, however, that at that time Poland was not producing any formally innovative films. On the contrary, the 'experimental' element has been an important driving force behind the development of documentary film in Poland in the post-war period. If one is to define the nature of such experiments and their relationship to what is generally understood as 'avant-garde film', the most coherent approach is to speak of the presence of certain elements in the Polish documentary film between 1945 and 1989. In 1958 Konrad Eberhardt, one of the most eminent of all Polish film critics, referred to Polish documentary films as 'the poetry of facts' (*poezja konkretu*), emphasising the artistic dimensions of the cinema of facts as its crucial elements.[2]

In the Polish nationalised film industry, filmmakers hardly had to worry about funding their films. Filmmakers in the West created their films within a democratic free economy – that is, under conditions that were utterly different from those in the Polish People's Republic. Western documentary films were usually commissioned, produced and aired on TV, especially after the late 1950s. Their filmmakers often used the cheaper technologies of the 16mm film. In the Polish People's Republic until the 1980s, even short films were made on more expensive 35mm film and were largely designed for cinema distribution. Thus Polish filmmakers did not have to be concerned with the laws of free-market economy; they did not feel the pressure to make films that would attract thousands of viewers. For them the challenge was not the achievement of success in the commercial mainstream, but the necessity of making films that were in accordance with the ideology of the producer, the State. Finally, the Western model of documentary filmmaking was often aligned with journalism (16mm was used extensively for reportage during World War II), whereas in Poland documentaries were being made by film-school trained professional directors.

The most important pieces in the history of Polish documentary films were made after World War II. In the 1920s and 1930s, international documentary films began incorporating avant-garde ideas, largely under the impact of Soviet filmmakers like Sergei Eisenstein and Dziga Vertov. The makers of such films included film poets and painters Joris Ivens, Walter Ruttmann and Jean Vigo. However, there were no Polish documentary filmmakers among them.[3] During World War II, Polish film units created documentaries that portrayed Polish troops fighting arm in arm with the Allies France, Britain, the USA and the Soviet Union. In the occupied country there was suddenly an increase in the number of documentary films and an increase in the status of the professional documentary filmmaker, as well as this type of film. Documentary chronicles of the Warsaw Uprising in 1944 were presented to the Polish soldiers in the Palladium cinema in the liberated part of the capital, shortly after the battle sequences were shot from the barricades. This is a unique example of the efficiency of the underground army filmmakers in World War II. The Polish Army Film Studio, created by the First 'Tadeusz Kościuszko' Division in the Soviet Union in 1943, produced several battlefield reportages. One of the first documentaries from the liberated concentration camps was *Majdanek, cmentarzysko Europy* (*Majdanek: The Cemetery of Europe*, Aleksander Ford, 1944), with in-front-of-the-camera interviews with prisoners and captured SS guards. After the war, Poland was under the influence of the Soviet Union, and in the late 1940s Communist order was imposed, and its independence was limited.

The Communists nationalised the cinemas and film industry. In their eyes, film was to become, as in the Soviet Union, a tool of national propaganda.

Nonetheless, among these filmmakers, who from the very beginning were creating post-war Polish cinematography, were the most talented directors, who in these new production conditions, free from the pressures of the free market, saw a chance to realise their dream of art cinema, supported by a giant patron – the State. These filmmakers were not interested in fulfilling the ideological needs of the Communist Party, and from very early on, they searched for ways to work around the censorship. One of the ways to achieve this was to experiment with the form of documentary film, widening its field of expression and finding solutions that would allow it to create content through allusions and metaphors, thus making censorship more difficult.

One of the key strategies here was the Polish documentary filmmakers' distrust of words, especially in voiceover commentary, which was considered easy to censor. The aesthetic experiments of the Polish documentary film-makers thus moved towards creating and perfecting – in the first instance – the visual aspect in a filmic, non-fiction narration, and sound elements like music, acoustic effects, dialogue and off-screen monologue. To this day, original commentary, written especially for the purpose of a documentary, remains a device rarely used by Polish documentary filmmakers. It could be argued that after the early post-war years, in their search for new narrative connections between film image and music, Polish documentary filmmakers were closer to the tradition of avant-garde film – Walter Ruttmann's city symphonies, the films of Alberto Cavalcanti, or Joris Ivens – than to the socially engaged cinema of facts, represented by such figures as John Grierson and Pere Lorentz, or to the anthropological documentaries of Robert Flaherty.

In the following part of the essay I shall discuss the key periods in the history of Polish documentary film, which can be characterised as a wave of experimentation led by anti-propagandist and anti-commercial ideas. Since the creative output of Krzysztof Kieślowski and the approach of his generation of documentary filmmakers in Poland has been discussed in a number of books published in English, my presentation of documentaries by this director will be limited.[4]

SYMPHONIES OF THE RUINED CITIES (1946–1948)

As already remarked, under Communism, documentary film became a propagandist tool in Poland. In Warsaw, a large production company for documentary films (Wytwórnia Filmów Dokumentalnych, or WFD) was established in 1949, and this, until the change of political system in 1989 and the introduction of a free economy, was the central institution for the production of documentary films, mainly aimed at cinemas. Immediately after the end of the war, in the years between 1945 and 1949, there existed a small margin of freedom that allowed Polish documentary filmmakers to create a selection of innovative films, films that were artistically interesting and original, and which can be characterised as having many experimental elements. Among these films are *Ballada f-moll* (*F-Moll Ballad*, Andrzej Panufnik, 1945), *Suita warszawska* (*Warsaw Suite*, Tadeusz Makarczyński, 1946), *Kopalnia* (*Coal Mine*, Natalia Brzozowska, 1947) and *Powódź* (*Flood*, Jerzy Bossak, 1947). As in Georges Franju's *Le sang des betes* (1949), in the above films, Polish documentary filmmakers attempted to comment on the tragedy of war but not in a direct, journalistic fashion.[5] Instead, they made use of metaphors and symbols removed from any associations with the war. But only at first glance. In these films there was no commentary and the dominant role on the soundtrack was given to music.[6] On the visual level, the image was often subjected to a variety of experiments, such as deformations through the employment of different filters, additional lighting and the extensive use of close-ups. The rhythm of montage was related to music, and, on the whole, these devices linked film more to painting than to photo-reportage, thus distancing them from the required stylistics of film chronicles and propagandist documentaries.

In all of the aforementioned films we see a certain narrative structure, which can be described as the journey 'from extermination to rebirth', as in *F-Moll Ballad* and *Warsaw Suite* in particular, as they talked about the ruined Warsaw. In Panufnik's film he juxtaposes Chopin's music with the images of ruins, without people or any signs of life within the film frame. A pretext for using Chopin is a poem by Cyprian Kamil Norwid, 'Fortepian Chopina' ('Chopin's Piano', 1863), at the start of the film. This well-known poem by a leading Polish Romantic poet was inspired by the events of 1863 and the January uprising, when the Russian soldiers, who at that time occupied Polish territories, threw Chopin's piano out of a window. The ruins were filmed by Adolf Forbert, with the use of filters that soften the image at its very edges. Overhanging rocks and mountain ranges are filmed as creations of abstract art, as if they were some strange sculptures which in no way brought to mind images of old cities seen in the few pre-war photographs, which are included in the film for a comparison. Chopin's calm, moody ballad 'F-Moll' was juxtaposed with the corpse of the city, a depopulated heap of rubble.

In his *Warsaw Suite* Tadeusz Makarczyński used an original, especially composed soundtrack by Witold Lutosławski. In this film, music builds a sound narration, which also gives a tempo to montage, as well as adding tonality to the whole story – from the first and downbeat part one, which depicts the ruins of a deserted Warsaw in a manner similar to Panufnik's film, through part two, which deals with the restoration of the city, and finally to the last part, which is upbeat and shows the city awakening to life in spring. This is somehow reminiscent of Joris Ivens's *Rain* (1929). Similarly to Panufnik, who called his film a ballad (*Warsaw Suite* is composed of three parts: *Adagio – Disaster, Andante – Return to Life*, and *Allegro – Warsaw Spring*), Makarczyński also refers to music, emphasising its special place as the film's narrator. Both films can be referred to as 'symphonies of ruined cities', marking their place in relation to the documentary city symphonies of the 1920s, and I will return to this point later.[7]

In Brzozowska's *Coal Mine* (1947), an expressionistic and high-contrast lighting dominates, reminiscent of German Expressionism-like aesthetics, or the first horror films. People are placed within the film frame to create precise compositional combinations. Shots are built up rhythmically through montage compositions. Music substitutes acoustic effects as it imitates the sounds of miners at work, the drama of the underground gas explosion, or the sounds transferred through telephone wires when help is called for. Images of the miners attempting to escape the explosion and of the miners returning to work after the rescue operation are all put together into a form of 'mechanical ballet' of shadows.

Jerzy Bossak's *Flood* is a film made over a period of many months from various fragments shot by camera operators from the Polish Film Chronicle (Polska Kronika Filmowa). The reels were part of a weekly newsreel that was screened in cinemas all over Poland. This footage was used to create a conventional news report, with an off-screen commentary, screened under the title *Lody ruszyły* (*The Ice Is Moving*, 1947). Using the same footage, with additional material, Bossak, together with the editor Wacław Kaźmierczak, made a documentary symphony about a flood and the world recovering after the catastrophe. The way of composing film material in the first few sequences of the film, which show the melting snow and the merging of the mountain tops into a fast river, brings to mind scenes from Viktor Turin's *Turksib* (1929) and Pare Lorentz's *The River* (1937). Bossak's film, once again, has no commentary, and as in the films discussed above, music plays an important role in dramatising the events and creating the overall mood. However, the most innovative aspect of this film relates to the way the scenes were edited together: on the one hand, the scenes constitute a detailed narrative about the flood catastrophe in Poland, but on the other hand, through the use of various symbols such as a bridge, a river, a house, bread and a ploughman, they evade literalism and instead become a universal narrative about people's struggles with natural catastrophes, and about the power of hope and solidarity. The most memorable scene of the film depicts the destruction of a bridge by a strong river of ice floes. This scene exemplifies the dominant role of the image over sound in Polish documentary film of the post-war era.

All the aforementioned films by Bossak, Panufnik, Makarczyński and Brzozowska[8] can be characterised as 'catastrophic symphonies', because in different ways they refer to the 'city symphony' films of avant-garde cinema of the 1920s, such as Ruttmann's *Berlin: Symphony of the Big City* (1927), Ivens's *Rain* (1928) and Alberto Cavalcanti's *Rien Que Les Heures* (*Only the Hours*, 1926). The main difference is that in the latter films the rhythmic, 'musical' imagery of contemporary cities was a homage to the modernist metropolis, whereas, in tone, the Polish films were more like a bitter critique of a modernity that had brought destruction to the world on a previously unseen scale.

This tendency to search for more artistic and individual forms of expression in film, focusing largely on the relationship between music and image, was continued throughout the 1950s in the work of Makarczyński and Andrzej Munk, who both took their artistic experiments further, avoiding replicating the filmic patterns of Polish documentary films of the late 1940s. Here I would like to discuss two films: Makarczyński's *Życie jest piękne* (*Life Is Great*, 1957) and Munk's *Spacerek staromiejski* (*A Walk in the Old City of Warsaw*, 1958). Makarczyński called his film 'a scream of protest', as in his films he wants 'the spectator to have an experience similar to his'.[9] The film is a warning against a nuclear disaster and war in general. This short, black-and-white documentary is sophisticated in its counterpoint deployment of music and visuals. The director begins with a sequence of shots fragmenting Pieter Bruegel's famous canvas *Children's Games* (1560) and *Dull Gret* (1564) and then introduces a medieval wall painting of a *danse macabre*, which becomes the key motif of the film. In the later part of the film, Makarczyński introduces a surprising and, at times, even shocking juxtaposition of music and image. Fragments of documentary films depicting street carnivals, parades and fancy-dress dances are contrasted with downbeat, funeral-like music. On the other hand, when we see horrific images of human remains and half-dead prisoners from Hitler's concentration camps,[10] the soundtrack plays fragments of popular contemporary tunes from the 1950s in English, French and German. This is the contemporary Dance of Death from the 'peaceful' Cold War era:[11]

The *Milong Tango* is played to bomb craters, *C'est si bon* to a nuclear explosion. This was shocking at the time. We can meet them used later as a means of expression or a cinematic device. Later cinema deprived them of the power of influence but there are still parts of Makarczyński's film that make an impression today. There is a vast square filled to the horizon with people in white.

The sound of an approaching plane. And when this whole crowd kneels we hear sounds of falling bombs. Today none would dare do anything of the like; it would be seen as utterly kitsch.[12]

It is a pity that Makarczyński's original film, a sophisticated anti-war essay, and an isolated piece of work in the Polish context, did not initiate a new tendency or trend in Polish cinema.[13]

One of the most important Polish documentary filmmakers of the 1950s, Andrzej Munk,[14] betrayed a particular interest in experimentation in connecting visual narration and music.[15] *A Walk in the Old City of Warsaw* is the last and most successful of three experiments in this area by the director. The other two were *Poemat symfoniczny "Bajka" Stanisława Moniuszki. Koncert w Klubie Fabrycznym Zakładów "Ursus"* (*Stanisław Moniuszko's Symphonic Poem Fairy-Tale: A Concert in the Ursus Tractor Factory Club*, 1952) and *Niedzielny poranek* (*One Sunday Morning*, 1956).

Fig. 8 *A Walk in the Old City of Warsaw* (Andrzej Munk, 1958)

Munk's last documentary short is also the most experimental of all his films. Two elements make *A Walk in the Old City of Warsaw* – in a sense – like *Ballad F-Moll* and *The Warsaw Suite*. The main theme is that of the rebuilding and rebirth of Warsaw. The other theme relates to the film's aesthetics and Munk's desire to experiment with sound effects and music within the film's narrative structure.[16] In Munk's film the city that arises from its ruins is not the only hero. Munk utilises aspects of a staged documentary by employing non-professional actors. The main hero here is a teenage female student, who walks through the streets of the ruined part of Warsaw (Old City). The idea for this film was suggested by the composer, Andrzej Markowski – who composed music for Makarczyński's *Life Is Great*. This is a tale about a young girl, whose internal feelings and how she relates to and interprets the reality that surrounds her (i.e. the city ruins through which she wanders), is depicted through a construction of an inner musical monologue. In Munk's film, the soundtrack mimics street sounds in such a way that the viewer perceives the depicted world in a very subjective manner, just as it is heard by the young girl, a music student, who is particularly sensitive to external sounds. As Michael Brooke notes, the film 'works just as well as a fictional psychological study of a young violin student whose studies have made her hypersensitive to the creative potential of the sounds that she hears during an otherwise routine walk between lessons'.[17] For the girl everything becomes music. She listens to 'the city symphony' on every step of her walk, whether she looks at a man sweeping the courtyard with a besom broom, or enters a church, where the organ is being installed, or plays on bottles on the windowsill of a cobbler's shop, or looks at the military frescoes from the Warsaw barbican. Markowski's music was used to create a sensory feeling about different places in Warsaw's old quarter, as experienced by the girl of 'hyperactive aural imagination'.[18] *A Walk in the Old City of Warsaw* is a rare piece in Poland, but unlike Makarczyński's film, it had an impact on the ways in which 'creative documentary' filmmakers perceived formal experiments in documentary film, as discussed later in this chapter.

THE BLACK SERIES (1955–1957): RADICAL BREAK-THROUGH

At the same time as Munk and Makarczyński were making their films, a new phenomenon in Polish culture appeared, one that had a much wider reception. The appearance of this new series of short documentary films became one of the most distinguished events in the history of Polish documentary film. In order to fully comprehend the meaning and impact of these films, we need to go back to 1949, when the political situation in Poland worsened.[19] It was a period of the Stalinist regime, when citizens' activities were limited, access to Western culture was cut off and creative activity was uncompromisingly fettered by the impact of Socialist Realism and censorship. This situation lasted until 1956, when Stalin was denounced by Khrushchev at the Twentieth Congress of the Communist Party of the Soviet Union.

A real break-through took place in October 1956, when the country's fate was in the hands of the Communist liberals who were keen on introducing important changes within Poland. In effect, the October Thaw period meant the end of the Communist totalitarian regime in its worst shape for Poland. The ice of the Stalinist winter began to break and melt, oppression began to loosen up, political prisoners left prisons, Cardinal Stefan Wyszyński, the primate of the Catholic Church in Poland, was freed and the Soviet officers who had previously been ruling the Polish army left for Moscow. The press and radio began depicting the image of the truer world, a world that was far from the propagandist fiction. Shelves of bookshops were being filled with previously forbidden titles – translations from contemporary international literature, as well as Polish authors. The period of Socialist Realism in its most orthodox shape was slowly becoming history. Playing and listening to jazz were finally allowed. Cinemas were full of Western feature films that had previously been inaccessible to Polish audiences. A very important and widely discussed phenomenon were the new innovative, anti-propagandist Polish documentary films, surprising in their realist short reportages, that rendered visible the darkest sides of reality, which previously had not been filmed. These films were referred to as the 'black series'. They constituted a manifesto of the young Polish cinema. This cinema was formed largely by young film school graduates who stood at the forefront of documentary filmmaking.[20]

Most of these documentaries offered a pessimistic view of Polish youth as a 'lost generation', deprived of prospects and cheated by Communist propaganda. Its most important titles are *Uwaga chuligani!* (*Look Out, Hooligans!*, 1955) and *Dzieci oskarżają* (*The Children Accuse*, 1956) by Edward Skórzewski and Jerzy Hoffman; *Gdzie diabeł mówi dobranoc* (*Where the Devil Says Goodnight*, 1956) and *Ludzie z pustego obszaru* (*People from an Empty Zone*, 1957) by Kazimierz Karabasz and Władysław Ślesicki; *Miasteczko* (*Little Town*, 1956) by Jerzy Ziarnik; and *Paragraf Zero* (*Article Zero*, 1957) and *Warszawa 1956* (*Warsaw 1956*, 1956) by Jerzy Bossak and Jarosław Brzozowski (the directors of the last two films represent the older generation of filmmakers).

Filmmakers in the Warsaw Documentary Film Studio (Wytwórnia Filmów Dokumentalnych, or WFD), fascinated by Italian neorealism and put off by the falseness of the cinema of Socialist Realism, used the Thaw period as an opportunity to express their disappointment with social problems: crime, prostitution and alcoholism – subjects that until then were submitted to heavy censorship. Their cameras looked beyond the surfaces of rebuilt government buildings, known from popular propaganda films, to show that there were still many people who remained living in the ruined buildings, as if the war had only just ended. These 'black films' made a clear distinction between good and evil, presenting evidence that supported the filmmakers' thesis that the conditions of living in post-war Poland needed drastic improvement. More important than a certain directorial finesse was the act of an enthusiastic destruction of the picture of fake reality that Polish society had been fed for many years. These films became the symbol of rapid political and cultural changes. Wherever possible, as they were still limited by technology and skills, these filmmakers searched for new ways to depict their subjects.

The hallmarks of Hoffmann and Skórzewski's films were rapid montage and solid narration. Karabasz and Ślesicki's cinema was innovative in the ways they used sound effects, as well as in their approach to 'capturing life unawares', showing non-staged scenarios from real life, as a CCTV camera does. This method was completely new in Poland and was characterised by a high level of spontaneity, previously unseen in Polish documentary films. In Wlodzimierz Borowik's *Paragraph Zero*, candid camera shots were used, as by the militia, in conjunction with interviews with Warsaw prostitutes. The main innovative quality of all the 'black films' rested primarily in the ability of the filmmakers to tell the truth without hiding any details. These filmmakers revealed events that many people did not know even existed, because, before 1956, the majority of films were controlled by Communist censorship, so only an image of Poland seen through rose-tinted glasses, with a booming economy, was allowed to reach the public.

When it comes to the form of these documentaries, the filmmakers attempted to revolutionise the 'old' poetics of Polish documentary cinema, instead of refusing it entirely. For example, they used audio commentary, but they tried to make it fresher and give it the impression of everyday speech rather than establish it as 'the voice of God', as in previous propaganda documentaries. It is worth mentioning here that these filmmakers knew of almost no Western productions, as in film schools they mainly watched Polish and Soviet films, next to the very few examples of the British cinema of the 1930s.

Look Out, Hooligans! was the film that initiated the black series. 'Today it is difficult to believe', stated Karabasz many years later,

<blockquote>
but this film constituted an authentic 'discovery' – and not only where the content is concerned, but also in terms of form and ways of seeing [...] It was [...] a complete novelty [...] And the awareness of this was very important for us, because it created unrest – and confirmed our desire to search for more than is around us. It was with this awareness that we began our first job at no.21, Chelmska Street, in WFD, which was the making of *Where the Devil Says Goodnight*.[21]
</blockquote>

The most interesting of all these films were made in the capital: *Warsaw 1956*, *Look Out, Hooligans!*, *People from an Empty Zone*, *Where the Devil Says Goodnight* and *Article Zero*. They all show the city as a phantom – full of ruins, among which there are hooligans, young gangs and prostitutes, shacks inhabited by 'Warsaw troglodytes'. Thus in terms of their subject matter these films were linked to ones which I described as 'symphonies of the ruined cities' made in Poland in the late 1940s. However, 'black films' were not so much about the architecture of destruction, which was the ruined city, as about people living in poverty, among the ruins, as an result of the country being ruled by the Communist authorities. This depressing, indeed black, picture of reality was powerful. It offered a bitter truth, which worked as an antidote for the viewers who were fed with the sickening sweetness of unrealistic Socialist Realist documentaries. The 'black series' was famous beyond Polish borders.

Erik Barnouw, the British film historian, used the expression 'black film' to describe all films made in Eastern Europe at that time.[22] *Where the Devil Says Goodnight* and *Article Zero* were presented as part of a programme entitled 'Polish Voices', presented in London in September 1958, included in Free Cinema film programmes organised by young British filmmakers.

THE SCHOOL OF KARABASZ:
TOWARDS THE CINEMA OF DOCUMENTARY OBSERVATION

The 1960s was the time of 'the school of Karabasz', a tendency in Polish documentary film that constituted a step in a new direction, slightly away from the achievements of the 'black series'. This new way of filmmaking was about searching for innovative ways of depicting reality, but without staging it, without using commentaries. This new tendency was interested in more direct cinema, similar to that of the Americans Richard Leacock, D. A. Pennebaker and the Maysles brothers. The difference was that Polish filmmakers did not make films for TV on 16mm, but on 35mm and for cinema release.

The late 1950s and early 1960s in Poland are often referred to as a period of 'little stabilisation', when documentary films no longer constituted such a radical critique of economic, social and political reality, as was the case with the 'black series'. Documentary filmmakers began perfecting methods to record the everyday lives of ordinary people, concentrating more on the depiction of their traditions and habits than on challenging the political order. Here the leading role belongs to Karabasz's film *Muzykanci* (*The Musicians*, 1960).[23] This piece is a brave formal experiment, a successful attempt at merging a poetic documentary with a more factual approach of observation and filming real, non-staged events. This film about the conductor of an amateur brass band was innovative, as Karabasz made it without any pre-prepared scenario. He took risks in trying a completely new way of filming, based on a long observation process, mixed with recordings of the orchestra. The filmmaker spent a few weeks filming this amateur orchestra composed of tram drivers, and in a pioneering way, he registered fragments of non-provoked, non-scripted dialogue between the conductor and other members of the orchestra. Moreover, he used a new type of lighting. Stanisław Niedbalski, the cinematographer, did not employ heavy lamps on tripods, which seriously limited camera movements, but instead hung a row of light bulbs on the ceiling. This type of top lighting revolutionised the way of lighting sets in Polish documentary films of that decade, even though in the beginning this idea was seriously criticised by technicians from the film studio because of its radicalism.

Unlike some feature documentaries made around the world at that time, which used lighter cameras and sound equipment and new methods of synchronising image with sound, namely *Primary* (Leacock and the Maysles Brothers, 1960) in America and *The Chronicle of a Summer* (Jean Rouch and Edgar Morin, 1961) in France, *The Musicians* was made by employing old and cumbersome equipment, as at that time Polish documentary filmmakers did not have access to the technology used by those working in direct cinema or *cinéma vérité*. Karabasz's following films kept improving his method of detailed observation of characters – ordinary people – with which he composed narratives that can be referred to as 'state of things' narratives.[24] Karabasz's films influenced other filmmakers, who in the 1960s began adopting similar subject matter and formal innovations. These filmmakers were often called 'the school of Karabasz'. Made in 1965, Karabasz's *Na progu* (*On a Doorstep*) is the first Polish film that was self-referential and dealt with the dilemmas of a documentary filmmaker trying to make better documentary films. Karabasz filmed a group of eighteen-year-old Polish girls, after their A-level exams. Particular sequences in the film were made using different documentary methods, from non-staged improvisation and observation, filming young women in public spaces, and interviews in front of cameras, to a sequence of still photographs accompanied by excerpts from letters sent by teenage girls to a popular weekly magazine, *Przyjaciółka* (*Girlfriend*). Each of these sequences has a critical commentary by the director, who demonstrates the limitations of these methods.

Karabasz's next film was perceived as an innovative experiment. *Rok Franka W.* (*Frank W.'s Year*, 1967) is a feature-length film which upset the commonly held belief that a documentary film is incapable of showing the life of an ordinary individual. To challenge such beliefs, the director spent a year observing the life of Franek Wróbel, a young man from the Voluntary Work Regiments. The film shares the spirit found in the early works of the French New Wave, particularly François Truffaut and Jean-Luc Godard.[25] The only difference is that Karabasz's hero is not acting out a carefully prepared scenario, but remains in front of the camera, which records his life, thus providing Karabasz with the material to construct a film that is a non-staged and non-scripted narrative.

Many Polish documentary filmmakers followed Karabasz's approach. Władysław Ślesicki observed and filmed for several months one of the last Gypsy caravans, to make a unique portrayal of the nomadic life of the Roma people in Poland, in *Zanim opadną liście* (*Before Leaves Fall*, 1964). Danuta Halladin in her *Moja ulica* (*My Street*, 1965) depicted everyday life in one of the Warsaw districts, combining the observation technique of filming with multi-voice off-screen narration by children commenting on life on their street. Even the young Krzysztof Kieślowski composed his documentary debut of several sequences from city life, collecting observed situations from streets and factories in his *Z miasta Łodzi* (*From the City of Łódź*, 1968). From then on, a lengthy and patient observation of subjects and reality became a key approach to documentary. We see more films that carefully register important gestures, looks and moods of the moment, all of which are given another dimension in the final edited product – a process similar to writing a poem.[26] Karabasz, who according to Roger Sandall was considered 'a major postwar documentary artist', is a central figure in the history of Polish documentary film.[27] He has the same status in Polish documentary that John Grierson did in British documentary and Dziga Vertov did in Russian documentary. Karabasz's vision of documentary film constituted an important and influential point of reference for many documentary filmmakers in the 1960s.

CREATIVE DOCUMENTARY

A new generation of documentary filmmakers who became leading figures in the production of Polish non-fiction cinema of the 1970s and 1980s manifested their artistic approach to the methods of depicting reality at the National Short Film Festival in Cracow in 1971. This was a moment of another political change in the Communist government, after the bloody pacification of workers' riots on the Polish coast in December 1970. The disappointment of the Communist rule paved the way for underground independent political organisations of the 1970s that preceded the birth of the Solidarity social movement in 1980. The filmmakers from the Warsaw Documentary Film Studio, like Krzysztof Kieślowski, Tomasz Zygadło, Marcel Łoziński and Grzegorz Królikiewicz, made films much more politically and socially engaged than those of their predecessors, although employing and developing filmmaking methods practised in the cinema of the 1960s. The main artistic purpose for making these films was to give a true description of social and political reality in contemporary Poland[28] by depicting micro-worlds of different institutions such as schools (*Szkoła podstawowa / Primary School*, Tomasz Zygadło, 1971), hospitals (*Szpital / Hospital*, Krzysztof Kieślowski, 1976) and hotels (*Moje miejsce / My Place*, Marcel Łoziński, 1986).[29] These films were allegories of and metaphors for Poland, something that was quite obvious for a Polish audience 'skilled in Aesopian reading and perpetually hunting for messages written in an invisible ink'.[30] The most formally innovative branch of this trend was 'dokument kreacyjny' ('creative documentary'),[31] represented by films made mainly in the Educational Film Studio (Wytwórnia Filmów Oświatowych, or WFO) in Łódź by Wojciech Wiszniewski, Bogdan Dziworski, Andrzej Papuziński, Piotr Szulkin, Józef Robakowski and Andrzej Barański. Declining the production methods employed in the Warsaw Studio, documentarians from WFO often made use of means typical rather for fictional or experimental cinema, including staging, set design constructions, elaborate sound and an expressive visual style.

Wojciech Wiszniewski remains the most recognised film artist from the circle of 'creative documentary' makers. Out of nine short documentary films he directed himself, three constitute his most important titles: *Wanda Gościmińska włókniarka* (*Wanda Gościmińska: A Weaver*, 1975), *Elementarz* (*The Primer*, 1976) and *Stolarz* (*The Carpenter*, 1976).[32] Because of his radicalism in applying methods more characteristic of fictional than non-fictional cinema, it is sometimes questioned whether Wiszniewski's films can be labelled 'documentaries'.[33] Wiszniewski deconstructed the audio-visual vocabulary of the Social Realist 'factual' cinema, transforming particular elements of the propaganda language in surrealistic manner. Proletarians, the characters from *The Primer* and *Wanda Gościmińska: A Weaver*, are transformed into monuments when filmed in low-angle shots or standing motionless in front of the camera in long takes. *Wanda Gościmińska: A Weaver* is a travesty of Social Realism, a portrait of a leader of labour. The propaganda message is ridiculed and discredited with hyperboles, as in the scene where Gościmińska is literally floating in front of members of a Communist Youth Association and in the scene in which propaganda newsreels are screened in the background of Gościmińska and her family celebrating at a table overflowing with food and drinks. The off-screen monologue of the weaver is ostentatiously artificial in form. Wiszniewski consequently demystifies the falsehood of filmic newspeak.

Bogdan Dziworski, a photographer and cinematographer, employed an original audio-visual style in his short documentary films made for WFO. Sports and artists, his favourite subjects, seem to be no more than a pretext for his formally extravagant documentaries, where the time and space of presented events are never precisely defined. The director avoids any verbal narration in his films, to elevate the visual to greater importance, shooting with wide-angle lenses, using tricks, over-cranking and under-cranking, cross-cutting and positioning the camera unusually to enhance the visual effect. Dziworski often uses sound effects to draw our attention to a certain action in the background that could otherwise go unnoticed by the audience.

Kilka opowieści o człowieku (*A Few Stories About Man*, 1983),[34] a lyrical portrait of handicapped man Jerzy Orłowski, joins two main motifs from

Dziworski's creative output: sport and art. Orłowski, who has no arms, is depicted here as a superman, more fit and adroit than many an able-bodied person. He can jump on skis or from a diving tower and draw exquisite sketches with a pen held with his neck. The film soundtrack, without dialogue or voice-over narration, is filled with music and selected sound effects. A typical 'Dziworski scene' is the one in which Orłowski jumps into the river from a bridge. This one-take scene is a long shot in slow motion. The ship approaching the bridge dominates the frame. The jumping of a tiny silhouette of the man is underlined by the sound of an aerial bomb falling down. The image brings to mind Pieter Bruegel's famous painting *Landscape with the Fall of Icarus* (c. 1560s). The situation of jumping down is reversed in the final scene, where Orłowski impressively jumps up from the floor and out of the roof window followed by one of the sketches, which flies up following its creator.

The 'creative documentary' trend appears to be the most avant-garde of Polish documentary trends of the 1970s and 1980s. The few titles presented above could be supplemented by no less important works like *Bykowi chwała* (*Glory to the Bull*, 1971) by Andrzej Papuziński, *Rynek* (*Market Square*, 1971) by Józef Robakowski, *Nie płacz* (*Don't Cry*, 1972) by Grzegorz Królikiewicz, *Życie codzienne* (*Everyday Life*, 1975) and *Kobiety pracujące* (*Working Women*, 1978) by Piotr Szulkin, *Kostka cukru* (*A Cube of Sugar*, 1986) by Jacek Bławut, and *Szczurołap* (*The Rat Catcher*, 1986) by Andrzej Czarnecki. The Communist system in Poland was gradually collapsing in the 1980s. Documentary makers made films that were more and more openly critical of the political system. The popularisation of video equipment enabled production and distribution of films in the underground, without censorship and outside the official studio system. The strategy of making poetic documentaries operating with visual metaphors and symbols became less and less popular and almost vanished after the collapse of Communism. The free-market economy elevated television to the position of the leading producer of documentaries for the mass audience. Making creative or experimental documentaries became difficult or hardly possible.

Polish documentary developed throughout the following decades up to the present time, but the above account sets out the key aspects of the documentary during an important period, from the end of World War II to the late 1980s, when more radical approaches to form and content were forged by filmmakers. The innovations of Western avant-garde, art and independent film, as I have argued, were often paralleled and sometimes influential, especially when during the Thaw greater access to international work became possible. There is no doubt that the documentary movement was a key one in the radicalisation of cinema during the period discussed here.

1   'Using avant-garde in its more encompassing sense, to include all experimental films, we can say that such films are considered "advanced" in that they deny the traditional narrative structure and techniques of commercial films by seeking to explore new modes of visual and emotional experience.' Ira Konigsberg, 'Avant-Garde Cinema', *The Complete Film Dictionary* (Harmondsworth: Penguin Reference, 1997), p. 25.

2   Konrad Eberhardt, 'Poezja konkretu', *Ekran*, no. 2, 1958, p. 20.

3   On the pre-war Polish avant-garde film, see Marcin Giżycki, *Awangarda wobec kina. Film w kręgu polskiej awangardy artystycznej dwudziestolecia międzywojennego* (Warszawa: Wydawnictwo Małe, 1996).

4   See Krzysztof Kieślowski, *Kieślowski on Kieślowski*, Danusia Stok, ed. (London: Faber and Faber, 1995); Paul Coates, *Lucid Dreams: The Films of Krzysztof Kieślowski* (Trowbridge, Wiltshire, England: Flicks Books, 1999); and Annette Insdorf, *Double Lives, Second Chances: The Cinema of Krzysztof Kieślowski* (New York: Hyperion, 1999).

5   Jeanette Sloniowski, 'It Was an Atrocious Film: George's Franju's *Blood of the Beats*', Barry Keith Grant and Jeannette Sloniowski, eds., *Documenting the Documentary: Close Readings of Documentary Film and Video* (Detroit: Wayne State University Press, 1998).

6   A certain exception to the rule is Andrzej Panufnik's *F-Moll Ballad* (1945), at the beginning of which the director placed a fragment of a poem by the Polish Romantic poet Cyprian Kamil Norwid, *Chopin's Piano*. The film is discussed later in the text.

7   We can see the important context for Panufnik's and Makarczyński's films about Warsaw in ruins in Eugeniusz Cękalski's avant-garde documentary. In 1937 he shot *Trzy etiudy Chopina* (*Three Etudes of Chopin*), an impressionistic visual illustration of Chopin's music. When this black-and-white experimental documentary was destroyed at the beginning of the war, Cękalski made its Eastmancolor remake, *Colour Studies of Chopin* (1944, USA).

8   Next to *Coal Mine*, Brzozowska's other important film from that period is *Muzyka* (*Music*), in which she also does not use voice-over narration. See Wacław Świeżyński, 'Film dokumentalny', Jerzy Toeplitz, ed., *Historia filmu polskiego*, vol. 3 (Warszawa: Wydawnictwa Artystyczne i Filmowe, 1974), p. 139.

9   Bożena Janicka, 'Man and Ape', Bożena Janicka and Andrzej Kołodyński, eds., *Chełmska 21. 50 lat Wytwórni Filmów Dokumentalnych i Fabularnych w Warszawie* (Warszawa: WFDiF, 2000), p. 70.

10 Makarczyński merges these scenes with close-ups on the pilots' faces, as they sit behind the steering wheels of modern bomber planes. The director shockingly juxtaposes historical documentary depictions of the Auschwitz prisoners behind barbed wire with images of the atomic bomb explosion, as if to suggest that the prisoners are seeing it, thus witnessing yet another tragic war.

11 Tadeusz Makarczyński helped collect footage for Lionel Rogosin's anti-war feature documentary, *Good Times, Wonderful Times* (1965).

12 Janicka, 2000, p. 70.

13 Makarczyński continued experimenting with form, making lyrical documentaries, such as *Szlembark* (1946, with music and commentary added in 1956), *A Canticle of Wood* (*Kantyczka z drewna*, 1958) and *Night* (*Noc*, 1961).

14 Andrzej Munk was one of the leading Polish filmmakers of the 1950s. His documentary films such as *Kierunek Nowa Huta* (*Destination Nowa Huta*, 1951) and *Kolejarskie słowo* (*The Railwayman's Word*, 1953) might now seem similar to Social Realist propaganda. However, at the time of their release these films attracted viewers by novelty of detail. See Marek Hendrykowski, *Andrzej Munk* (Poznań: Wydawnictwo Naukowe UAM, 2011), p. 57. Translated by Peter Langer.

15 Hendrykowski, *Andrzej Munk* (Warszawa: Biblioteka Więzi, 2007), pp. 78–79.

16 The city arising from the ruins of the Old City in the capital of Poland had already been presented in Jerzy Bossak's *Return to the Old City* (*Powrót na Stare Miasto*, 1954).

17 Michael Brooke, 'Polish Documentaries: *A Walk in the Old Town of Warsaw* (1958)', *Kinoblog*, http://filmjournal.net/kinoblog/category/directors/munk-andrzej/.

18 Ibid.

19 For more detail, see Norman Davies, *Heart of Europe: A Short History of Poland* (Oxford; New York: Oxford University Press, 1986), p. 8.

20 Ibid., pp. 1–62.

21 Kazimierz Karabasz, 'Rok przełomu – rok startu', *Kamera*, no. 1, 1970.

22 See Erik Barnouw, *Documentary: A History of the Non-Fiction Film* (New York; Oxford: Oxford University Press, 1993), p. 263.

23 The leading Polish documentary filmmakers of the 1970s and 1980s, like Krzysztof Kieślowski and Marcel Łoziński, declared *Musicians* their favourite and most praised documentary film. Kieślowski wrote in 1994: 'It's rare for a short film to express so much, in such a beautiful and simple manner, about the fundamental human need to create.' Kieślowski, '*The Sunday Musicians*', Kevin Macdonald and Mark Cousins, ed., *Imagining Reality* (London; Boston: Faber and Faber, 1996), p. 216.

24 The term 'poetic narration' is mainly associated with a lyrical form. This form consigns to the background the action with its events and its heroes' active and dynamic needs. In Polish documentary film discourse this is often referred to as 'the state of things' (*stan rzeczy*) – the term borrowed from the Czech director Ivan Passer. See Roger Crittenden, *Fine Cuts: The Art of European Film Editing* (Amsterdam: Elsevier, 2006), p. 211.

25 Karabasz, similarly to Truffaut, not only makes documentary films, but also publishes his views on film. His books and articles are a unique theoretical record of his practices as a practitioner. See *Cierpliwe oko* (*A Patient Eye*; the title became a synonym for his filmmaking method); *Bez fikcji – z notatek filmowego dokumentalisty* (*Without Fiction: From the Notes of a Documentary Filmmaker*, 1985); and *Odczytać czas* (*Reading Time*, 1999). In these books Karabasz merged elements of his artistic manifesto with some practical observations, theoretical reflections and interviews with other documentary filmmakers.

26 Experimenting with new documentary strategies and techniques continued in the Polish documentary studio in Warsaw for the whole decade of the 1960s. Jan Łomnicki transformed so-called 'production reportage' into a visual poem, *Narodziny statku* (*A Ship Is Born*, 1961) – a short documentary depicting the constructing and launching of a cargo ship. Władysław Ślesicki made several lyrical ballads about people living far from industrial regions of Poland, close to nature, almost in wilderness. These were *Płyną tratwy* (*Drafts Are Floating*, 1962), *Rodzina człowiecza* (*Family of Man*, 1966) and *Zanim opadną liście* (*Before the Leaves Fall*, 1964), all inspired by films of Robert Flaherty.

27 See, for example, Roger Sandall, 'Seven Polish Shorts', *Film Quarterly*, vol. XV, fall, 1961, p. 54.

28 'At that time, I was interested in everything that could be described by the documentary film camera. There was a necessity, a need – which was very exciting for us – to describe the world. The Communist world had described how it should be and not how it really was. We […] tried to describe this world and it was fascinating to describe something which hadn't been described yet. It's a feeling of bringing something to life, because it is a bit like that. If something hasn't been described, then it doesn't officially exist. So that if we start describing it, we bring it to life.' Kieślowski, quoted in Danusia Stok, *Kieślowski on Kieślowski* (London and Boston: Faber and Faber, 1993), pp. 54–55.

29 This method of depicting various institutions as metaphors for the whole system reminds one of the films of the American direct cinema filmmaker Frederick Wiseman, who made films like *High School* (1968), *Hospital* (1970) and *Welfare* (1975).

30 Marek Haltof, *The Cinema of Krzysztof Kieślowski: Variations on Destiny and Chance* (London; New York: Wallflower Press, 2004), p. 11.

31 See Mirosław Przylipiak, 'Amongst the Statues', Tadeusz Sobolewski, ed., *Polska Szkoła Dokumentu. Wojciech Wiszniewski* (Warszawa: Polskie Wydawnictwo Audiowizualne, 2008), p. 8. Translated by Aneta Uszyńska.

32 The artificiality of documentary style is demonstrated in *The Carpenter*. Vicissitudes in the life of the title character of this faux documentary are presented in the off-screen narration using the recognisable voice of the popular actor Jan Himilsbach. The individual story of a Warsaw carpenter is precisely interwoven with the crucial moments of Polish history from the twentieth century. Wiszniewski questions the petrified style of biography documentaries, where a personal confession is juxtaposed with archive footage of the 'official' history. The library shots from this film are ordered into single clips repeated several times before they give way to other images. When shots of a newspaper boy on a Warsaw street from the 1930s, Hitler dancing in his mountain residence of Berghof, or Polish cavalry bathing horses in the river are repeated, they are not presented as unquestionable evidence of history, but rather reveal the constructed nature of the film. *The Carpenter* could be called mock-documentary. On the one hand, the director challenges the documentary form by demonstrating how it is constructed; on the other, he does not refrain from presenting certain moments from history.

33 For more details see Przylipiak, 2008, p. 9.

34 In 1990 Dziworski turned out the prequel to his *A Few Stories About Man* for Channel 4. *The Prisoner* is a portrait of Jerzy Orłowski when he served a long-term sentence. The film was shot in the style of the original documentary – without dialogue and off-screen narration.

AVANT-GARDE AND THE THAW:
EXPERIMENTATION IN POLISH CINEMA OF THE 1950s AND 1960s

Marcin Giżycki

The 1958 Expo Exhibition in Brussels included an international competition for experimental films. Never before, or after, was there a festival that gathered together works of such diverse artists as Kenneth Anger, Stan Brakhage, Robert Breer, Shirley Clarke, Maya Deren, Georges Franju, Abel Gance, Claude Gorretta, Yoram Gross, Hy Hirsh, John Hubley, Ian Hugo, Lewis Jacobs, Lawrence Jordan, Nelly Kaplan, Peter Kubelka, Len Lye, Willard Maas, Marie Menken, Stan VanDerBeek, Jean Mitry, François Reichenbach, Alan Tanner, Agnes Varda and John Whitney. All together, a hundred and thirty-three films from twenty-nine countries were shown, with the American film being represented by the highest numbers: thirty-seven directors and fifty-seven films. France entered seventeen films, England presented twelve works, Germany showed nine films, Belgium and Sweden, six. It must have come as a surprise to many Western candidates that as many as seven Polish films were presented in the competition. Aside from the one film entered by Yugoslavia, these were the only productions from the Communist countries. It was a revelation that avant-garde films too were being made behind the Iron Curtain. Even more consternation was caused when the Grand Prix and the two additional awards were granted to Polish artists.

In 1958 Poland was not a country without an avant-garde tradition in film. The roots of the Polish film avant-garde go as far back as 1913, when one of the first European film theorists, the writer and critic Karol Irzykowski, wrote:

If we can imagine that painters might be supplying their own pictures for cinematographic shows one day... then cinema would become the 'true art' and we would receive overwhelming impressions from it, of which today we get only the slightest taste when seeing contemporary films of fantasy and wonder.[1]

A few years later, a friend of Irzykowski, a journalist and philosopher named Feliks Kuczkowski, spun ideas about a 'visionary film', made without any scenario and out of materials created by the filmmaker himself. He even attempted to enact such ideas. In the 1920s Polish Constructivists – Mieczysław Szczuka, Teresa Żarnower and Henryk Berlewi – created projects for unmade films. Finally, in the next decade and during World War II, a few proper avant-garde films were made. Among these were seven films made by Franciszka and Stefan Themerson, the most important representatives of the Polish film avant-garde. Worth noting here, because of its abstract elements, is a film by Eugeniusz Cękalski, *Colour Studies of Chopin* (1944), made in America.[2] The film consists of numerous abstract moments (reflections of light on water, flames and clouds moving in the sky), and finishes with a short sequence, which was scratched directly in the film's emulsion.

The war, and the nationalisation of the cinema industry, as well as the imposition of the Socialist Realist doctrine on Poland's artistic endeavours, put a temporary end to this type of artistic expression. However, during the Thaw period, which arrived with the change of government in 1956, a symptom of Stalin's death (in 1953), film became one of the key practices of the reawakening Polish avant-garde. Polish cinema at that time, particularly when compared with that of other countries of the Soviet bloc, contained the strong presence of experimental, avant-garde tendencies within the state cinematography, as well as outside of it – a characteristic unheard of in neighbouring countries. A decisive date is 1957. During this year the following films were made: *Kineformy* (*Kineforms*) and *Tam i tu* (*There and Here*) by Andrzej Pawłowski; *Somnambulicy* (*Somnambulists*) by Mieczysław Waśkowski; and *Był sobie raz* (*Once Upon a Time*) by Jan Lenica and Walerian Borowczyk.

The first three films deserve special attention because of their connection to Tadeusz Kantor, the leading representative of Polish *art informel* and alternative theatre. Before *Kineforms* became a film, it was an improvised spectacle, which was first shown to the public in Kantor's theatre programme 'Cricot 2'.[3] One of the critics participating in the spectacle at the time wrote:

     THE STRUGGLE FOR FORM

Fig. 9 *Kineformy* (Andrzej Pawłowski, 1957)

Forms appear on the screen. Fantastical, dreamlike, indescribable, emerging from a hazy abyss, coming and going, coloured or black and white, exceptionally beautiful. They did not represent anything and could thus be associated with anything, utterly abstract, organic, alive in an inexplicable and urgent way, coming to life and dying the most real death, dramatic to the point of breathlessness.[4]

The device for creating *Kineforms* was a box, equipped with primitive dials, with a mechanical system that would set in motion lenses and small objects, made out of paper and cellophane, all lit up with a spotlight. In the front of the box there was a screen made out of tracing paper, onto which the images created inside were projected from behind.

Kineforms the film and its continuation, *There and Here* (also made in 1957), preserved many features of the original project, with the exception of spontaneity. The images were carefully selected and put together, with the accompaniment of Adam Walaciński's synchronised music. These mobile forms appearing and disappearing off the screen are so unique, and phantom-like, that they do not resemble anything else seen before. To this day they give an impression of something unearthly which is becoming and lives its own real life during the projection. It is worth noting here that Pawłowski's films discussed here were in fact independent productions, although they were filmed by the state-funded film collective Zespół Filmowy 'Po prostu'.

Inspired by Tadeusz Kantor's paintings and made the same year as *Kineforms* was another abstract film, Mieczyslaw Waśkowski's *Somnambulists*. Kantor familiarised himself with Surrealism, and new tendencies in abstract painting that derived from it, during his visits to Paris in 1945 and 1955. From this moment on, chance effect, as a 'co-creator of the work', became a crucial element in the creative method employed by the future author of *Wielopole, Wielopole*.[5] Waśkowski, together with the camera operator Antoni Nurzyński, decided to create a filmic equivalent of Kantor's Wielopole, Wielopole that would also refer to the subconscious. Waśkowski's film is composed of close-ups of paint of various colours, applied using Jackson Pollock's method. The paint dribbles, then creates a bigger puddle, which then forms a large bubble. The film's very title, *Somnambulists*, did not leave any doubt as to its connection with dreams, Surrealism and Freud. Numerous critics perceived the multi-coloured spots covering the screen as images of an 'unhardened crust of some planet filled with active volcanoes'.[6]

Kineforms and *Somnambulists* were shown in Brussels, and the former film was awarded a distinction. A few more Polish films were part of the same competition: *Dom* (*House*, 1958) by Jan Lenica and Walerian Borowczyk, Roman Polański's *Dwaj ludzie z szafą* (*Two Men and a Wardrobe*, 1958), *Perdu...* by Rostandré (Borowczyk's pseudonym), *Warszawa '56* (*Warsaw '56*, 1956) by Jerzy Bossak and Andrzej Brzozowski, and *Życie jest piękne* (*Life Is beautiful*, 1957) by Tadeusz Makarczyński. The last two films can be considered creative documentaries. About *Perdu...* one can only reiterate what the exhibition catalogue states, as the film is now lost:

The film depicts a man being at a crossroad of his life; he is surprised at a moment when he realises that he wasted his last chance. The external, real world, as well as the imaginary world are both represented from the main character's point of view.[7]

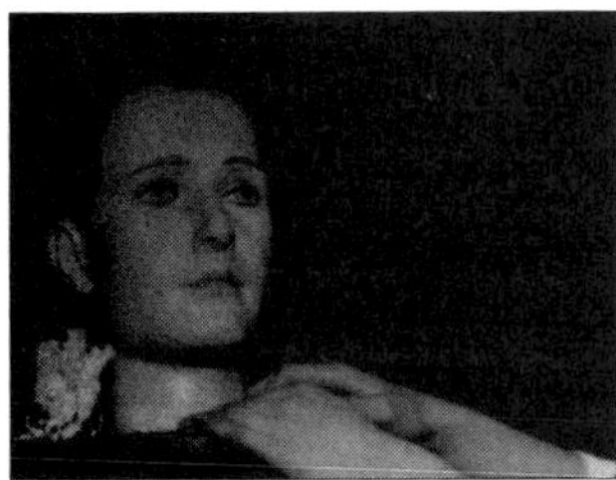

Fig. 10 *House* (Jan Lenica and Walerian Borowczyk, 1958)

Lenica and Borowczyk's *House* was awarded the Grand Prix in Brussels. A year earlier they entered their experimental, improvised debut film, *Once Upon a Time...*. This animated collage is made out of small scraps of old prints and coloured pieces of paper, with a few excerpts copied from newsreels and elements of deliberately amateur hand drawing. The film's slight narrative – the adventures of a small black spot, which wanders through graphic details and

THE STRUGGLE FOR FORM

Fig. 11 *One Upon a Time* (Walerian Borowczyk and Jan Lenica, 1957)

takes up different shapes to finally become a part of an abstract canvas that hangs in a museum – was in fact only a pretext. Lenica and Borowczyk's next project, *Nagrodzone uczucie* (*Love Required*, 1957), was another film made out of a collection of *ready-made* elements, mainly fragments of paintings by a naive painter, Jan Płaskociński, which contributed to the creation of a story in 'the best style of novels for boarding school girls'[8] kept in the conventions of silent cinema with inter-titles. Lenica and Borowczyk's interest in Płaskociński was analogous with the Surrealists' fascination with primitive and naive art, in which they saw a pure expression of the artistic spirit. The directors of *House* never hid the sources of their inspiration. In one interview they stated: 'Film died with the death of the French film avant-garde. We would gladly return to Méliès.'[9] Many years later Lenica added:

I think that the Surrealists had the greatest impact on cinema. Their first films have completely torn down the barrier between reality and fiction, between the realm of the visible and the imaginary. Surrealism was instrumental in the development of cinema; film, which naturally gravitated towards theatre, finally found a narrative inaccessible to the latter. The camera could not only capture the real world in a manner that was out of reach of the eye, it could also demonstrate the processes of the unconscious, making the invisible perceptible. Although spare and hermetic, the Surrealist films had a significant influence on ways of seeing and perceiving and, consequently, on forms of visual narrative. Thirty years later, their influence on the development of cinema is unquestionable, just as unquestionable as the influence of Surrealism on all aspects of the visual arts.[10]

There is no doubt that *House* is the closest to the Surrealist ideal not only in the work of Lenica and Borowczyk, but also in the whole of Polish cinema. The film is not abstract, yet it is devoid of a conventional narrative, filled with visual associations, and has undertones of eroticism. In *House* we find such typically Surrealist props and motifs as a mannequin and *l'amour fou* (for the actual mannequin), old prints, photographs, postcards and bizarre, because taken out of context, objects from a junk room (a wig sucking milk from a bottle and then swallowing a piece of paper). All of this is free from the terrors of cause-and-effect logic, all associations being close to psychic automatism, as most parts of the film were improvised in front of the camera. *House* is made out of loosely combined scenes, which take place in numerous rooms of an old secession block of apartments. What links all the elements is a return-ing motif, like a refrain, of a woman lifting and lowering her head. The woman is the observer of the events in the film. In one of the aforementioned scenes the wig becomes alive and drinks milk from a bottle; in another sequence two fencers from an old photograph are depicted in a battle; in another a woman kisses the mannequin's head…

Roman Polański's *Two Men and a Wardrobe* – another film from the Brussels competition, which won the third prize – represents yet another Surrealist grotesque, characteristic of the Polish cinema of the Thaw period. The origins of this tendency can be found in a film by Franciszka and Stefan Themerson, *Przygoda Człowieka Poczciwego* (*The Adventure of a Good Citizen*, 1937). Other representatives of this type of grotesque are *Rondo* (*Rondo*, 1958), *Kapelusz* (*Hat*, 1961) and *Szpital* (*Hospital*, 1962) by Janusz Majewski; *Hamleś* (*Little Hamlet*, 1960) by Jerzy Skolimowski and *Ssaki* (*Mammals*, 1962) by Polański. One of the recurring motifs in all of these films is an absurd, pointless journey that leads nowhere and loosely alludes to the odd marches from *Entr'acte* (René Clair, 1924; a speeding funeral march) or *The Seashell and the Clergyman* (Germaine Dulac, 1928; a priest walking on all fours). In *Two Men*, as in the Themersons' film, the characters carry a ward-robe to an unknown destination. They come out of the sea, to which they eventually return. In *Rondo* a waiter unexpectedly leaves the premises and takes off towards the far-off fields, while an astounded customer follows him. In *Mammals* two men walk through heavy snow carrying a sledge, only to disappear somewhere in the far white distance. In *Hat* a father takes his Boy Scout son for a walk without any purpose. In addition, *Rondo* and *Hospital* share a Kafkaesque atmosphere of distrust for public institutions that are on the one hand ordinary and on the other hostile (a restaurant and a hospital). A similar mood would later become a mark of the Czech and Polish cinema prior to the Prague Spring. It can be found in films such as *Postava k pod-pírání* (*Joseph Kilian*, 1963) by Pavel Juráček and Jan Schmidt and *O slavnosti a hostech* (*The Party and the Guests*, 1966) by Jan Němec. Certain formal connections to the Czech cinema can also be found in *Hat*, because in its artistic conventions – the actors in drawn, flat decorations – it resembles *Vynález zkázy* (*The Fabulous World of Jules Verne*, 1958) by Karel Zeman. A similar approach can also be seen in other Polish films of that period which combine artificial sets with actors, namely the films of Antoni Radzinowicz, *Allegro vivace* (1965) and *Harivari* (1967).

This atmosphere of close-to-Surrealism oddity characterises many other Polish films of that period: Polański's *Lampa* (*The Lamp*, 1959) and *Gdy spadają anioły* (*When Angels Fall*, 1959), as well as Tadeusz Makarczyński's *Czarodziej* (*The Sorcerer*, 1963). In *The Lamp*, which is a study on the life of objects inside a doll-maker's workshop, there is the Surrealists' fascination (as well as Bruno Schulz's) with mannequins. *Angels*, on the other hand, shows a close spiritual link to Jean Renoir's *La petite marchande d'allumettes* (*The Little Match Girl*, 1928). Both films, in addition to their visionary character, are connected by a similar ironic sentimentalism, as well as the main character being supported by alms. In both films the assumed artistic conventions allowed for the replacement of the city with a tacky model. In Polański's film there is also an unusual gallery of types visiting the main place of action, namely a public toilet.

The Sorcerer by Makarczyński, one of the most neglected of all Polish directors, is a separate piece of work. The film is grotesque and shocking at the same time in its attempt to bring back the nightmare of World War II. Once again, the film's conventions belong to the Kafkaesque and Surrealist traditions. An empty beach, with an absurd shooting range, minded by a farcical officer. Children who come to visit are given machine guns to shoot the 'enemy': plush animals and dolls. As a reward, the children are given school bags and are sent marching towards… their own execution. A sentimental officer now plays his violin while waiting for the next group of children. Makarczyński managed to turn the absurd of *Entr'acte* into a moving metaphor, which touches on the nature of genocide.

An entirely separate position within Polish cinema of the early 1960s is occupied by Kazimierz Urbański, who experimented with form in the most consistent fashion. From the very beginning of his career it was clear that Urbański had little regard for the classical division of genres and film techniques. What interested him was the nature of cinema, the movement of forms on the screen, their visual expression, their relationships to each other: in other words, everything which inspired the makers of so-called 'pure cinema'. Urbański made documentary impressions (*Gips – romanca / A Plaster Romance*, 1960; *Diabły / Devils*, 1963), as well as animated films (*Igraszki / Games*, 1962; *Materia / The Matter*, 1962), and a mixture of both poetics (*Słodkie rytmy / Sweet Rhythms*, 1965). He used new materials (wool yarn in *The Matter*) and experimented with new techniques, such as thermic impact on film emulsion (*Sweet Rhythms*). The critics, who often could not handle the unique and innovative nature of Urbański's films, criticised him for weak narrative and the prominence of form over content, as if the poetry of movement could not exist in its own right and for itself. For the director himself, the largest burden was the fact that his films were expected to have some connection to 'life'. But the times were such that a film which, at least in the opinion of the decision-makers, did not express anything had little chance of seeing the light of day. Nonetheless, *Games*, *The Matter*, *Moto-gas* (*Moto-gaz*, 1963), *Sweet Rhythms* and *Tren zbója* (*Brigand's Train*, 1967) are highly original pieces, which create a separate category within Polish animation.

House, *Two Men* and *Kineforms* were not the only Polish films that were noticed during the 1958 Expo in Brussels. In the feature film competition, a debut film by the well-established Polish author Tadeusz Konwicki (*Mała Apokalipsa*, 1979),[11] *Ostatni dzień lata* (*The Last Day of the Summer*), received the award for the best experimental film. *The Last Day* was yet another phenomenon in the Polish cinema of the Thaw period.[12] Made in the summer of 1957 by a crew of only five people, and outside of the structures of the Polish film industry (although officially promoted, like *Once Upon a Time...* and *House*, by the film collective Zespół Filmowy 'Kadr'), this largely improvised auteur film is a work that predates John Cassavetes' *Shadows* (1959). *The Last Day* had no equivalent in Polish cinema until the emergence of so-called 'off-cinema' ('kino offowe') in the 1990s. According to Mateusz Werner:

> *The Last Day of Summer* was so far ahead of its time that there was no response to it. A ground breaking movie which appeared by some chance, unexpectedly, it caused no ferment, sowed no seeds of rebellion, founded no school.[13]

Konwicki's film tells the story of an impossible love, as two people marked by the experiences of war meet on a deserted beach after the tourist season. She is older than him and lost her loved one in the war. She is thus unable to open up to new feelings. He keeps trying to overcome her distance, while guarding his own secret. The characters' alienation is reinforced by the desert-like dune landscape and the vastness of the sea. Six hours of the life of the protagonists are condensed into sixty-six minutes of screen time, during which not much happens in the sense of a conventional narrative.

As was the case with *The Last Day of the Summer*, which was not followed by any comparable works, all of the aforementioned films remain a separate phenomenon in Polish cinema. They did not create a unified front, and neither did they establish a movement. By and large, these films were not appreciated by Polish critics. They are, nonetheless, a characteristic document of the epoch: the time of the post-Stalinist Thaw.

Translated by Kamila Kuc

NOTES

1 Karol Irzykowski, 'Śmierć kinematografu', *Świat*, no. 21, 1913; Marcin Giżycki, 'Irzykowski, Kuczkowski, and the Tradition of "Visionary Film" in Poland', *Afterimage*, no. 13, 1987, p. 84.

2 This film was released on a DVD, together with other films concerning subjects related to Chopin, to commemorate the composer's 200th birthday anniversary: *Chopin: Film Motifs* (Warszawa: Filmoteka Narodowa, 2010, DVD 3).

3 Before this the artist was showing them to his friends in his flat.

4 Juliusz Garztecki, 'Andrzej Pawłowski', *Ty i ja*, no. 6, 1963; Jan Trzupek, 'Wprowadzenie', *Andrzej Pawłowski 1925–1986* (Katowice: Galeria Sztuki Współczesnej BWA, 2002), p. 15.

5 Wiesław Borowski, *Tadeusz Kantor* (Warszawa: Wydawnictwa Artystyczne i Filmowe, 1982), p. 41 and after.

6 Jan Krzysztof Malkiewicz, 'Kolorowy eksperyment', *Ekran*, no. 5, 1957, p. 4.

7 *Competition du film experimental*, 2–7, IV (Brussels: Cinémathèque de Belgique, 1958), pp. 72–73: 'Le film présente un être humain à un tournant de sa vie, le surprend au moment où il se rend compte de sa dernière chance perdue. La convention spécifique dont se sert le réalisateur consiste à présenter le monde extérieur, réel ou imaginaire comme vu par le héros.'

8 Rafał Marszałek, 'Maszyny na rykowisku', *Jan Lenica w Kwancie* (Warszawa: Centrum Klubowe Politechniki Warszawskiej 'Riwiera-Remont', 1976), p. 53.

9 Stanisław Janicki, 'Rozmawiamy z J. Lenicą i W. Borowczykiem', *Film*, no. 31, 1957, p. 6.

10 Jan Lenica, 'Film i formy narracji wizualnej', *Projekt*, no. 6, 1970. See also Giżycki, 'The "Red Wall of Surrealism": Experimental and Animated Film After the Thaw', Kamila Wielebska and Kuba Mikurda, eds., *A Story of Sin: Surrealism in Polish Cinema* (Cracow-Warsaw: Korporacja Ha!Art, 2010).

11 Tadeusz Konwicki, *A Minor Apocalypse* (New York: Farrar, Straus, Giroux, 1983).

12 The film was also awarded the Grand Prix in the category of experimental film in the International Documentary Short Film Contest in Venice in 1958.

13 Mateusz Werner, 'A Rebellion a la Polonaise', Łukasz Ronduda and Barbara Piwowarska, eds., *Polish New Wave: The History of a Phenomenon That Never Existed* (Warsaw: Centre for Contemporary Art, 2008), pp. 8–9. See the reprint of Werner's chapter in this collection.

CHAPTER FIVE

AVANT-GARDE EXPLOITS:
THE CULTURAL HIGHS AND LOWS OF POLISH ÉMIGRÉ CINEMA

Jonathan L. Owen

WESTERN PROMISE

A memorable running gag in Walerian Borowczyk's 1967 animated feature *Le Théâtre de M. et Mme. Kabal* (*The Theatre of Mr. and Mrs. Kabal*) concerns the voyeuristic exploits of Mr. Kabal. Confined to a barren Absurdist nowhere with his formidable, Ubuesque wife, the diminutive Kabal brings himself some relief by peeping through binoculars at bikini-clad girls – live-action and full-colour apparitions whose appeal can only be enhanced by their onto-logical superiority over the cartoon, monochrome Kabals. Such scenes may evoke the shopworn image of the Eastern bloc citizen peering in from a world of drabness and stringency at the sensuous beauties and freedoms of 'the West': Borowczyk, the Polish émigré, in that respect reprises the gaze of the elfin young Roman Polański at the distant Paris skyline in his own Absurdist fable of oppression *Le Gros et le maigre* (*The Fat and the Lean*, 1961), a longing look all too easily glossed as the migratory fantasy of another future émigré (autobiographical insinuation is of course the default critical position with Polański). Mr. Kabal is likewise a sneaking witness to that sexual revolution that Polański would experience first hand through his Playboy Club carousals in 1960s London. Yet Kabal's scopophilic pleasures are only permitted for so

Fig. 12 *The Theatre of Mr. and Mrs. Kabal* (Walerian Borowczyk, 1967)

long, as in each of the titillatory tableaux he espies, a short straggly-bearded old man reveals himself, to repel Kabal's gaze in a fury and sully these lush pin-up shots.

The apparition of this grotesque beau at once halts voyeuristic gratification and harshly denies a proffered erotic enjoyment, a reversal or disappointment that might be seen satirically to note the failures of 'Western promise', the façade that is the free world's garish declamation of liberty and satisfaction. Alternatively, a psychoanalytic reading might cast these vignettes of erotic frustration as a scenario of Oedipal, and pre-Oedipal, rivalries: the old man indeed suggests the woman-hoarding primal father of Freudian myth, something that makes him a hirsute and buffoonish variant of Noah Cross (John Huston) from Polański's *Chinatown* (1974) (the binocular-wielding Kabal standing as a lewder Jake Gittes). Or do these abortive openings into live-action rather expound the Lacanian message of an intrinsically impossible enjoyment, of blocked access to 'the real'? Brimming with interpretive possibilities, Borowczyk's offhand gag displays several of his cinema's most noteworthy qualities: glimmers of barbed satire and psychic penetration, grave sexual competition, visual incongruity, pessimistic humour, even the mooted union of art and reality. At the same time, these titillatory and 'commercial' images of bikini girls, parodic and hastily sabotaged though they may be, constitute a signal, ominous if one likes, of Borowczyk's ultimate 'descent' into softcore pornography and sexploitation. To what extent is Mr. Kabal's lechery an image of Borowczyk himself, the émigré filmmaker peering through his viewfinder at 'Western' excesses?

Peeping and voyeurism are dominant motifs in Polański as in Borowczyk, and even crop up in the work of a less notorious, if equally critically unstable, Polish émigré filmmaker, Jerzy Skolimowski: one strange encounter in *Moonlighting* (1982) has the displaced Polish builder Nowak (played by Jeremy Irons) catching sight of a topless woman in a London shop window, an image that suggestively fuses (female) sexuality, distance, emigration and commodification, not to mention a Surrealist sense for the fortuitously apprehended marvel. Above all, though, such images are significant as both the admission of prurient or exploitative tendencies and the expression of the distanced gaze, the 'outsider' status that is arguably indispensable to the true avant-garde artist. Polish émigré cinema unites the excesses of 'high' and 'low' culture, the extreme demands of avant-garde formal articulation and bleak, dogged philosophical investigation and what may seem the grossly 'insider' phenomena of sensational affect, submission to generic conventions and an unabashed handling of the body that ranges from the sensuous to the horrific by way of the vulgar. Andrzej Żuławski's *Possession* (1981) presents the apex and summation of that fusion in its female protagonist's sibylline disquisition on the warring sisters of faith and chance, a discourse capped by the metaphor of mud-wrestling women. Żuławski's film, like Borowczyk's *La Bête* (*The Beast*, 1975) or Polański's *What?* (*Che?*, 1972), is far from respectable arthouse fare, yet do sensational or 'commercial' elements necessarily vitiate the avant-garde qualities that have been claimed for these filmmakers? Might 'respectability' itself comprise a greater threat to the latter? And can these filmmakers' straddling of (or falling between) the various stools of acceptability be considered an avant-garde strategy in itself, even a concordance with that 'Outsider Art' proper that the historical avant-gardes so valorised, creative expression conceived as oblivious and obsessionally self-pleasuring?

This chapter aims to explore that tangle of high and low influences, of the recondite and the reviled, that informs Polish émigré cinema, along with the extent to which these filmmakers uphold the avant-garde's radical, disruptive ambitions. By 'Polish émigré cinema' I refer here to Borowczyk, Polański, Skolimowski and Żuławski: if animator Jan Lenica, another émigré and an early Borowczyk collaborator, is relatively neglected here, this is not because I consider Lenica's work less interesting or accomplished, but rather because it reveals less negotiation with the characteristic modes and imperatives of capitalist production and thus raises fewer questions regarding the coincidence of the avant-garde and the commercial, Surrealism and sensationalism (Lenica's corporate patronage as a poster designer perhaps tells a different story). Discussing these filmmakers specifically as émigrés under the West's impact entails the difficulty of cleanly separating their 'Polish' and 'Western' periods. Their initiations into Western film production generally preceded emigration proper: Polański made *The Fat and the Lean* in France before leaving Poland in 1963, while Skolimowski was invited to make *Le Depart* (1967) in Belgium, before a political storm over *Ręce do gory* (*Hands Up!*, 1967/1981) forced his own emigration. Nor did emigration spell an end to working in the socialist system: Borowczyk and Żuławski would be invited back to Poland for *Dzieje grzechu* (*The Story of Sin*, 1975) and, unhappily, *Na srebrnym globie* (*On the Silver Globe*, 1976/1988). Communist authorities proved strangely susceptible to West-established reputations, and the notion of mutually hostile and enclosed blocs belies how far East and West were 'communicating vessels' with regard to cultural product. It is claimed that the 'high output of aggressively artistic films' by Communist Europe was 'a response to demand from Western markets', with the scooping of some prestigious American or West European prize (such as the Brussels Experimental Film Festival's Grand Prix, awarded to Borowczyk and Lenica's *Dom* (*House*, 1958)) a major boost to a Czech or Polish director's stature and comfort back home.[1] This implies a partial determination of East European film production by Western fashions, the people's democracies' dancing to the cultural tune of their nominal enemy. The filmmakers discussed here were themselves culturally cosmopolitan figures prior to emigration, boasting concrete affiliations with Western countries, especially France (Polański was born in Paris; Żuławski studied at the French film school IDHEC). They were thus always already shaped – 'corrupted' – by a Western context, intensely transnational before the term became academic common currency. For such reasons this chapter, while focused on Western avant-garde and commercial influences, will not confine itself to films of literal Western provenance.

With that said, distinctions can still be drawn in more than one of these cases between Poland-based and émigré careers. Skolimowski's Polish films, for instance, are distinguishable from those he made abroad on account of their stylised dialogue and richly composed travelling shots, a complex orchestration of poetic effects that edges into the abstract and oneiric. This Polish period is easily the more 'avant-garde' to the extent that the latter term chiefly signifies such dense, anti-realist formalism. While the rich formal language of Borowczyk's animated shorts survived intact its relocation to France, his Polish-made work is the more overtly avant-garde at a temperamental or attitudinal level. *Był sobie raz* (*Once Upon a Time*, 1957), made with Lenica, is self-consciously redolent of avant-garde iconoclasm, right down to its title, an allusion to the opening inter-title of Buñuel's *Un Chien Andalou* (1929) and a mocking prelude to the demolition of established narrative forms and professional artistic standards. A 'story' of the peregrinations of an identity-shifting black blob across a white background adorned only with cut-out illustrations, geometric shapes and sparse, infantile scrawls, *Once Upon a Time* merrily exhibits a scorched-earth, zero-point negativism, and is only ever a few jumbled figures away from the key avant-garde trope of the 'blank page'.[2] Similarly, Skolimowski and Żuławski assumed the bellicose, refusenik stance of the angry young man in both their work and persona while in Poland, a stance that Skolimowski, at least, did not preserve in the West but translated into a less bumptious, more haunted and embattled outsiderdom. Skolimowski's young protagonists are at once adrift in a pragmatist contemporary Poland and alienated from a self-romanticising older generation, the latter attitude cruelly endorsed by the director in the 1966 *Bariera* (*Barrier*), with its clownish, paper-hatted chorus of self-proclaimed war veterans. Skolimowski even translated this iconoclastic stance into *nouvelle vague*-style cinematic Oedipalism through his insolent attack on Andrzej Wajda, veritable 'father of Polish cinema', over Wajda's script for *Niewinni czarodzieje* (*Innocent Sorcerers*, 1960). Żuławski, a firebrand in any context, has never been more scathing than in his broadsides against other Polish filmmakers: his denunciation of the Cinema of Moral Concern, Polish film's dominant trend of the 1970s, as a '*coup d'etat* against cinema' approximates Artaud's invectives against a text-bound French theatre in both import and ferocity.

It is impossible to speculate how these filmmakers' careers would have developed had they stayed in Poland, or whether this would have better

Fig. 13 *Hands Up!* (Jerzy Skolimowski, 1967/1981)

profited the 'avant-garde' character, generally speaking, of their art. Yet it is very probable that they would have faced continuing difficulties with censorship. For all that Skolimowski played out his Young Turk irreverence in a more forthright manner while in Poland, we should remember that his emigration was a forced choice sealed by the satirically loaded poster image of a four-eyed Stalin in *Hands Up!* together with Skolimowski's intransigent refusal to cut the offending scene. Żuławski endured similar run-ins: his eighteenth-century-set second film, *Diabeł* (*The Devil*, 1972), widely considered an allegory of the officially provoked student revolts of 1968, was banned, nominally for its violence, while production on his super-baroque science-fiction epic *On the Silver Globe* was shut down just before completion, the film interpreted by Poland's new Vice-Minister of Culture as a coded depiction of anti-Stalinist struggle. Thus, if we consider subversive critique, contemporaneity and profound meditation on one's socio-historical circumstances as avant-garde characteristics, the cases of Skolimowski and Żuławski attest to state socialism's limiting of options for the avant-garde artist. The fiasco of *On the Silver Globe*, a densely layered work that prompts multiple interpretations along with outright bewilderment, further illustrates the problems faced by complex, unconventional aesthetic practices in a political culture for which opacity spelled masked subversion.

It is true, however, that the checks and blows of socialist officialdom have their capitalist counterpart in the scuppered projects that litter these filmmakers' Western careers, even that of the 'bankable' and household-famous Polański: the artistic potential of such unrealised works as a Polański's *Master and Margarita* or a Borowczyk's Sade biopic makes their non-existence agonising (by contrast, *On the Silver Globe* does at least exist in some form, and Żuławski's insertion of present-day *vérité* footage into the released version, patching over the lacunae of the sabotaged shoot, ironically makes it an even more fragmentary, dislocated and 'avant-garde' work than originally intended). As for the crassest commercial corners into which the Western marketplace might force a filmmaker, it is doubtful that Borowczyk would have succumbed to the nadir of *Emmanuelle 5* (1987) had he remained in Poland. Then again, he would probably not have made his great anti-totalitarian fantasy *Goto, l'île d'amour* (*Goto, Island of Love*, 1968). Moreover, Polish Communist cinema was itself awash with 'safe' and substandard commercial fare by the time Martial Law ended.[3]

Yet I do not wish to characterise Polish émigré cinema's excursions into genre or even exploitation cinema as the inherent corruption of an exemplary artistic purity. Commercial assignments and genre exercises may have yielded uninspired work, from the clumsy comedy of Skolimowski's *The Adventures of Gerard* (1970) to Polański's soporific horror-noir *The Ninth Gate* (1999), yet at their most successful such engagements have entailed the imaginative and subversive rewriting of familiar genres and ensured wider exposure for the troubling preoccupations of Surrealism and the Absurd. More importantly, as I intend to demonstrate, Polish émigré filmmakers' syntheses of nominally high and low cultures have served to emphasise the shared concerns of avant-garde and popular cinema, a destabilisation of cultural boundaries that in itself reflects vanguard developments in Western art cinema during the 1960s and 1970s. Such syntheses also act to foreground the mix of subtlety and vulgarity, of the extroverted and obscure, that was present in these filmmakers' works from the start. But this encounter with the West was far from simply a collision with the commercial, for these filmmakers partook no less of a post-war West European avant-garde and modernist scene whose resurgent energies broadly coincided with their own early, trailblazing years. It is with an overview of these less contentious inputs that I shall proceed, before entering the 'perilous' waters of sleaze and sensation.

ART, LIFE AND REVOLUTION: WESTERN AVANT-GARDE CONNECTIONS

Individualists by temperament, none of these filmmakers properly belonged to any of the avant-garde groupings that I shall discuss here. It is not even known whether all the groups mentioned exerted a direct influence. Loose, personally grounded connections do abound, including Borowczyk's close friendship with the Surrealist writer André Pieyre de Mandiargues (himself only ever on the fringes of André Breton's group) and such tidbits as the youthful meetings of Polański's long-time co-writer, Gerard Brach, with Breton and another Surrealist luminary, Benjamin Péret. Yet what I am principally concerned to chart is a shared engagement in the same artistic practices, anxieties and problematics, most important among the latter perhaps being the key avant-garde concern with dissolving the boundaries of art and life.

Surrealism and the Theatre of the Absurd are the movements with which these four filmmakers are most commonly associated. Such affinities are conspicuous from their earliest films: thus, Borowczyk and Lenica's *Dom* and Polański's *Dwaj ludzie z szafą* (*Two Men and a Wardrobe*, 1958), aptly garlanded in the eminent Surrealist locale of Brussels, strike us as vintage Surrealism and Absurdism respectively. Considered by Parker Tyler a '*ne plus ultra* of concentrated avant-gardism',[4] *House* is visually immediately assimilable to classic Surrealism – with strong shades of Dada – as well as standing as a work that penetrates to the movement's morbid core, beneath the Bretonian carapace of 'love and liberation'.[5] A Victorian playbox of ravenous objects, automated minds and bodies, jerky Muybridge duellists and male mannequins that splinter upon erotic contact, *Dom* is a domain pervaded by destructive desire, psychic compulsion and uncanny confusions between life and death, the animate and inanimate. *Two Men and a Wardrobe* is a fable of random cruelty and social hostility towards the outsider that evokes Ionesco's critique of conformity, while the constantly carried wardrobe is a 'Sisyphean' burden that inevitably recalls Camus. Polański even frames his film with a gesture of existential reductivism whereby the succession of pricks and kicks comes to embody life itself: the protagonists are first 'born' from the sea and finally vanish back into it, a return to the peace of oblivion. Unsurprisingly, given the close identities of the two movements, Surrealist and Absurdist influences are seldom exclusive in these directors' films, as this example shows: Polański's wardrobe equally suggests a Surrealist burden of transgressive desire (comparable to the ubiquitous sack of Buñuel's *Cet obscur objet du désir* (*That Obscure Object of Desire*, 1977) or the phantasy-filled wardrobe of Jan Švankmajer's *Žvahlav aneb šatičky slaměného Huberta* (*Jabberwocky*, 1971)), a reading that chimes with interpretations of the film's protagonists as a gay couple.[6]

While Surrealism never had an official outpost in Poland, the Absurd was well-rooted there: Sławomir Mrożek, Poland's most celebrated Absurd dramatist, arguably looms large over the work of Polański, Skolimowski and Borowczyk, with the hooded figures and deathly stakes of *Goto*'s forced combats an overt echo of Mrożek's parable of oppression *Striptease* (1961). One might also argue that Polański, say, adheres more closely to Eastern Europe's more grounded variant of the Absurd, centrally concerned with authority, power struggles and social dysfunction, than to the metaphysical enquiry of a Beckett, despite the strong presence of Beckettian tropes (as well as Beckett stalwart Jack MacGowran) in such films as *Cul-de-Sac* (1966). Even such a flamboyantly supernatural and psychologically focused work as *Rosemary's Baby* (1968) also tackles social manipulation and venal complicity. It is worth addressing here the risks of accommodating to Western models works whose real inspirations lie elsewhere: Daniel Bird[7] has suggested that what we identify as 'Surrealist' in Borowczyk or Żuławski actually represents the influence of Poland's long tradition of Romanticism. If such an argument is over-totalising, and Borowczyk's approving acquaintance with Surrealism on record, it is nonetheless plausible that the Polish Romantic heritage of dreams, morbid loves, occultism, passionate individualism and formal heterogeneity has helped shape these filmmakers (Breton in any case famously declared

Surrealism 'the prehensile tail' of Romanticism, so the boundaries between the two movements are already considerably blurred).[8]

Yet these filmmakers also significantly distance themselves from the Romantic tradition, broadly conceived, with Polański's and Skolimowski's early work in particular comprising a cynical dialogue with the idealising, martyrological and heroic traditions of Polish culture. The aforementioned indictment of bogus heroism in Skolimowski's *Barrier* suggests, for instance, that it is a short step from the Romantic to the romanticised. In another striking image from *Barrier* – the protagonist 'jousting' a car with an antique sabre he has inherited – Skolimowski at once parodies the notorious wartime myth of Polish cavalrymen battling German tanks and suggests the anachronistic status of Romantic nobility. Romantic tropes and gestures are indeed 'Absurd' in a world where cynical self-interest prevails and utopian ideals have been diverted into consumer promises, although Skolimowski is hardly unsympathetic to such a legacy: Polish or otherwise, his heroes are creatures of quixotic gestural extravagance, Romantic activism translated into the Surrealist *acte gratuit*. The pathetic George in Polański's *Cul-de-Sac* might be considered a crueller skewering of Romanticism, something implicitly signposted by George's reverence for Sir Walter Scott, the Scottish Romantic writer in whose ancient seat George resides. In an unmistakeably 'Polish' touch of self-mythification, George has even misled his wife into believing he was in the cavalry rather than a tank division during the war. Yet George's utter inability to act heroically perhaps only reiterates in harsher fashion the partition-era Romantics' fixation on their own revolutionary impotence. Generally speaking, however, Polański's and Skolimowski's self-conscious 'modernity' and demystifying cynicism separate these filmmakers from the less ambivalently Romantic 'Polish School' of the 1950s and align them with contemporaneous cinematic and cultural developments in Western Europe.

One key difference from the Polish cinematic mainstream concerns the representation of World War II and the Holocaust. Unlike, say, Wajda, these four filmmakers have rarely addressed the war and its atrocities directly: such realities rather inhabit their films in a manner both oblique and sensorially oppressive, even when Occupation-era Poland comprises the literal locale, as in Żuławski's *Trzecia część nocy* (*Third Part of the Night*, 1971). Concentration camp allegory is often signalled only in resonant objects and spaces, from the trucks and trains of *Hands Up!* and Żuławski's *L'Amour braque* (*Limpet Love*, 1985) to the widespread use of 'concentrationary' space in Skolimowski, Borowczyk and Polański. Raymond Durgnat has highlighted the persistent invocation of the 'concentration universe' and the 'terrible building' by such French 'Left Bank Group' directors as Alain Resnais and Chris Marker,[9] and indeed a work like Resnais's great Holocaust documentary *Nuit et brouillard* (*Night and Fog*, 1955) is specifically comparable to the oneiric allegory of twentieth-century atrocity in Borowczyk's *Les Jeux des anges* (1964) and *Goto*. Similarly to Borowczyk, Resnais mines a fearful Surrealism from traumatic reality, producing a vision that abounds in uncanny confusions and eerie part-objects (the piles of teeth and hair) and reveals the grotesque imposition of ordering and classification. As I have argued elsewhere,[10] Borowczyk can be considered an honorary member of the French *nouvelle vague*'s 'Left Bank' wing – just as Skolimowski, so devoted to energy and autobiography, is an affiliate of its better-known *Cahiers du cinéma* faction.

This most famous of film waves might be considered too 'mainstream', institutionally and artistically, to constitute a 'true' avant-garde, yet it did comprise a vanguard in commercial art cinema and one that influenced more 'orthodox' avant-gardists in Britain and the USA.[11] If the *Cahiers* companions indulged in the brash polemics typical of twentieth-century avant-gardes, the Left Bank filmmakers were more absorbed in the non-cinematic avant-garde developments of post-war France, evident for instance in Resnais's collaboration with *nouveau roman* exponent Alain Robbe-Grillet. The Surrealist influence on Marker, Resnais and Georges Franju is well-established, yet these filmmakers' concern with systems and classification aligns them with a more contemporary 'structural turn' in French avant-garde culture, as exemplified by the permutation of limited elements in both the *nouveau roman* and Boulez's serial music.[12] Borowczyk is similarly fascinated by structures and taxonomic principles, as is evident in the animated shorts *L'Encyclopédie de Grand-Maman en 13 volumes* (*Grandmother's Encyclopedia in 13 Volumes*, 1963) and *Le Dictionnaire de Joachim* (*Joachim's Dictionary*, 1965), structured around the eponymous classificatory forms. If Borowczyk is often associated with anarchic Surrealism and perverse eroticism, he also explores the Surrealist perversity of all attempts at organising reality,[13] and the playfulness with which he simultaneously establishes and sabotages order links him closely to the experimental French literary circle OuLiPo.[14]

The OuLiPo writers founded their literary endeavours on structural and linguistic constraints, most famously the lipogram (the avoidance of a particular letter), a tactic that perhaps finds its parallel or inversion in *Goto*'s restrictive use of names beginning with the letter 'G'. *Grandmother's Encyclopedia*, an alphabetical exposition of early forms of travel, ends after a mere three entries, a refusal of completion that accords with Georges Perec's insistence that any system requires 'some play', some 'creaking',[15] and compares with Raymond Queneau's decision to leave his celebrated *Exercises de style* (*Exercises in Style*, 1947) at 99 variations of the same anecdote, rather

                                          THE STRUGGLE FOR FORM

than 100. Such incompletion asserts the provisional and imperfect nature of the systematising attempts evoked, and suggests also a deferral to the spectator's own imaginative and enumerative powers, a means of inspiring our own additional encyclopedic entries and volumes. This gesture, along with Borowczyk's deployment of 'ready-made' alphabetical structures and his dependence on the combinatory, relatively artless method of collaged cut-outs, presents a striving towards those ambitions that, in Peter Bürger's strict definition, distinguishes the authentically avant-garde from 'neo-avant-garde' imitation: the will to integrate art into social life, turning the spectator into a collaborator and transforming creative production from elite activity into common practice.[16] OuLiPo's own concern to erode the barriers between art and society prevents us from considering it yet another 'institutionalised' neo-avant-garde movement. Borowczyk also shares with OuLiPo his fascination with games and play: *Goto*, which depicts a society where mortal contests between prisoners replace trials and a governor's election is decided by spins of a shoe-cleaning implement, is specifically comparable to Perec's novel *W, ou le souvenir d'enfance* (*W, or the Memory of Childhood*, 1975) as a vision of cruel yet ludic dystopia. Menacing and perverse games abound equally in Polański and Skolimowski.

Another grouping with links to Polish émigré cinema is *Panique*, a loose artistic affiliation founded in Paris in 1962 and, like OuLiPo, tangential to the Surrealist movement. Two of *Panique*'s three founders, Chilean director Alejandro Jodorowsky and Spanish playwright Fernando Arrabal, were themselves émigrés; the other, illustrator and writer Roland Topor, was the child of Polish Jews. Émigré status and national or ethnic otherness are clearly conducive to avant-garde preoccupations and tropes, the conflicted belonging and contested, multiplicitous identity of the émigré underpinning, for instance, the fractured, hybrid, transnational non-places that haunt Absurdist drama and much of this cinema, from *Goto*'s mash-up of Stalinist austerity and frayed Victorian pomp to the de-literalised Berlin Wall locale of Żuławski's *Possession*, actual 'no man's land' rent asunder by a hubbub of international accents. Polański's *Le Locataire* (*The Tenant*, 1976), adapted from a novel by Topor, can be seen as a reflexive comment on the resonances between 'avant-garde' anxieties and the fears of the émigré or outsider. The tale of a retiring man of Polish origin, convinced his neighbours are plotting to turn him into the suicidal former tenant of his Paris apartment, *The Tenant* ingeniously fuses major themes of the Absurd and the Surreal: the terrorising community and interpersonal dysfunction from the former, self-alienation and psychic dissolution from the latter. The protagonist Trelkovsky's ultimate transformation into his female predecessor, along with the film's nightmare intimations of corporeal fragmentation, vividly dramatise the crises, fractures and negotiations of identity undergone by the émigré. Yet *The Tenant* is also an allegory of persecution with subtle historical echoes and implications of Jewishness,[17] and Trelkovsky's transformation and loss of self-identity might themselves be considered the internalisation of a socially despised otherness, the point at which Trelkovsky becomes 'other' even to himself. Trelkovsky's final, abased masquerade of femininity not only presents, or pre-empts, authorial insecurities about sexual identity, but also heightens the abject image of national or ethnic otherness as perceived by its host culture.

The Polish émigré auteurs are additionally linked to *Panique* by a playful and relativist stance towards ideological and philosophical positions. *Panique* cultivated bad taste, visceral shock and scatological outrage in its theatrical events, and proclaimed its acceptance of all cultural forms, including comics, television, rock music and pornography: tendencies with supreme relevance for these often notorious filmmakers. Jodorowsky propounded happening-style events (*éphémères*) that would 'eliminate the spectator' and 'take theatre out of the theatre',[18] thus aligning *Panique* with key practices and concerns of the 1960s theatrical avant-garde: rejection of the bounded space of the stage, attempted breakdown of the distinction between performers and spectators, and integration of the latter into a common project of creation and self-realisation. Like Richard Schechner, the Living Theatre and the widely influential Polish director Jerzy Grotowski, Jodorowsky exemplifies a post-Artaudian tradition that subordinates text to gesture and invests theatre with therapeutic and utopian goals, the promise of individual and collective transformation. That tradition thus maintains the extra-artistic ambition of the historical avant-gardes, while its transcendence of hermetic stage space and merging of spectators with professional performers again recall Bürger's formulation of the authentic avant-garde project, 'the sublation of art into the praxis of life'.[19] As in the work of *nouvelle vague* filmmaker Jacques Rivette, theatre and its integration into life remain a recurring point of reference for Polish émigré cinema. Jodorowsky's insistence that theatre might be made in an express train, an abattoir or a gay bar finds reinforcement in the extempore stageless performances that occur in these films, from the cattle-truck psychodrama of *Hands Up!* to a whooping, cavorting, Disney-masked bank robbery, complete with chorus-line coda, in *Limpet Love*. The fusion of performance with life is intensified by serious stakes and consequences, although, as with the games played throughout these films, these are often grave: arrest and violence are risked in *Limpet Love*, while the male protagonist of Borowczyk's *Cérémonie d'amour* (*Love Rites*, 1988) is physically lacerated and symbolically stripped of his identity at the hands of a play-acting erotic partner.

Such mergings of theatre and real life could hardly be described in ideal terms, and these films offer little suggestion of the positive or utopian possibilities of theatre, or art in general. Experimental theatre and its political ambitions are directly addressed in Skolimowski's *Success Is the Best Revenge* (1984), whose autobiographically conceived protagonist is Rodak (Michael York), an émigré Polish director mounting a polemical production about Martial Law. Yet Rodak's elaborate theatrical piece might be considered a reduction of the avant-garde's integrative ambitions to hollow, tricksy formalism, for no real action is permitted on the part of the spectators, who are driven through the large-scale 'happening' in a London bus (a scuffle between 'protestors' and 'militias' might be genuine, but this is unclear). Moreover, as Rodak's wife implies, there is little prospect that this production will have any further real-world impact, beyond preventing Rodak from ever returning to Communist Poland (the piece thus suggests another flamboyant, futile Skolimowski gesture). If Żuławski, unlike Skolimowski, derives much of his own directorial approach from Artaud and Grotowski, his work no less pessimistically rejects the utopian commitments of this theatrical tradition. The performances Żuławski elicits from his actors, as convulsive and as disciplined as the Balinese theatre of Artaud's encomium, lurch towards art-life integration in the most ferocious fashion, their excesses a form of headlong spectatorial assault that seems to smash the confines of the screen, along with the boundaries of acting and authentic expression. Yet the annihilatory visions that end several Żuławski films pervert the millenarian motifs of Artaud and his followers, suggesting a bleak variant on Grotowskian scenarios of 'rebirth' or the revolutionary and regenerative 'Apocalypse' of the Living Theatre's *Frankenstein* (1965).[20] Isabelle Adjani's notorious subway breakdown in *Possession* is a terrifying 'workout' (for character and actress alike) that spawns a literal monster and perhaps precipitates the film's apocalyptic climax: an unholy 'immaculate conception' lacking the redemptive flavour of Grotowski's own Christian-inspired conceits.

If Polish émigré cinema problematises the revolutionary capacity of art, this may comprise less a reflection on art's own limits than the expression of a broader pessimism regarding political change. *Possession*'s subway scene also intimates the monsters born from psychic derepression, a cautionary display that runs counter to much avant-garde libertarianism. Yet such warnings are ironically situated in a cinema that has frequently been condemned and censored for its own licentious image-making. My next section deals precisely with this cinema's complex negotiation of the licentious, the 'exploitative' and the disreputable, aiming ultimately to illuminate the secret affinities between avant-garde and commercial cultures.

This section examines how these filmmakers destabilise cultural boundaries and question established aesthetic values. One could thus do worse than begin with reference to Polański's *What?*, arguably the most maligned, unpopular and un-seen film of Polański's career (in a close race with *Pirates*, 1986). Sometimes taken for sexploitation or even pornography (and theatrically marketed as such), *What?* is actually a parodic reiteration of such forms that fuses 'high' and 'low' cultural tropes in a spirit of conscious outrage: even the film's nubile, *Candy*-esque heroine, who spends most of the film half-dressed and with one leg painted bright blue, is a synthesis of sex object and *objet d'art*. *What?* indulges a penchant in Polish émigré films for unorthodox meditation on the functions of art and its relation to commerce and titillation, a questioning itself evocative of avant-garde assaults on dominant aesthetic norms and proprieties. 'Great art' is a concrete presence in *What?*, in the form of the famous canvases that improbably clutter the film's plush villa locale. Yet this literal integration of art into reality makes for an abuse of art, the paintings besmirched by contact with the sordid and perverse pursuits of the villa's inhabitants. *What?* thus elaborates the suggestion made by fugitive criminal Dicky (Lionel Stander), in *Cul-de-Sac*, that George's (Donald

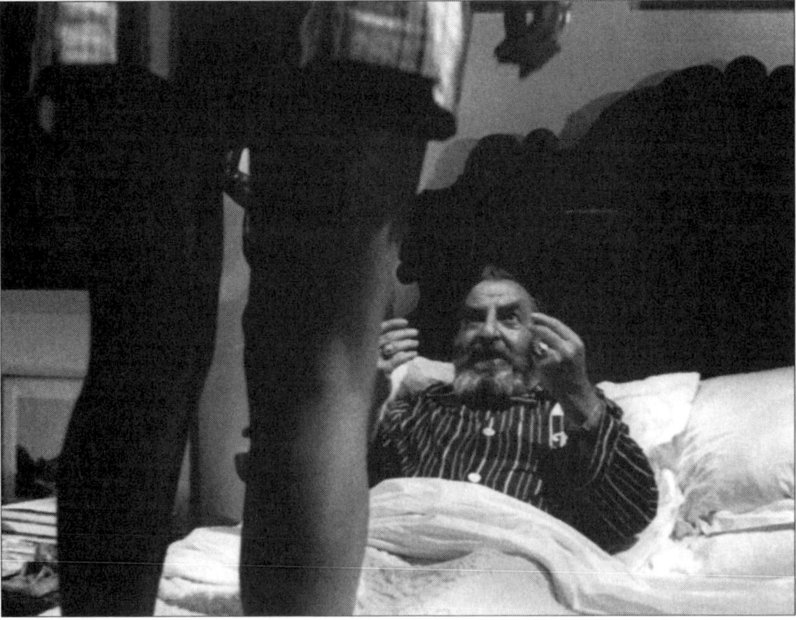

Fig. 14 *Che!* (Roman Polanski, 1972)

Pleasance) castle would be the perfect setting for wild orgies: Walter Scott forced to accommodate Sade. Polański's ultimate aim, however, is perhaps to refute Arnoldian associations of art and edification, of high culture and the high-minded. Noblart (Hugh Griffith), the aged, wheelchair-bound art collector who presides over *What?*'s villa, is himself – as his jokey name implies – an unflattering caricature of high culture in its prestige, seclusion and impotence. Yet Noblart has himself come to value the 'real thing' over its artistic representation: as another character explains, Noblart would now 'rather eat an apple than look at a picture of one'. As if to validate this twilight epiphany, the 'real thing' proves, tragically, more powerful than any painting: it is the unsimulated vision of Nancy's (Sydne Rome) nude breasts and genitals that finishes off the dying patriarch. If art is derided as but a 'feeble substitute for the experience of reality',[21] does the unadorned, desublimated character of pornography render this the superior form? *What?*'s teasing mimicry of pornographic codes, which evokes the genre only to withhold the explicit sex act, might be said to foreground the frustrations of pornography itself in failing to deliver 'the real' – however conceived – in any but the most superficial or attenuated sense. Pornography might thus be identified with art 'proper' as merely a more extreme variant of the latter's simulations.

Borowczyk links art and pornography in an equally provocative manner. A ribald drawing by Rembrandt, its signature conspicuously displayed, features among the erotic artefacts of *Une Collection particulière* (*A Particular Collection*, 1974), a reminder of the difficulties of clearly demarcating the artistic and the pornographic. The Renaissance-set first segment of *Heroïnes du mal* (*Three Immoral Women*, 1979) contains lusty thumbnails of Raphael and Michelangelo, the former shown to be erotically involved with his model, a duplicitous baker's daughter. Borowczyk hints at the libidinal and 'impure' origins of canonised culture, in the vein of critic Stephen Bayley's assertion that Botticelli's sitter for his *Birth of Venus* was a 'Florentine hooker', 'painted nude to titillate his client'.[22] Not only scandalous in itself, this linkage of art with sexual need also presents a model of engaged artistic reception at odds with the traditional view that art should invite 'tranquil, detached' contemplation.[23] If 'great art' can titillate, so can commercial culture express authentic emotion: the unironic use of well-worn 1970s pop songs in Borowczyk's *La Marge* (1976) seems intended to emphasise this, aptly enough for a story about the queasy junctures of commercial sex and romantic obsession. If Skolimowski, in *Success Is the Best Revenge*, suggests a firmer sense of the oppositions and antagonisms between 'serious' culture and sleazy commerce, he also implies their interdependence. The funding of Rodak's theatre piece is completed by the pornographer Montecurva, who turns up late into the performance and prompts the crowd of extras to burn the IOUs Rodak has given them: a redemptive final image of paper torches blazing in darkness is thus impelled by a sleaze merchant. That Montecurva, like Rodak, is himself an émigré serves to remind us that commercial success is one way of not being an outsider.

Such commentary of course reflects back on these filmmakers' own careers, all of which have strayed into territories beyond 'orthodox' arthouse material. Rather than striving, well-meaningly, to wrench these films out of their commercial contexts and dismiss the charges of pornography and 'selling out' laid at Borowczyk's or Polański's door, it should be acknowledged that these directors *do* belong to the sphere of commercial and exploitation cinema as much as that of European arthouse, at least at the level of production and packaging. It must be remembered that even the esteemed 'art-horror' of Polański's *Repulsion* (1965) was financed by a Soho company that made most of its revenue from a club showing 'timid soft-porn films' – ironically indeed for a work that perceptively rebukes the 'liberated' pleasures of so-called Swinging London.[24] Polański himself, moreover, conceived this film as a 'potboiler' that would ensure funding for the film that became *Cul-de-Sac*. Borowczyk's Franco-Italian co-production *Interno di un convento* (*Behind Convent Walls*, 1977) is an entry in the contemporaneous 'nunsploitation' genre, while *La Marge* was probably conceived as glossy softcore in the mode of the *Emmanuelle* films, as suggested by the casting of that series' lead actress, Sylvia Kristel (the film was even re-titled *Emmanuelle '77* in certain regions). To some extent, these filmmakers' absorption into an unsavoury nexus of schlock horror and Euro-sleaze was unintentional and retroactive, a matter of the imitations they themselves inspired: *Repulsion*, for instance, spawned the more overtly outrageous (if not uninteresting) knock-offs of José Bénazéraf's softcore *Frustration* (1971) and Mario Bava's *Shock* (1977), while Borowczyk's already sufficiently notorious *The Beast* saw its graphic equine couplings, furry priapism and 'star' Sirpa Lane redeployed in the Z-grade sci-fi-exploitation *La Bestia nello spazio* (*The Beast in Space*, Alfonso Brescia, 1980).

Yet the aura of sleaze and commercial excitement that surrounds these filmmakers was no mere imposition by calculating distributors or opportunistic rip-off artists, but rather reflects qualities genuinely inherent in their work, qualities evident, in fact, from their earliest and most 'respectable' films. *Nóż w wodzie* (*Knife in the Water*, 1961) and *Cul-de-Sac*, nominally among Polański's 'purest' and most original features, adopt the respective frameworks of the psychological and crime thriller, without forsaking those genres' tensions. The body-horror and monster-movie stylings of Żuławski's *Possession* alert us to how his earlier *The Devil* resembles a bloody Spaghetti

Western set amid the frozen plains of partitioned Poland. The early presence of generic, even sensational elements makes untenable the notion of some identifiable locus of commercial or exploitative 'decline' in these directors' careers – as does, conversely, the presence of ostentatiously avant-garde tendencies in their later work. To take one example, Borowczyk's last film, *Love Rites*, is a work of near-underground sensibilities, its cramped, crepuscular and often inscrutable images contrasting with its flights of baroque recitation and capricious, Godardian insertions of illustrations and texts. The characteristic presence of Borowczyk's own drawings and script further root the film in the artisanal aesthetic that has defined his work since the days of *Dom* (a word whose meaning, 'house', is appropriate to Borowczyk's home-made methods). Even the film's eroticism is a mix of visual reticence and final, tart savagery, and thus at odds with any conventionally titillatory aim.

This dense interweaving of high and low culture in Polish émigré cinema inscribes and foregrounds the surprisingly prevalent habit in post-war film exhibition of conflating and confusing the nominally distinct spheres of arthouse, B-movie and exploitation. As James Morrison asserts, the fare offered by American art house venues 'was notably various' from the late 1950s onwards,[25] and legendary theatres from New York's Elgin to London's Scala could accommodate under their rubric of hip marginalia a motley blend of the erotic and the esoteric, of scatological sensationalism, mystic pretension and outlandishly 'Surrealist' imagery. The confusion of artistry and base impulse was compounded by salacious marketing campaigns promoting the supposedly 'sexy' pleasures of canonical European art films (in which context the nude *Playboy* spreads promoting Polański's *Repulsion* and, bizarrely, *Macbeth* (1971), seem slightly less aberrant). If such fluid interchanges and blithely catholic programming practices had largely been effaced from cinemas with the start of the new millennium, that hybrid spirit was preserved, so Joan Hawkins observes,[26] by online bootleg retailers selling gore and Godard side by side, and it looks bound to persist in an era of downloads and video-sharing sites.

As Hawkins argues, such minglings may be less haphazard than symptomatic of the affinities that pertain between avant-garde or art cinema and the lowbrow 'body genres' of exploitation and horror. International art cinema took a determined plunge into explicit and transgressive material in the late 1960s and 1970s, a topic to which I shall return – yet it could be argued that art cinema has been marked by associations of scandal and disreputability throughout much of its history.[27] The same is even truer for the artistic avant-gardes, concerned with scandalising bourgeois opinion and committed to the galvanising, revelatory power of shock. *Un Chien Andalou*'s famous opening scene both exemplifies and expresses this programme, a metaphor of assaulted vision that is also the progenitor of cinematic gore: this iconic 'cut' must be situated in a lineage that includes not only Evelyn Mulwray's gaping eye-socket in *Chinatown*[28] but also the eye-piercing from Lucio Fulci's *Zombi 2* (*Zombie Flesh Eaters*, 1979). A vision of fragile tissue, viscous effluvia and violated boundaries, Buñuel's eye mutilation primarily provokes a visceral horror, the same affect-based response Artaud's 'Theatre of Cruelty' was designed to inspire. Yet it is precisely for eliciting such affective, non-cognitive reactions that critics have traditionally denigrated the 'body genres' of horror, comedy and pornography. Eroticism and excess are themselves a privileged terrain of the avant-garde, and if avant-gardists from Bataille to Philippe Sollers have been said to deploy 'erotic exhibitionism' as a metaphor for textual transgression,[29] such figurative use need not exclude affect or coarser involvements (nor is metaphoric potential absent from the unabashed porn products of, say, Michael Ninn).[30]

Comparisons abound between exploitation and avant-garde or modernist cinema at the level of form as well as content. The non-linear structures and lack of three-dimensional characters in Godard or Ruiz have their complement in the derisory plotting and artless construction of exploitation films, in pornography's noted refusal to adhere to the structure of 'beginning-middle-end' – or at least to put them in that order.[31] At the risk of sounding facetious, even European distributors' once-rife practice of inserting unrelated hardcore sequences into softcore films, a practice that mars such late Borowczyk films as *Ars Amandi* (*The Art of Love*, 1983), might be considered a contributor to 'avant-garde' qualities of fragmentation and stylistic discord, an unwitting 'poststructuralist' gesture of problematised authorship and broken unity. The flattened performances in much Borowczyk lead back to the anti-psychological acting style favoured by Bresson as well as to the deadpan silent comic or inexpressive porn 'star'. Conversely, the grotesque, overheated performances in Żuławski, which I traced back to Artaud and Grotowski, risk association with 'low' melodrama histrionics (hysterionics?) and 'kitsch'.[32] The crowded tradition of avant-garde praise for popular and disdained cultural forms – in which horror, pulp adventure and slapstick comedy figure highly – suggests that the avant-gardes themselves recognised such congruence with their own interests and practices. Surrealist critic Ado Kyrou, alert to the careless poetry of 'the fantastic and semipornographic', openly enjoined his readers to see 'the worst films'.[33]

If the connections I have just drawn seem rather general, I would like now to examine how one of these films relates to its specific cultural context, drawing out the 'avant-garde' aspect of particular popular forms. Skolimowski's

Fig. 15 *Deep End* (Jerzy Skolimowski, 1970)

London-based *Deep End* (1970), while preserving much of the visual formalism of Skolimowski's early Polish work, can also be linked to a number of popular British traditions and trends. One obvious intertext is Clive Donner's *Here We Go Round the Mulberry Bush* (1968), a film that, as Robert Murphy notes, 'generically attempts to combine the traditional humour of a British sex comedy with the psychedelic trendiness of a "youth" film'.[34] *Deep End* sits at a tangent to both the sex comedy and the modish youth film, and, like *Mulberry Bush*, presents a narrative of male coming of age set to a pop-rock score. With seeming irony for a film thus evocative of 1960s youth culture and its 'permissive' social mores, *Deep End*'s depiction of London counterculture is harsh and satirical, a vision of seedy lechery fondled and entreated by porn cinemas and strip-show barkers (*Deep End* was not alone, however, in its critique of 'swinging' chauvinism: the grosser character of a film like Val Guest's softcore sex comedy *Au Pair Girls* (1972) does not deny it similar perspicacity). At the same time, commodified sex is presented as mere simulation and substitution, as when the protagonist, virginal swimming-baths attendant Mike, caresses a cardboard cut-out of a stripper who resembles his beloved, unattainable Susan.

Most interesting is how *Deep End*'s uneasy yet farcical sexuality darkly echoes the male sexual anxieties at play in Britain's 'lowbrow' comic tradition, as represented by the saucy seaside postcard, the *Carry On* series and the contemporaneous *Confessions* comedies. In several scenes Mike (John Moulder-Brown) is confronted by actual or threatened sexual overtures from voluptuous older women. While such encounters might be seen to comment on Mike's 'Oedipal' attachment to the slightly older, more self-possessed

Susan (Jane Asher), they also connect to the powerful, 'castrating', often sexually voracious female figures of the British comic imagination.[35] The presence of an over-ripe Diana Dors, whose character virtually assaults Mike, is a particularly overt throwback to that tradition (and anticipates the dominatrix-dictator character Dors would play in *The Two Ronnies'* 'The Worm That Turned' sketches). Skolimowski appends to these fearful females such visual puns as an 'ejaculating' fire extinguisher clutched by the baths' matronly receptionist: the film thereby evokes the 'phallic mother' of Freudian and Kleinian theory, a psychic fantasy seen as alleviating, or actually embodying, infantile castration anxieties (if the mother with penis is one manifestation of Klein's 'combined-parent' imago, its counterpart, the 'pregnant father', is also evoked in the form of the Health Education Council's famous poster).[36] *Deep End* thus exemplifies how these maligned comic traditions explore difficult and distressing topics (if not necessarily in 'progressive' ways) and delve into the same psychic and sexual phenomena as the Surrealist movement.[37] The outrageous corporeality of, say, the scene with Dors demonstrates a carnivalesque excess that seldom found expression in mainstream British cinema outside of lowbrow comedy. Even Skolimowski's punning visual conceits, while close to the sexual metaphors of Surrealism, also approximate the bawdy sight gags of American comic filmmaker Frank Tashlin.

Skolimowski may engage cinematically with the 1960s' 'liberated' mores, and indulge a certain Rabelaisian ribaldry, yet his work does not display that tendency towards extreme explicitness and provocation that characterises a number of this period's most adventurous art filmmakers – this trend, not coincidentally, was synchronous with the newfound respectability of pornography or erotica in the USA and Western Europe, as well as the emergence of 'adult auteurs' like American filmmaker Radley Metzger. 'The Pornographic Imagination', a 1967 essay by the ever-prescient Susan Sontag, heralded this cultural sea-change. Sontag's recuperation of this most despised of genres strangely suggests how pornography is itself, like 'high' or avant-garde culture, a matter of elite access, with only the subtly prepared minority capable of handling the genre's mind-blowing transgressions. Similarly, the explicit sexuality of some 1960s and 1970s art films (for instance, Dušan Makavejev's *Sweet Movie* (1974) and Pier Paolo Pasolini's 'Trilogy of Life') was linked to a sexual-revolutionary 'vanguardism', conceived as expressing a Reichian or Marcusean politics of radical libidinal 'liberation'. The defence of pornographic films proper was itself often couched in wider principles of healthful liberation and sexual progress. All this represents one point, then, where the avant-garde, the 'disreputable' and the revolutionary – the topics I have explored throughout this chapter – fuse in the most self-conscious manner.

Yet Borowczyk, who embodies art cinema's 'erotic turn' more than any of the other Polish émigrés (especially in *Contes immoraux* (*Immoral Tales*, 1974) and *The Beast*), does not espouse such an uncomplicatedly libertarian view of sexuality. In fact his films are little more assertive of 'liberation' than those of Polański or Skolimowski. Many of Borowczyk's depictions of erotic activity take place under the shadow of repressive authority – notably the Catholic Church, whose representatives are sometimes the very perpetrators of sexual transgression. While such representations are no doubt intended in part as a satirical comment on ecclesiastical hypocrisy, they also tend to stress the symbiotic character of license and authority, transgression and taboo. Such is the import of *A Particular Collection*, the short study of antique erotic curios that commenced Borowczyk's foray into explicit cinema: in emphasising how these mechanisms conceal, obfuscate and gradually disclose their 'shameful' erotic contents, Borowczyk inscribes the very interdictions he aims to upset. His work thus aligns itself with the vision of Bataille, for whom the sin and its prohibition remain bound together in a relation of mutual reinforcement.[38] Alternatively, we might detect here a Foucauldian insistence on how the Church and other institutions are engaged less in repressing sex and sin than in *producing* them as objects of knowledge: witness, for instance, a perversely erudite discourse on bestiality given by the visiting Cardinal at the end of *The Beast*. Even when eroticism seems detached from authority and institutions, it comes to constitute a repressive and often violent institution unto itself, confined to enclosed, forbidding spaces and ordered into rules and rituals. There is, as Bataille put it, 'no liberty' in transgression,[39] and no return to animal spontaneity, although Borowczyk's artifice-ridden erotic scenes might suggest a further means of integrating art and life, as per the ideals of the avant-garde.

For all their points of contact with avant-garde and commercial culture, these Polish émigré filmmakers are (or were) committed outsiders who never fully adopted any one movement, trend or genre. Surrealism is the possible exception to this, at least in Borowczyk's case, yet that is in part a reflection of Surrealism's extreme elasticity with regard to formal practice. Moreover, Borowczyk, like the other filmmakers, espoused a dark, unredemptive version of Surrealism at odds with the movement's established (and Breton-promoted) image. Polish émigré cinema seldom endorsed the socially revolutionary or utopian aspirations of many avant-garde movements, and actively exco-riated those media-hyped Western 'scenes' (such as Swinging London) that proclaimed their own rebellious liberation. These filmmakers do, however, gesture towards the avant-garde's parallel commitment to the integration of art and life. As noted, Skolimowski attained such integration in the modest sense of blending his films with his current life in both artistic and practical terms; Żuławski has also insisted that his work and his life partake of one another, while Polański will never divest his *oeuvre* of such parallels and confusions, much as he might wish to. These filmmakers' engagement with popular genres might itself be considered a means of fusing art with life, in the sense of adopting the commercial forms most prevalent in daily existence. Yet even as 'commercial' directors, to a greater or lesser extent, these filmmakers remain assimilable to the notion of Outsider Art I broached at the beginning of this essay. None of these accomplished figures could be compared to George, the inept 'Sunday painter' of *Cul-de-Sac*. Yet they assume something of the amateur artist's freedoms, at once displaying fidelity to their interests and obsessions and retaining their right to the capricious gesture or shocking departure.

NOTES

1   Daniel Bird, *Roman Polański* (Harpenden: Pocket Essentials, 2002), p. 15.

2   Marianne DeKoven, *Utopia Limited: The Sixties and the Emergence of the Postmodern* (Durham: Duke University Press, 2004), p. 203.

3   Geoffrey Nowell-Smith, *The Oxford History of World Cinema* (Oxford: Oxford University Press, 1996), p. 637.

4   Parker Tyler, *Underground Film: A Critical History* (Harmondsworth: Penguin, 1974), p. 163.

5   Hal Foster, *Compulsive Beauty* (Cambridge, MA: Massachusetts Institute of Technology Press, 1993), p. 4.

6   Elżbieta Ostrowska, 'Knife in the Water: Polański's Nomadic Discourse Begins', *The Cinema of Roman Polański: Dark Spaces of the World*, John Orr and Elżbieta Ostrowska, eds. (London: Wallflower Press, 2006), p. 70.

7   Bird and Jeremiah Kipp, 'Outsiders, Shamans and Devils, Part 1: A Discussion of Central European New Wave Cinema with Film Writer Daniel Bird', *Slant Magazine*, 2009, http://www.slantmagazine.com/house/2009/03/outsiders-shamans-and-devils-part-1-a-discussion-of-central-european-new-wave-cinema-with-film-writer-daniel-bird/.

8   André Breton, *Manifestoes of Surrealism* (Ann Arbor: University of Michigan Press, 1972), p. 153.

9   Raymond Durgnat, 'Borowczyk and the Cartoon Renaissance', *Film Comment*, January–February, 1976, p. 42.

10 Jonathan L. Owen, *Avant-Garde to New Wave: Czechoslovak Cinema, Surrealism and the Sixties* (London; New York: Berghahn Press, 2013).

11 Michael O'Pray, *Avant-Garde Film: Forms, Themes and Passions* (London; New York: Wallflower Press, 2003), pp. 69–70.

12 David Bordwell, *Narration in the Fiction Film* (Madison: University of Wisconsin Press, 1985), p. 26.

13 Michael Richardson, *Surrealism and Cinema* (Oxford: Berg, 2006), p. 109.

14 As Matthew Coniam suggests, Borowczyk also anticipates here the ludic yet obsessive embrace of structures and taxonomies in the films of quasi-avant-garde British filmmaker Peter Greenaway. See Matthew Coniam, 'Angel Games: The Early Films of Walerian Borowczyk', Matthew Black, ed., *Necronomicon Book Two* (London: Creation Books, 1998), p. 83.

15 Warren F. Motte Jr., 'Introduction', *Oulipo: A Primer of Potential Literature* (Dalkey Archive Press, 1998), p. 20.

16 Edward Lintz, 'Difficiles Nuage: Gertrude Stein, OuLiPo and the Grammar of the Avant-Garde', Dietrich Scheunemann, ed., *European Avant-Garde: New Perspectives* (Amsterdam: Rodopi, 2000), p. 200. See also Peter Bürger, *Theory of the Avant-Garde* (Manchester: Manchester University Press, 1984).

17 Herbert J. Eagle, 'Power and the Visual Semantics of Polański's Films', John Orr and Elżbieta Ostrowska, eds., *The Cinema of Roman Polański: Dark Spaces of the World* (London: Wallflower Press, 2006), p. 48.

18 Alexandro Jodorowsky, 'Vers l'éphémère panique ou Sortir le théâtre du théâtre', Fernando Arrabal, ed., *Le Panique* (Paris: Union générale d'éditions, 1973), p. 82.

19 Bürger, 1984, p. 53.

20 Monique Borie, *Mythe et théâtre aujourd'hui: Une quête impossible? Beckett, Genet, Grotowski. The Living Theatre* (Paris: Librairie A.-G. Nizet, 1981), p. 159.

21 James Morrison, *Roman Polański* (Urbana: University of Illinois Press, 2007), p. 88.

22 Stephen Bayley, 'Britain Has Become Indifferent to Beauty', *The Observer*, 22 March 2009.

23 Susan Sontag, *Styles of Radical Will* (New York: Farrar, Straus and Giroux, 1969), p. 39.

24 Roman Polański, *Roman by Polański* (London: Heinemann, 1984), p. 180.

25 Morrison, 2007, p. 37.

26 Joan Hawkins, *Cutting Edge: Art-Horror and the Horrific Avant-Garde* (Minneapolis: University of Minnesota Press, 2000).

27 Hawkins, 2000, p. 21.

28 Kamila Kuc, 'A Cruel Imagination: Roman Polański's Short Films', Kamila Wielebska and Kuba Mikurda, eds., *A Story of Sin: Surrealism in Polish Cinema* (Kraków: Ha!Art, 2010), p. 60.

29 Susan Rubin Suleiman, *Subversive Intent: Gender, Politics, and the Avant-Garde* (Cambridge, MA; London: University of Harvard Press: 1990), p. 13.

30 Hawkins, 2000, p. 196.

31 Sontag, 1969, p. 87.

32 Marek Haltof, *Polish National Cinema* (Oxford; New York: Berghahn Books, 2002), p. 123.

33 Ado Kyrou, 'The Marvelous Is Popular', Paul Hammond, ed., *The Shadow and Its Shadow: Surrealist Writings on the Cinema* (San Francisco: City Lights Books, 2000), p. 71.

34 Robert Murphy, *The British Cinema Book* (London: British Film Institute, 2009), p. 253.

35 Bart Moore-Gilbert, *The Arts in the 1970s: Cultural Closure* (London: Routledge, 2002), p. 233.

36 Glen O. Gabbard and Krin Gabbard, *Psychiatry and the Cinema* (Washington, DC: American Psychiatric Publishing, 1999), p. 295.

37 Richard Dyer, *The Matter of Images: Essays on Representation* (London: Routledge, 2002), p. 92.

38 Shadia B. Drury, *Alexandre Kojève: The Roots of Postmodern Politics* (London: Palgrave Macmillan, 1994), p. 116.

CHAPTER SIX

THE MECHANICAL IMAGINATION –
CREATIVITY OF MACHINES:
FILM FORM WORKSHOP 1970–1977

Ryszard W. Kluszczyński

1.

Today, Polish art of the 1970s produces various reactions. All too frequently, opinions on the subject are not based on research, and sometimes are extremely subjective based on mere likes or dislikes. In addition, some historians and critics intellectually linked to the avant-garde paradigm of the 1960s have constructed through the use of very selectively gathered materials a rejection of the different, radical, inelegant and iconoclastic actions of artists who reigned in the following decade. Unfortunately, they rarely state clearly which type of artistic activity they prefer; rather, one art rather than the other is simply closer and dearer to their hearts. They maintain that the former is the real art, the actual avant-garde, and the latter is pseudo-avant-garde, devoid of any value. Such lack of respect for the critical body does not allow one to take such opinions seriously. Others do not undertake any study of the period in Poland as they believe that more interesting and more valuable tendencies developed abroad, while here in Poland we witnessed merely uncreative attempts at adapting these tendencies to local conditions.[1] Others discredit the art of the 1970s for political reasons, claiming that through their actions, 1970s artists provided an alibi for a quasi-modernist ideology promoted by those in power in Poland at the time. Such opinions have been formulated without serious study of the decade and with no real knowledge of the art of the 1970s, of its essence, of its achievements or of the new and strong elements it introduced in Polish art. Attempts to understand (or misunderstand) this period use inappropriate tools. They are attempts to understand or to grasp the phenomena of one paradigm using the categories and instruments from another one.

Within Polish critical, historical and theoretical writing on recent art in Poland, there is still no work that undertakes a serious reflection on this period, which contrasted so much with what went before. A work is needed that attempts to address the importance of the nature, scope and breadth of the breakthrough of 1970s Polish art. This breakthrough, in general, means a TRANSFORMATION FROM AN AVANT-GARDE ART STILL ROOTED DEEPLY IN CLASSICAL WAYS OF THINKING ABOUT ART (IN CATEGORIES OF FORM, STYLE AND VALUE) TOWARDS A NEO-AVANT-GARDE (CHARACTERISED BY DE-MATERIALISATION, DE-FORMALISATION AND SELF-ANALYSIS), FROM REPRESENTATION AND EXPRESSION TO ACTION AND COMMUNICATION, FROM THE OBJECT TO FUNCTION, AND FROM FINE ART TO MEDIA. [Upper case in original]

There is a real need for research into this period of Polish art, a need to verify the large number of ideas that were hurriedly formulated, a need to establish a good foundation for future constructions. Many important exhibitions have not been organised and many artistic facts have been neither discovered nor interpreted. Many artists still await their monographs. At the end of the century we have reached a point for summing up, and any history of Polish contemporary art or art of the twentieth century without an adequate, true picture of the 1970s would not be complete. In my opinion, a review of the art of the Film Form Workshop brings up material which may serve to change the views of new art in Poland, as well as show how significant a role the media plays in the transformational processes of art culture and allow for an examination of the scope of conceptual tendencies and the shaping of avant-garde tendencies, and also, importantly, an examination of the significance and value of the 1970s art to the general image of contemporary art in Poland.

2.

Formed in 1970 as a section of the Scientific Society at the State Film, Television and Theatre School in Łódź, the Film Form Workshop was one of the groups which, as it later turned out, had a decisive impact on the art of the times, raising important issues and problems and giving them original and discernible forms. The name drew attention primarily towards film as an art phenomenon, and the group gathered a large number of highly skilled filmmakers interested in the character and properties of their field. However, despite its name, the group was open to any creative individual ready to make art for its own sake, in any of its kinds and manifestations, on the condition that there was no commercial aim. In short, a readiness to link artistic practices with meta-artistic reflection is the best proof of the workshop character of the group. As the Workshop's formative manifesto states:

Fig. 16 Group photo of Film Form Workshop, 1973: Janusz Połom, Wojciech Bruszewski, Wacław Antczak, Jacek Łomnicki, Tadeusz Junak, Antoni Mikołajczyk, Lech Czołnowski, Zdzisław Sowiński, Józef Robakowski, Paweł Kwiek, Kazimierz Bendkowski, Andrzej Różycki, Ryszard Waśko, Zbigniew Rybczyński

> WORKSHOP realizes films, recordings and TV transmissions, sound programmes, art exhibitions and different kinds of events and artistic intervention... Workshop also carries out theoretical and critical activity. It studies and has the ambition to broaden the possibilities of audio-visual arts.

Thanks to the open formula of the group's activities, besides filmmakers there were also photographers, poets, musicians, sculptors and performers among its members. Even those who had completed their film education or were studying in the Camera or Direction department at the Academy did not limit their activity to film. Some of them, including Wojciech Bruszewski, Antoni Mikołaczyk, Józef Robakowski and Andrzej Różycki, had in fact previous non-film experiences, for instance with the practice of Toruń art groups such as 'Zero 61' and 'Krąg' ('Circle'). As a result of the multitude of disciplines practised, and the versatility of artistic concerns of the participants of the Film Form Workshop, the scope of the group's artistic activity included most art fields and transgressed boundaries, invading public space itself. The latter arena of activity (like all others) took various forms. One example was a furniture sale at Łódź Red Market Square where Józef Robakowski's action centrally involved Wacław Antczak, a cult figure of the Łódź avant-garde in the 1970s. Other examples involved various 'interventions' or 'actions' decomposing institutions or art scenes with the aim of revealing the sloppiness of the representatives of the art and film world, for instance those undertaken at the Festival of Films on Art in Zakopane in 1972. One should not forget their participation in the amateur theatre play *Kariera i śmierć Adolfa Hitlera* (*The Career and Death of Adolf Hitler*), staged by Edward Kowalski's troupe.[2]

Given the character and beginnings of the group, its outcomes would obviously be significant, but two of these in particular are worth discussion. Firstly, because the core of the Workshop was constituted by filmmakers, film and media played a prominent part in the group's programme and practice. This was evident not only in the number of film, photography and video works produced and their accompanying manifestos, but also in types of work in other disciplines that had been shaped through reference to film and other media, for instance Ryszard Waśko's 'Hypothetical' films and photographs, exhibited as schemas and notifications; Józef Robakowski's *Light Theatre* (1973); and a number of Andrzej Różycki's projects using photography with the dimensions of time, for instance the 1975 photographic board *Ikar – Projekt uruchomienia obrazu fotograficznego* (*Icarus – A Project of Moving Photographic Image*). Moreover, as a result of the media origin of the group, the problem of communication immediately became one of the most important issues.

Secondly, the professional film education of the Workshop founders and their equally professional standards of working, for example their use of professional 35mm cameras, a result of the group's functioning within the film academy, turned out to be a specific distinction from the international film avant-garde. In the USA and in Western Europe one witnessed artists emerging from other art disciplines, who were not acquainted with film work, transferring to the area of film. This led to the transformation of film through non-filmic influences and the process of the amateur, who typically used 16mm or even 8mm cameras.[3] On the other hand, Polish artists of the Film Form Workshop, due to their film education, have transformed from the inside – they have experimented on film with the aim of purging it of other art forms, particularly literature.

3.

The open, informal character of the group was the prime reason why so many artists participated in its activities, in spite of the fact that not all of them belonged to the group. One should therefore differentiate between circles of the Film Workshop. The first circle was formed by artists whose work was the strongest, and they were connected to the Workshop for the longest period. They constituted the Workshop, although they joined it at different times. In alphabetical order: KAZIMIERZ BENDKOWSKI, WOJCIECH BRUSZEWSKI, PAWEŁ KWIEK, ANTONI MIKOŁAJCZYK, JANUSZ POŁOM, JÓZEF ROBAKOWSKI, ANDRZEJ RÓŻYCKI, RYSZARD WAŚKO. [Upper case in original]

The second circle comprised other artists (including film technicians), who also participated in the Workshop's presentations.[4] They primarily worked in cooperation with the artists of the first circle.[5] Such people as Lech Czółnowski, Jan Freda, Ryszard Gajewski, Tadeusz Junak, Marek Koterski, Ryszard Lenczewski, Jacek Łomnicki, Ryszard Meissner, Zbigniew Rybczyński and

Zdzisław Sowiński should be included here. In the Workshop's final period of activity, artists from the younger generation such as Janusz Kołodrubiec, Tomasz Konart, Andrzej Prauzel, Janusz Szczerek and Piotr Weychert could be found within the scope of the Workshop group. Soon they founded their own art group, 'Grupa T' ('Group T'), partially in opposition to the Workshop but rooted in its activities. The third circle consisted of artists who because of the nature of their art, their project or their art stance appeared at the Workshop actions or had an artistic dialogue with the group, although they were never members of the group. In this context important artists in contemporary Polish art such as Zbigniew Dłubak, Andrzej Partum, Jan Świdziński and Zbigniew Warpechowski should be mentioned. These circles of artists as well as critics and curators, such as Gerard Kwiatkowski and Janusz Zagrodzki, together with some institutions who supported their activities (usually private galleries), created a wide and dynamic artistic movement, which due to its scope and scale, novelty, originality and importance gave the 1970s its artistic character, participating in the creation of its neo-avant-garde profile.

The Film Form Workshop activities came to an end in the second half of the 1970s. The development of individual projects and the evolving practices of the members of the group led to its unity waning. Although some signs of disintegration could have been seen earlier, it is usually assumed that participation in Documenta in Kassel in 1977 was the last group activity.[6] After the Kassel show, the artists, now limited in number, participated in two international avant-garde film shows in Koeln and London. What remains is the Workshop's visibility and influence in various forms in the subsequent activities of its members.

4.

A review and analysis of the works produced within the Film Form Workshop shows that conceptual and analytical tendencies were a priority in its projects. Regardless of an artist's discipline and the nature of any particular work, whether it had cognitive, meta-discursive or transgressive intentions, it always tended to disturb the boundaries between the arts. It is worth pointing out the multiplicity of boards present in the artistic production of the Film Form Workshop. This multiplicity didn't result only from the need to document art events or present ephemeral works (for instance, installations realised only once at a particular place) or from the desire to remember actions or performances. The boards were created simultaneously with the films, video tapes and installations, or they presented concepts and ideas unmaterialised. Boards, schemes, drawings and notations such as those created by the Workshop are classical instruments of conceptual art.

As well as the conceptual and analytical character of the Workshop's approach, one should not forget another trace, that of the anarchist, neo-Dada or Fluxus type of irony, play and deconstruction. This Dadaist and Fluxus dimension is no less important than the Workshop's conceptual element. This deconstructive quality of works with analytical and conceptual aspects foregrounded indirectly reveals the irony and humour of the Fluxus impulse. Combining these two aspects endowed the Workshop's activities with an exceptional originality.

5.

The Workshop films, as well as their other works, are analytical in character in the various ways they take up the problems of representation or time and space construction in film, the relation between film and reality, and the study of the relationship between film and photography, plus the significance and function of the relationship between image and sound. They also address issues such as the psychology and physiology of perception. They also question the role of language and the role of cultural conventions in their relationship to reality.

This analytical aspect of Workshop films locates the group within the framework of the conceptual art movement, which in film took the form of so-called structural[7] or materialist film.[8] Given its origins in the conceptual art era during which structural film was developing, the Film Form Workshop was naturally allied with artists who rejected aesthetics for the cognitive approach. Workshop members established their own relationship to the conceptual art movement, drawing on traditions emanating from the Polish and Soviet avant-gardes of the 1920s and 1930s. The ideology and practice of Constructivism became an important source of artistic and theoretical inspiration. This is especially visible in the work of Robakowski, Waśko and Bruszewski.

Initially, the Workshop made an effort to eliminate elements taken from literature, theatre and narrative film. Robakowski's early films in particular resemble specific experiments to analyse the perception of film and the links between various levels of film structure, thus attempting to eliminate the conventions of literary-type perception. In his *Rynek* (*Market Square*, 1970) he intervened in the flow of time through frame-by-frame photography. In such a way, he condensed time, simultaneously giving an impression of a continuous recording of events. The problem of the film's internal time in relationship to the recording of reality is the issue being examined here. In *Test* (1971), made without a camera, Robakowski studied afterimage and, indirectly, the physiological condition of reception. In *Zapis* (*Record*, 1971), made by

Robakowski and Mikołajczyk (photographs by Andrzej Jaworski), the differences between filmic and photographic representation were analysed, and in *Test II*, the bi-lateral influence of image and sound and its significance for film was explored.

In 1971, in a programme note, 'Jeszcze raz o czysty film' ('Once More for Pure Film'), Robakowski wrote:

> Working currently with the Film Form Workshop at the Łódź Film School I have been given the opportunity to carry out practically unlimited tests and experiments on the boundaries of other people's perceptions of my films [...] the theoretical and practical are undertaken with the aim of finding and acknowledging film's specific qualities. I do believe that film, as well as music, poetry, ballet, painting and architecture, have to dispose of the superfluous burden of literature.[9]

Later, Robakowski concentrated on the relationship between the mechanical character of equipment and the psycho-physiological nature of its user. In his approach, the influences are bilateral, in other words: the psychological state (though physiologically conditioned) of the cameraman shooting a film also involves revealing unknown elements unnoticed previously by the cameraman, which influences his choices about the world filmed. Films such as *Idę* (*I Am Going*, 1973) and *Ćwiczenia na dwie ręce* (*Exercises for Two Hands*, 1976) are the result of these experiments. Mechano-biological records have, in their turn, led to a subsequent phase in Robakowski's art, the personal 'cinema of my own'. This began with the film entitled *Z okna* (*From my Window*, 1978–1984). This trend in the later post-war Workshop period, represented by *O palcach* (*About My Fingers*, 1981) and *Kino to Potęga* (*Cinema Is Power*, 1985), for instance, is characterised by a dominant subjectivity in relation to the author.

Figs. 17 & 18 *From My Window* (Józef Robakowski, 1978–1984)

A fundamental problem raised by the Workshop, already present in Robakowski's early works as well as being researched by Waśko and Bruszewski, is the issue of the mutual relations between reality and its audio-visual representation, and between the viewer and reality and its representation. This problem was explored by Bruszewski, who transposed these analyses to video with exceptional insight. Bruszewski underlined particularly the duality of the concept of reality, differentiating between its material (the reality itself) and the mental dimension (how we experience reality). He treated the latter as a cultural product, one of conventional rules regulating perceptual data input. This led to the thesis that our contact with reality is not direct but is mediated by language. Bruszewski also noticed that mechanical and electronic media (photography, film, video, etc.) act, to some extent, independently from our minds, and that the image of the external world communicated through these media is equal to our conceptions of it, which in turn are subordinated to customary rules of conduct. According to Bruszewski, the perceiving brain is eager to use exclusively the part of its experience of the media which does not infringe on these conventional regulations. Bruszewski's, Waśko's and Robakowski's films, through their analysis of the relationships between reality and its representations, was an attempt to adapt the mind to an image of the world created by new, emerging technologies.

The Workshop's films often raised the issue of the relationship between image and sound, in a number of different ways. Bruszewski, in his many audio-visual experiments, for instance *Yyaa* (1973) and *Łyżeczka* (*A Spoonful*, 1976), and in *Pudełko zapałek / Eksperyment audiowizualny* (*Match-Box / Audio-Visual Experiment*, 1975), attempted to show that the relation between the acoustic and visual perception is more an illusion produced by the human mind than a constant, independent fact. Similar experiments in film were carried out by Waśko, but here issues concerning sounds were combined with the context of the articulation of space in film. Bendkowski's films *Obszar* (*Area*), *Koło* (*Circle*) and *Punkt* (*Point*), all dated 1973, analysed the possibilities of narration and expression resulting from various combinations of image and sound. Compared to the minimalist works of Robakowski, Bruszewski and Waśko, Bendkowski's films are distinguished by the more complex structure of internal relations.[10] In subsequent years Bendkowski also began to work in video, in which his work is characterised by a minimalism and a tendency to create basic, essential structures.

Janusz Połom also carried out a number of experiments, where he confronted sounds and their respective images. As Robakowski was releasing the image from human domination by allowing the camera to run without using the viewfinder and thus avoiding the influence of cultural codes, Połom similarly by translating sounds into images in a direct way gave autonomy back to images and transgressed or at least problematised their traditional representational character. To attain this end he used various tools, including an oscylograph, with which he made his film *Alfabet* (*ABC*, 1974). He undertook a large number of projects with the aim of directly visualising sounds.

Waśko's films constitute an analytical approach towards the medium of film, and an intertextual tendency to transgress genre boundaries. *Kłódka* (*A Padlock*, 1972) constructs the filmic narration using photography – static frames impose that quality on the film image. *Rejstracja* (*Record*, 1972) manipulates the space through various uses of counterpoint, building sequences of images which appeal to the viewer's imagination and finally deceive her or him with a vision of an impossible space. The above film tries to localise the viewer in the scope of the constructed space. This is done according to its media constitution, despite the discourse being much indebted to photography. *Ściana* (*The Wall*, 1972) processes a direct film record by its achronological montage of very short pieces and counterpoint use of soundtrack. In *Chodnik* (*Pavement*, 1972), again, intertextual reference to photography is used when movement appears as a result of the linking and dividing of static images obtained with frame-by-frame exposure. *Układ I – VI* (*System I – VI*, 1973) is an analysis of the relationship between image and sound, which – as is evident from the above analysis – plays the role of media intertext in so many of Waśko's and other Workshop artists' films. *30 Sytuacji Dzwiękowych* (*30 Sound Situations*, 1975), in turn, studies these relationships in reference to perception more than to ontology of film. In these, and all of Waśko's other film works, one can clearly notice an analytical interest in the spatial dimensions of cinema, whereas *Chodzę pomiędzy* (*I Walk Between*, 1975) transfers film into the domain of performance art. To a lesser extent, the same happened with *30 Sound Situations*. This is just one of the paths which Waśko's films take, as does his photography, in leaving their areas of origin. The analytical attitude has much in common with conceptualism and structural cinema, as it draws attention to, first and foremost (if not exclusively), the elements of media, neglecting the expressive function of art and form in its simplest understanding. This also refers to film and photography. In Waśko's work in both media, the image is gradually de-objectified. Representative function is here replaced by abstract analytical discourse. A number of photographic and film projects were given completely to issues Waśko found interesting, such as the relation between the surface (a photograph, a screen) and multi-dimensional space.

Paweł Kwiek's film concepts were of a completely different character. He made a few documentaries in line with these concepts, where the protagonists played an active, creative part. Explaining his theory in the text *Dokument obiektywny o człowieku* (*Objective Document on Man*), Kwiek wrote:

> Documentary strives to deliver the truth on Man. Both for art's and science's needs. Until now however no one could avoid the deformation of that truth resulting from the influence of the producer on the work. In the history of film, once in a while people tried to get rid of this influence [...] The effects were, however, unsatisfactory [...] I claim that the truth of a man can be a product of a face to face contact, regardless of what s/he would like to say [...] In film the situation is present when all the decisions [...] are taken by a person, or a group, which is the subject of the film. That means that s/he will make the film on herself/himself, or in other words s/he would be allowed to make a free realization on any subject.[11]

6.

Zbigniew Rybczyński took a separate position, far exceeding the standards of analytical cinema in the Film Form Workshop. To a much lesser extent than its other members, he was concerned with media problems and concentrated on formal image organisation, orchestrating and harmonising it with music. However, his visualisation of musical structures was by no means the final aim of his experiments. It merely formed a frame for more detailed researches.

Using an optical printer, colour filters, a transfocator and frame-by-frame exposure, and combining traditional animation with transformed actor shots (live action), Rybczyński built in his own, original style something very difficult to imitate. Up until 1980 and *Tango*, simultaneously, he broke the boundaries of the linearity characteristic of the medium of film (therefore adopting a meta-artistic strategy), which became one of the main forms of experimentation defining the area of his creative search.

At first Rybczyński carried out his idea by the means of the classic repertoire: a closed or circular composition – the ending is the return to the starting point; multiple exposure (*Kwadrat / A Square* and *Take Five*, both 1972). They were quite often – especially *A Square* – presented during the group presentation of the Film Form Workshop. In his later films, made outside of the Workshop, Rybczyński

Fig. 19 *Tango* (Zbigniew Rybczyński, 1981)

introduced new technologies and concepts. In *Nowa książka* (*A New Book*, 1975) he divided the screen into nine parts, took the action from one part to another and showed simultaneously a multitude of events taking place at the same time. It is a specific unification of successive and simultaneous narration. Here also we encounter a closed, circular composition. This type of structure was also used in *Tango*, which granted Rybczyński international fame. He won the American Film Academy Award for best animation in 1983.[12]

7.

Structural film – one of the fundamental paradigms for the Workshop artists – modified the character of the avant-garde cinema in a substantial way. Until its appearance, the model of avant-garde film in its variants (abstract, poetic, direct, etc.) generally persisted. The model had been shaped in the classical period of the avant-garde in the 1920s and it consisted of the co-existence of two discourses, the artistic and the meta-artistic. Such work still maintains a formal character. The tension between the two discourses resulted in a particular aspect of avant-garde art situated between destruction and construction, between anti-art and new art, and finally between discourse and meta-discourse itself.[13] In structural film, however, art discourse is significantly minimalised. It is just an excuse for meta-artistic analysis, or it is merely the direct product of the analysis. In the borderline cases, the two discourses are equalised, the art discourse absorbed by the meta-artistic. Structural film diverts the viewers' attention from the formal aspects, as well as from the subjective element, that is, the expression, while it invites them to reflect on the nature of cinema.

8.

In spite of their common approach to art and the similarities of the works created individually, the artists of the Film Form Workshop are characterised by developed qualities which endow their films with original features, reflecting the individual needs and approaches of the authors. Exploiting areas between reality and its audio-visual representation, Bruszewski, for instance, expressed, if between the lines, a complete mistrust of any message, any broadcast, any form of communication, any value. He presented a prevalent relativism, which is on an everyday basis camouflaged by endowing the conventional rules with autonomic values. Bruszewski believed that media art was to play a de-mystifying role, and was to reveal the conventional perception of reality. Such an approach led him to the notion of a self-generating text as an unlimited source of multiplying the senses, which do not communicate anything in the traditional sense of the word, because they do not represent anything.

Kwiek came up with the vision of an open cinema, undefined, negating norms and conventional rules, and opening a view to the unknown. He continually moved on the edge of film, directing himself towards the other arts or – something especially worth underlining – towards other subjects, to potential users of the medium, questioning their various notions and concepts, the concept of the author among others.

Waśko's art, as a whole, can be characterised as exploring inter-media relations. His works open a network of intertextual relationships both on the level of general structural and ontological signs and on the level of types of perception and interpretational rules. In other words, to grasp a work of a given discipline in its specific character, one has to appeal to its non-characteristic features, those belonging to other disciplines. When Waśko's work might be classified under disciplines other than film (photography), film plays the role of the intertext. In the case of film works, the process of intertextual referencing is carried out through references to other media.

Waśko's cinema spans internal analysis of the medium, studies of its mathematical logic, and external analysis of its relationships and links. External intertextual functions, in the case of film, are performed through other media, which in various ways and to various extents are present in the very film structure. Photography, sonoristics (the knowledge of sound) and performance are examples of art disciplines which participate in deconstructing the film medium. Their active appearance, internally and externally, in the film medium therefore questions the opposition between the 'interior' and the 'exterior', such that transgression and trans-medialism become the main qualities of the artist's work.

A similar quality can also be found in some of Robakowski's films. In foetal form it can already be seen in *Prostokąt dynamiczny* (*Dynamic Triangle*, 1971), and then in a more developed form in *Idę* and *Mój film* (*My Film*, 1974). This quality involves treating the human camera operator and the camera as a unit, where the camera reveals and transfers the psychophysical emotions, temperament and awareness of the artist onto celluloid. Having chosen the above strategy, Robakowski consciously headed towards its consequences, which in the case of many other authors happens more unintentionally, or even against their will. The above process was complemented by a number of experiments which revealed the nature of a medium perceived as a fully autonomic instrument. What Robakowski did was to broaden the perspective of analysis, and concentrate on those film qualities which allowed him to combine the character of the medium and his own art project.

9. [...]

10.

Besides structural film works which activated in various ways the relationships between film and other visual arts (and were enriched by various forms of activism, such as performance, happenings and art objects), the production process and photography appeared within the scope of the Film Form Workshop. Here I will be referring to them as inter-media films. They are neither pure cinema nor traditionally perceived films on art. They are located in the area between cinema and other art disciplines, having integral links, rather than only loose connections.

Among the problems raised by the Film Form Workshop, it seems that the problem of inter-media relations was introduced, more than anyone else, by Kwiek. To some degree, Rybczyński can be included here too. Kwiek pioneered video experiments, which he transformed into multi-media, combining drawing, video and photography. This can also be seen in the work of Zofia Kulik, Przemysław Kwiek and Jan Wojciechowski, group work done by cooperating artists and directors of photography. The film *Forma otwarta* (*Open Form*, 1970–1971) was one of the results of such endeavours. Similar actions were also undertaken within the scope of the Workshop itself, whose interdisciplinary make-up guaranteed the possibility of versatile cooperative projects. The main type of film activity of the Film Form Workshop was, however, medialism (analytical film).

Inter-media cinema is a modification of a more general phenomenon, the so-called expanded cinema. Around the world it has taken a great variety of forms: computer films, film-performances, light shows, shadow theatre, and so on. In Poland however, it appeared especially as inter-media film – as a result of a reciprocal interaction between film, video, photography, visual arts and actionism. In this kind of film, one witnesses a clash of several art approaches. These are group works which lead to very complex constructions in terms of form. A sub-group of inter-media cinema emerged as a result of experiments: films created by many artists, each one producing chosen parts committed to their care. *Kinolaboratorium* (*Cinelaboratory*, 1973) by Kwiek and Robakowski's *Żywa galeria* (*Living Gallery*, 1975) and *Konstrukcja w procesie* (*Construction in Process*, 1981) belong in this group.

An interesting, though later form of inter-media work, especially where film was replaced by video, were multi-media installations composed of many parts. Constructed, besides video, from art objects, photographs and light projections, such realisations-exhibitions were presented by Robakowski and Antoni Mikołajczyk, among others.

11. [...]

12.

Artists of the Film Form Workshop were pioneers in Poland in their use of video. The early tapes and installations by Bruszewski, Mikołajczyk, Robakowski and Waśko, while they continued their film work, showed new directions for experimentation in this new medium. Analytical video works brought about an interest in the strategies of television's functioning and in what its social and artistic meanings and functions were.[14] It is worth mentioning that video enabled the Workshop artists to give new shape to their work on reality, which they had carried out from the beginning of their artistic work; that is to say, video broadened their analysis of media, and what should be emphasised is that the technological and ontic relationship they had with television enabled them to present the meaning of communication as an art process.

It was at that time that the first works studying the various aspects of television's functioning drew attention to the television programme and its place in everyday life (e.g. Andrzej Różycki's *Seans telewizyjny* / *Television Programme*). They analysed the very nature of the phenomenon of direct transmission (e.g. a group work by the Workshop artists, *Transmisja telewizyjna* / *An Objective TV Transmission*), and finally concentrated on the television set as a new fetish of mass culture (Kwiek). All the above actions were carried out in 1973 during an endeavour entitled 'Action Workshop' in the Museum of Art in Łódź, marking the beginning of video art in Poland in the form of installations. The first work produced on magnetic tape was Piotr Bernacki and Bruszewski's *Pictures Language*. It was an attempt to translate abstract language signs into definite object images (for instance, 'A' stood for sand, 'B' for a stone, 'C' for a road, etc.).

In 1974 Bruszewski and Kwiek accomplished their subsequent works. They concentrated here on the notion of space articulation (Bruszewski's *Transmisja przestrzenna* / *Space Transmission* and Kwiek's *Sytuacja studia* / *Studio Situation*). Kwiek's work resulted from his reflection on the parallel phenomena of the structures of the mind and the media, their feedback, and the social outcomes they created. In the following years Kwiek produced a number of works of exceptional importance for the development of Polish video art (*Video C*, 1975; *Video*; and *Video i oddech* / *Breath/Video*, 1978), which combine not only various media but also different ontological dimensions of artistic communication. Bruszewski, in turn, drew on his observation of narration, registration and transmission, leading to the constitution of 'the unrecognizable situation'.[15]

The artists in the Film Form Workshop made various forms of creative use of video, including those which widened the scope of possibilities of expression in other art disciplines (besides cinema). This was the result of the above-mentioned open and multi-disciplinary approach of the Workshop artists. Finally, in addition to the most popular forms – tape works and video installations (the latter were produced exceptionally often by Bruszewski, Mikołajczyk and Waśko) – video performance appeared at this point with equal frequency and versatility.

Waśko in his video installations (such as *Róg / A Corner* and *Powiększenie / Enlargement*, both from 1976) continued with the problem he had previously both addressed theoretically and realised on film – the problem of space and construction through and in media. He disclosed the relativity of the reciprocal of real space and its (audio-)visual image, as well as the relative and illusionary nature of the representation itself. In the installation *A Corner*, he problematised the phenomenon of direct transmission and examined simultaneously the relationship between reality and its representation, and between the real and the represented space. An important and emphasised aspect of this work is the spatial character of the installation itself, that is, the monitor – the point where the real space meets the represented. Therefore the installation, besides deconstructing the medium of video, opens up to the intertextual relationship between sculpture and environment art. The problematic nature of space represented in video art, with intertextual reference not only to spatial arts but to performance as well, returns in a video-performance installation titled *Przestrzeń poza* (*Space Behind*, 1976). The video performance *Zmęczenie mojej nogi* (*Tiredness of My Leg*), from the same year, creates the position of the artist as a subject of involuntary inferences in the work's structure and theme, which subsequently shows the work itself (according to Marshall McLuhan's theses) as a continuation of psycho-physical human activity. Waśko examines the problem of inference in the medium within the work's structure in the already-mentioned *Enlargement*.

Antoni Mikołajczyk, in turn, in a number of video installations, for example *Obraz brawny, obraz czarno-biały* (*Colour Image, Black and White Image*, 1975), *Obraz pozorny* (*Illusory Image*, 1976) and *Rzeczywistość – Obraz rzeczywistości* (*Reality – Image of Reality*, 1976), worked through the use of photography (his original medium) to multiply and complicate the processes of recording and transmission (for example, he registers a register transmitted as an image of reality). Mikołajczyk reveals here, in this way, the relativity of information communicated by the media and how it manipulates reality (or the image of reality) and its status. In another installation from the same period, *Zapis świetlny* (*Light Record*, referring in its character to his earlier works produced in other media), the future basic type of his art is already anticipated: the art of light in its many forms. Using a number of instruments, such as photo cameras, video cameras, lasers, welding machines and electric lamps, Mikołajczyk created virtual forms of light interacting with the universe of solid and permanent entities. In this way, he continued on another level his games with reality (and its illusionary representations, which are manipulated), something which was characteristic of his video installations. Treating light as material and simultaneously as an instrument,[16] Mikołajczyk problematised the borderline between reality and its illusion, as he created spaces where the mind experiences both transgression and infinity.

A concern for the media aspect of video marked all three types of video art produced by the Workshop artists who developed cognitive characteristics. In many cases, analytical works were a continuation in this new medium of the scope of experiments and approaches that had been previously undertaken in film. Many video tapes by Robakowski and Waśko's *Tiredness of My Leg* were rooted in the earlier filmic experience of mechano-biological feedback (these include Robakowski's *Prostokąt dynamiczny / Dynamic Rectangle*, 1971; *I'm Going*, 1973; and *Exercises for Two Hands*, 1976). Some tapes indeed repeat the subject matter of previous film works, with the use of the new means of expression. *Po linii* (*Along a Line*, 1977) by Robakowski and Waśko's *Pomiar* (*Measurement*) of 1976 may serve as examples.

The examination of video as a new artistic medium was connected at that time with the analysis of television, which in spite of its similarity to video on a technical level was perceived as its opposite. This reserve towards television was characteristic of Polish artists well into the 1980s. That the negation was then clearly ideological in nature, by the way, belies the thesis of the political indifference of the avant-garde of the 1970s.[17] 'Video art', wrote Robakowski in 1976, 'is an opposition which depreciates the usefulness of that institution [i.e. television – RWK], it is an art movement, which through its independence strips bare the mechanism of the steering of another man'.[18] Later Robakowski's words became a specific commentary on the above issue – they were filmed TV images that he manipulated, for example in *Pamięci Leonida Breżniewa* (*Tribute to Leonid Brezniew*, 1982–1988) and *Sztuka to Potęga!* (*Art Is Power!*, 1985). Earlier, from the mid-1970s, the artist consistently produced video tapes in which he minutely analyses the character of the electronic medium and its relationship to the author, the operator and the public. He studied different ways of registering reality and how the media had conditioned them, and also the new image of the world and its elements that was arising. He also studied the relationship between video works and the references of video tapes in the context of presentation, and so on.

As was the case with film, the problem in video of the relationship between reality and its audio-visual representation and the recipient dominated most

Workshop artists' work. Their video works revealed the relativity of perception mediated by the electronic image, the blurred boundaries between reproduction and creation and the resulting possibilities of the manipulation of reception. The confrontation of the 'electronic reality', combined with the knowledge of the world held by the recipient, provoked a reflection on the nature of the medium and its borders of cognition, its credibility, and the possibilities of communication. These issues were exceptionally potent in Bruszewski's video tapes and installations, as well as Mikołajczyk's installations. In a series of tapes titled *Dotknięcie video* (*Touch of Video*), Bruszewski analysed the same problems by referring to his ideas of the contradiction between direct experience and experience mediated through conventional codes, which regulate our cognisance and organise our knowledge. It is a paradox, but direct perception is possible here only because of the media, and the mechanical and electronic means of data transmission. So the works from the *Touch of Video* series, as Bruszewski intended, set traps for what exists, thus disclosing the conventionality of our perception and knowledge.[19] Both his video tapes and his installations, like *Outside* (1976) and *Instalacja dla Pana Muybridge'a* (*Installation for Mr Muybridge*, 1977), functioned in this way.

At the end of the 1970s and the beginning of the 1980s, Bruszewski produced a number of works which concentrated on sound. In some cases, they remained connected to the image, as in the installation *Telewizyjna kura* (*Television Hen*, 1979), where a sensor reacting to the changes of intensity of emission, attached to the screen of a monitor, controlled a 'cackling' sound generator. In other cases, sound partially gained independence, as in *Sternmusik* (1979), an installation where the sound camera reacted to the turning of Stern magazine pages. All these works on sounds finally gained complete autonomy in some installation-performances, later compiled in *Trochę Muzyki* (*A Bit of Music*, 1982). These examples, alongside Bruszewski's own theory on art communication, formed a basis for his radio installation *The Infinite Talk* (1988), performed in Ruine der Kunste Berlin, where the synthetic voices of a pair of virtual interlocutors held an infinite talk on air. The materials for the talk were fragments from classical philosophers' writings randomly chosen by a computer program.

13. [...]

14.

In addition to the media works (photographs, film and video), boards, artistic and programme publications, various objects and installations also found their place in the Workshop's activities. Some of them demanded activity on

the part of the viewer, thereby introducing the problem of the viewer's participation and interactivity. All of them combined to form a specific syndrome of
artistic activities and their product, whose character allows us today to perceive
the Film Form Workshop as a phenomenon as much modern as historical.
Representing the most interesting features of the new avant-garde art of the
1970s, and being closely related to the analytical and conceptual movement,
the Workshop – due to the media character of its activity, the concern for the
communicative aspect of art (it was the Workshop artists Połom and later
Bruszewski who started to use the computer as a specific, active instrument
of an art work) and its strategy of actively provoking the recipient – remains a
phenomenon related to modern interactive multi-media practices.[20]

*Originally published in Warsztat Formy Filmowej 1970–1977 (Warszawa:
Centrum Sztuki Współczesnej, 2000). An edited version of the original, with
some clarifications of the original English translation.*

NOTES

1 Daniel In the introduction to his book *O sztuce nowej i najnowszej*, Piotr Krakowski bluntly states: 'I have purposefully excluded Polish art because our art milieu does not play any special role as far as the newest trends and tendencies are concerned. Rather, it interprets and transforms ideas previously demonstrated and suggested by artists in the West.' See *O sztuce nowej i najnowszej* (Warszawa: Warszawa: Państwowe Wydawnictwo Naukowe, 1981), pp. 7–8.

2 See Lechosław Olszewski, 'The Activity of the Film Form Workshop as an Example of Art Strategy Towards the Polish Authorities in the 70s', *Artium, Questiones*, vol. IX, 1998.

3 See among others Stan Brakhage, *Scrapbook: Collected Writings 1964–1980* (New York: New Paltz, 1982), p. 168 and following.

4 Many film artists had been linked to the Workshop merely for the time of their studies, or shortly after graduating, before they moved to cinematography – the film production industry.

5 The above differentiation is not parallel to the initial membership at the founding of the Film Form Workshop, which included artists belonging to both groups, namely Wojciech Bruszewski, Ryszard Gajewski, Juliusz Janicki, Tadeusz Junak, Paweł Kwiek, Józef Robakowski, Andrzej Różycki and Zbigniew Rybczyński.

6 For example see Antoni Mikołajczyk's view in conversation with Jaromir Jedliński, *The Real and the Evasive Catalogue* (Poznań: Arsenal Gallery, 1995), pp. 14–18.

7 See P. Adams Sitney, 'Structural Film', *Film Culture*, no. 47, 1969.

8 See Peter Gidal, 'Theory and Definition of Structuralist/Materialist Film', *Studio International*, November 1975.

9 Józef Robakowski, 'Jeszcze raz o czysty film', *Polska*, no.10, 1971, unpaginated.

10 Bendkowski commented on his work: 'the possibilities of the dynamics of the film image and sound have been tested with the use of the following elements: the actor's account, the changes of focus with the constant recording of space; multiple copying of some recorded spaces; insertion of static elements into images of high dynamics; the increase of contrast; fragmentary record of space; the identification of an object and the human being; the fragmentary composition of human body parts; the dynamic editing of all relations.' *Galeria Współczesna*, no. 6, 1975.

11 Paweł Kwiek, *Dokument obiektywny o człowieku*, 1976, unpublished essay available in the Centre for Contemporary Art, Documentary Department.

12 See Kluszczyński's chapter 'Zbigniew Rybczyński albo ino jako wideo', *Film wideo – multimedia. Sztuka ruchomego obrazu w erze elektronicznej* (Warszawa: Instytut Kultury, 1999).

13 See Kluszczyński, *Awangarda. Rozwazania teoretyczne* (Łódź: Łódzki Dom Kultury, 1998).

14 Compare, for example, Robakowski's text *Video art – szansa podejscia rzeczywistości* (Lublin: Labyrinth Gallery, 1976).

15 See Tomasz Samosionek, 'Rozmowa z Wjciechem Bruszewskim', *Zeszyty Artystyczne*, no. 7, 1994.

16 Compare Hanna Wróblewska, 'Antoni Mikołajczyk – rzecz raz jeszcze w naturze swiatła',

Exit, no. 2, 1994.

17 See Piotr Piotrowski, *Dekada* (Poznań: Obserwator Publishers, 1991).

18 Robakowski, 1976.

19 Bruszewski, *Rozmowy o sztuce, poznaniu i języku* (Łódź: Warsztat Formy Filmowej, 1973–1974).

20 See also Kluszczyński, 'Od konceptualizmu do sztuki hipermediow. Rozważania na temat modelu sytuacji estetycznej w sztuce multimedialnej', Krystyna Wilkoszewska, ed., *Piękno w sieci. Estetyka a nowe media* (Kraków: UNIVERSITAS, 1999).

THE 1980s: INTRODUCTION

Michael O'Pray

In his brief but incisive snapshot of the 1980s, published in 1989, on the cusp of momentous changes in Poland, Ryszard Kluszczyński analyses many of the traits that identify much of the avant-garde moving-image work of that decade. It was a period of huge social and political upheaval marked by the Solidarity movement, the imposition of martial law in 1981 and the collapse of communism in 1989.

In relation to film, it witnessed the fuller emergence of video as a medium, adopted by many young artists and used more extensively by the older Film Workshop generation who had pioneered it from the mid-1970s on. However, in retrospect, it is now possible to see more clearly a further and extremely important development that was to have a huge impact especially in the post-1989 period, and that is of the role of women in avant-garde moving-image production and beyond. It needs to be said immediately that women had always been involved in the 1970s avant-garde. For example, Zofia Kulik, Natalia LL, Ewa Partum, Katarzyna Hierowska and Jolanta Marcolla, had all been very active in the 1970s. The myriad strategies and approaches of these women artists and others deserve a much more substantial account than an introductory book like this can supply. Needless to say, in their work the broader Polish and Western culture was explored from a radical critical position. For example, 'consumerism', sexuality and the 'body', were explored in Natalia LL's performance-inclined work (eg. *Consumptive Art*, 1973), and art as an open-structured and inter-media process, in Przemysław Kwiek and Zofia Kulik's (KwieKulik) work (eg. *Open Form*, 1971, with Przemysław Kwiek and Jan Stanislaw Wojciechowski).[1]

As in the UK and USA, the 1980s in Poland heralded new media, inter-textuality, social critique and more personal forms of representation, thus becoming an energetic cauldron of varied, often clashing, ingredients that would pave the way for its future art practice. In many ways, the Polish avant-garde moving-image work of the 1980s was confronting ideology, not from an 'objective' point of view but rather from that of subjectivity, that is of the subject's 'experience' within social, political and cultural ideologies and structures. These large, complex issues were to be developed more forcefully in subsequent decades by moving-image artists working within a pluralist art world, while engaging at the same time with Western ideas and practices involving, importantly for Polish women artists, feminism, gender and sexuality.[2]

NOTES

1   See, for example, Maxa Zoller, 'KwieKulik' Open Form Film: Polish Expanded Cinema?', A.L.Rees, Duncan White, Steven Ball and David Curtis, eds., *Expanded Cinema: Art, Performance, Film* (London: Tate Publishing, 2011).

1   See, for example, Izabela Kowalczyk, 'Feminist Art in Poland', ed. Katy Deepwell, *nparadoxa*, no. 11, October, 1999.

THE 1980s:
FROM SPECIFICITY TO THE NEW TRADITION – AVANT-GARDE FILM AND VIDEO ART IN POLAND

Ryszard W. Kluszczyński

The 1980s have brought with them many different artistic forms. The term 'pluralism' became the most widely used description of today's art. This, however, does not mean the birth of completely new creative forms or new media. On the contrary, we can observe a renewed interest in the styles and tendencies of the past, such as the return of expressionism and Surrealism or the Dadaistic poetry of scandal. Heterogeneous works now appear which embrace in their form elements and tendencies which formerly functioned separately.

In contemporary avant-garde cinema throughout the world, the return of these tendencies can be seen sometimes as evidence of helplessness and lack of direction, while at other times it signals an attempt to connect with a source of new inspiration through an exploration of avant-garde history; cinematic abstraction appears again in, for instance, some video work. An oneiric – expressionist cinema returns in some women's work – crossed with feminist ideology. Narrative experiments harken back to the *nouveau roman*, the lessons of structuralist cinema are renewed and remembered.

Such retro-references may also be found in Poland. Sometimes the sources of inspiration are found beyond the realm of cinema, as in the case of the work of Jerzy Truszkowski, who attempts to reactivate the image of the artist created by Stanisław Ignacy Witkiewicz. In films by Małgorzata Potocka we find traces of references to surrealistic oneirism, for instance, Bogustaw Schaeffer. The films of the group 'Łódź Kaliska' reactivate elements of Dadaistic poetry, and unite them with the experiences of the Happening and Performance Art. Nevertheless, techniques used in these films, for example *Robić sztukę* (*Making Art*) and *Freiheit, nein danke* (*Freedom, No Thanks*), including motionless camera, cutting in mid-movement and non-pristine images, all suggest that their authors have not forgotten the experiences of structural film. On the other hand, the group 'Yach Film' presents a fusion of the techniques of Performance and Happening with the new expressionist genre, recording their experimentation first on Super8 film and finally on video.

Most of the Polish works created in the last years have been recorded on video tape. Video art thus becomes the main medium of artistic statement for the independent film community in Poland. It has developed into two main streams. The first of these is rooted in the tradition of medialism (experimentation with the medium) and is most fully realised in the creativity of Józef Robakowski. In his works the subject and structure are treated in an intellectual way. In spite of their expressionist look, they are rationally constructed and minutely underlined: their intimate personal character often possesses an ironic inflection which demonstrates the author's reserve about his own image recorded on tape.

The second stream opposes the primacy of the intellect and bases itself on emotions and their irrational sources. Representing such an attitude is the work of Truszkowski, who stresses that in his works he submits to spontaneous and intuitive inspiration. His creativity belongs to the post-conceptual phase of the work. A similar, though distinctive, quality may also be found in the work of Zbigniew Libera; this artist limits the rule of the emotional factor, giving his films a contemplative-meditative character. The viewer is asked to see beyond the emotional measure of the work if she or he is to arrive at the message therein. This happens in the case of *Obrzędy intymne* (*Intimate Rites*). In this film, however, emotional reaction remains the basis for an understanding of it. Zygmunt Rytka's works also have a meditative quality. The rational element found

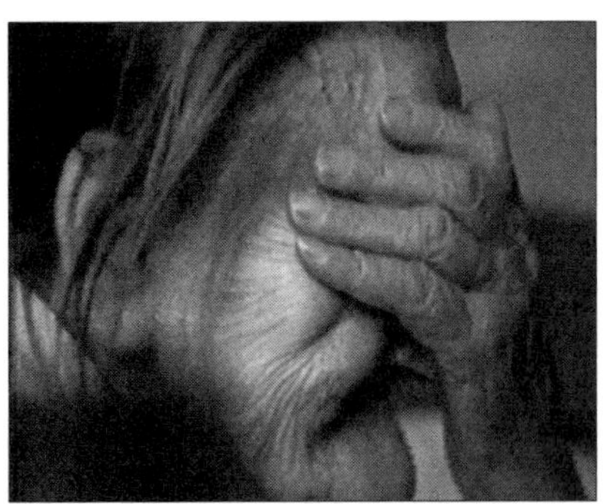
Fig. 20 *Intimate Rites* (Zbigniew Libera, 1984)

in them brings the author of *Obiekty chwilowe* (*Momentary Objects*) towards the stream represented by Robakowski. A lack of interiorised reserve places Rytka's work somewhere between the two tendencies.

A new situation, then, has arisen. Inasmuch as in the 1970s the domination of medialism imposed upon the Polish avant-garde film a depersonalised analytic character, the 1980s have brought with them the primacy of the subjective. However, the opposing terms 'medialism' and 'intermedialism', which described the dynamics of changes in Polish avant-garde film in the past decade, have not been replaced by the tension between rationalism (full control over the work, reserve and irony) and irrationalism (directness, emotionalism and meditativeness). This change does not destroy, however, the continuity between both facets of development of independent cinema in Poland; contemporary creativity is nurtured by the influences flowing from the recent past.

Film and video work in Poland in the 1980s has reactivated the classical mode of avant-garde art work. In part it is defined by the inner tension between the artistic and meta-artistic discourse (for instance the works of Truszkowski and Rytka), deepening, however, the extent of its subjective meaning. There have appeared also a number of films and video works whose structure is defined not by the tension between certain discourses but by the opposition of artistic languages. An example of this is the work of the group 'Łódź Kaliska' on the one hand, and of Józef Robakowski on the other. The films and videos of the Lodz group, work by Marek Janiak and Andrzej Kwietniewski, and the video works of Adam Rzepecki are based upon the collision of the language of medialism with the language of Dadaism, this juxtaposition being aimed by its authors against the ideology of medialism. Equally conflicting in character is the inner dialogue of artistic codes in the latest works of Robakowski. Here the medialistic language clashes with the language of the new personal expressionism, which remains the object of his deconstruction.

The transformations within Polish cinema and video art in the last years lead from the model based upon the coexistence of pure artistic and meta-artistic discourse, to a model in which pure artistic discourse loses its relative autonomy and in the 1970s becomes treated as a meta-artistic discourse, towards a model in the 1980s where the two artistic languages of a personal expressionism (or a neo-Dadaist language) and a structuralist language clash against each other in an attempt to parody, critique and deconstruct each other.

Originally published in Undercut, no. 18, 1989.

FILM FORM WORKSHOP:
MANIFESTO AND ARTISTS' STATEMENTS

Michael O'Pray

INTRODUCTION

As was also the case with other film movements and groups in Europe and the USA at the time, in the 1960s and 1970s, many members of the Film Form Workshop wrote fairly extensively about their work and explored ideas and theories about film and other media. Uniquely perhaps, they were also responsible for one of the few manifestos relating to experimental film in the post-war period. They also formed one of the few cohesive film groups to arise out of the period. Like the British filmmakers who centred their activities largely around the London Film-Makers Co-op set up by them in the late 1960s and early 1970s, the Polish filmmakers had a physical base in the Lodz Film School, where the workshop was initiated. However, probably more than other experimental avant-garde film groups, the Film Form Workshop generated a large amount of written material expressing ideas that were integral to articulating theory and, most importantly, the members' practice as artists. What follows is a collection of pieces, sometimes edited, mainly from the mid to late 1970s. It makes no claims to being a comprehensive collection; rather it is a fascinating snapshot of a moment of enormous creativity and intense questioning of the nature of film and filmmaking by the Polish film avant-garde. Finally, at times the theoretical and philosophical ideas being expressed in some of the artists' statements are ones often struggling for articulation and any difficulty in engaging with them is the result of encountering this struggle as it takes place. We have resisted any attempt to 'clarify' this important process, this struggle.

WORKSHOP MANIFESTO (1975)

There exists in art the poetically engaged tendency, or to define another of its aspects, the emotionally expressive one. This tendency is directed towards the presentation of the inner experience of the artist, his anxieties, eagerly making use of all uncontrolled, and thus 'authentic', impulses as the means of expression (that is where the favoured criterion of 'truth' comes from). It finds its relationship to tradition through references to the 'universal' ('final') problems, in some shades mystical, political, moral or didactic, in others, aesthetic or entertaining, and ultimately fatalistic.

The tendency appealing to the 'sensitivity' of the audience (aesthetic value) on the one hand, and to its 'sense of humanity' (the value of 'content') on the other, is generally understood and eagerly consumed. It expresses what the average spectator knows or feels, but is not able to express. Flattering the audience and sometimes befriending it is part of the ritual of this kind of activity, its very principle of functioning. This tendency, through its popularity, gives the impression that its values are beyond discussion. Seeing this kind of perspective before us, we undertake the para-scientific activity, cool and calculated artistic theory-practice, the activity which, in the eyes of poetically intuitive criticism, turns out to be a primitive, unworthy of 'critical reflection', crazy-aesthetes play-thing.

We ignore the 'evaluating verdicts' and 'explanatory sentences' of this criticism. The general re-evaluation of the art of the latter half of the twentieth century makes us acclaim, together with the whole tendency, as stale, existing only as the 'live' history of the past.

First

1. Entering the sphere of the mechanical means of transmission and ...., we reject all attempts to annex a part of this sphere to serve word culture. More precisely, we reject literary cinema.
2. We also reject all other functions taken from outside the essence of cinema, that is:
   Politicising
   Moralising
   Aestheticising
   and amusing the spectator.
3. We reject all that disables the breaking of tradition. This hinders the construction of a different picture of reality from the one imposed through

school and education.

We reject then the film language limited by strict codification and defined utility functions. We pay as much attention to the technical equipment as to the clear channel unblurred by external accretion. Our essential activity is thus unlearning everything produced by education and what we call the found culture.

4. Recognising that reality is received on the basis of transmission, we undertake its examination through the analysis of how the means of our contact with it function.

This activity (which renders the situations observed to their elementary states, 'contents' to commonplaces) is supposed to be central and absolutely adequate. There is no insight into the new spheres of reality without the equipment enabling this insight.

That is why, having no ambition to construct the picture of the world (as if completing the act), we try to find out what is to be constructed thanks to the phenomenon of film technique, its sphere and its boundaries, surpassing the possibilities of verbal expression.

We want to give another chance to the subjective in play with the objective.

ARTISTS' STATEMENTS

Kazimierz Bendowski
The Relativity and Objectivity of Visual Messages

Every day, we encounter the means of mass transmission, the visual message (TV, cinema, the press, photography, street posters, paintings in galleries and museums), all of which present information we cannot confirm personally. As to the possibility of such events, we cannot believe that they may have been prepared, falsified. Seeing a picture on TV or in the cinema for instance – pictures, say, showing the Gobi desert – one would find difficulty in saying that these were not pictures of the Sahara desert. The same is true in the case of differentiating between French and Spanish landscapes, German and Dutch. Only the spectator's faith in the honesty of the reporter, on the one hand, and the honesty of the institution producing the means of transmission, on the other, allows the acceptance of this message as a true one. Those creating visual messages – filmmakers, TV workers, press reporters, advertisement makers, etc. – realise fully how difficult it is to convince the spectator of the objectivity of events using visual media. In my studies in film, photography and television pictures, I have been interested in the divergence between reality and its picture, recorded by the latter media. Such a picture always differed from the real thing, stressing the inadequacy of recording using all the presently applied techniques. I witnessed many paradoxes by which a funny element of reality recorded on film was understood by most spectators as tragic.

The visual message consists of:

1. PICTURE – TV, cinema, the press, an exhibition etc. may be the carrier of a picture
2. ITS INTERPRETATION – written, spoken by a living creature or a machine.

The interpretation is also determined by the cultural location and the values and ideas of its inhabitants.

Wojciech Bruszewski
Traps

1. WHAT EXISTS – exists outside of me.
2. WHAT EXISTS is knowledge of what exists.

The knowledge exists from cultural pressure.

WHAT EXISTS – IS A CONVENTION

What I do in film, video or in the area of other techniques consists in nothing more than laying traps for WHAT EXISTS (1, 2).

The traps I lay are in the place of a contact between an object and an object, between an object and a subject. The functioning means of transmission supply that place.

The procedure systematically performed leads to the destruction of 'THE CONVENTION OF WHAT EXISTS'.

WHAT EXISTS (1) is the potential energy of destruction of WHAT EXISTS (2), but it cannot appear as an argument.

That is from here that the appearance comes stating that in this activity the objective factor does not participate at all.

It is just this factor indeed that gets into the game with the subjective one and as a result the traps are opened for something to fall in.

(1975)

Paweł Kwiek
WHAT DO I DO?

Lately, apart from my work with film, camera and photo camera, I am interested in situations in which, because of TV technology, there are possibilities of seeing new spaces of reality. I am trying to explore in them my possibilities and limitations.

TV technology provides possibilities for the construction of schemes that are transmitting picture reality in an impossible manner for man but complaisant with his attributes.

I am constructing such a scheme where the observed reality is a man whose picture of reality is his transmitted image.

There is the possibility of various constructions of these schemes, which have various degrees of dependence of ways of transmitting the observed man – therefore a different degree of dependence of himself on the reality picture, which he perceives.

On the other hand, the construction of such a scheme implies what a person, being a part, can point out, distinguish, define.

So here, we are dealing with the creation of intentional reality, physically existing and examining the function of a person in it through performing on them, plays in concrete operations.

This activity can be defined as the creation of meanings that enter our reality through TV technology, or as an examination of its structure.

The kind of work I undertook in my project *Video A–Z*.

It contains 24 situations of this type, out of which only 4 (A, C, M, N) were accomplished because of problems.

(10 July 1976)

Antoni Mikołajczyk
REGISTRATION

Making the penetration of reality, that surrounds us, we are not able to registrate all the changes that take place under the reality.

Through our curiosity we are able to registrate only a piece of this reality, which we interpret according to our idea, which becomes of our experience.

I am interested in the experiments that make the scope of our field of vision as wide as it may be possible and that theoretically would cover an unlimited number of possibilities in search and reality interpretations.

Record of reality is the method of experiment, which changes under the influence of mechanic change of visual angle of the camera and cinecamera.

Camera changes the angle in the relation to the vertical and horizontal level by using the constant angle distance. The horizontal registration is 15 and the vertical, 10.

(1975)

ANTONI MIKOŁAJCZYK

The material which I use in my work offers the possibility of penetrating regions of reality which verify established, interpretative stereotypes of the photographic picture, and shake the explicitness of reality. This explicitness of reality turns out to be an ambiguous or even a non-existent, apparent reality. Because of its ability to translate the multi-dimensional world reality into its two-dimensional recording, photography is not, in my opinion, an extension of the sense of seeing, but a factor creating a new reality which often only exists in our consciousness. Thus, the most important aspects of my studies are:

1. relationships between a real picture and an apparent image,
2. relationships between a photographic recording of reality and the photography of this recording,
3. relationships between motion and time, recorded by a video camera,
4. mechanical recording of reality encompassing its total space,
5. quasi-documentary description of reality with geometrical elements,
6. a photographic recording of reality by a luminar point.

Using a photographic camera, I make a recording of some definite space, attempting to record the concrete reality, such that it would encompass all of its possible elements.

The method I use involves making a series of photographs of the reality surrounding the cameras: the pictures are taken while the camera turns with an increasing angular value. In this way, the whole space available for registration has been encompassed, becoming a kind of disclosed geometrical figure whose edges would be the most distant points of this reality. It changes according to the surroundings in which the camera is placed. In my research of the possibilities of shaking the explicitness of reality as a medium of message, I also used a video camera. In the case of pointing a video camera at a concrete reality and recording a particular registration of this reality, the picture on the monitor created the impression of sameness. Introducing the elements of motion into the picture, feigning it or combining auditory effect with an immobile monitor picture I got the chance to interfere with the realness of the transmitted world of reality. A new non-real reality, the artistic reality, has been created.

In successive works I attempted to introduce into our consciousness a non-existent reality created through the combination of a picture of reality with new elements alien to it. I introduced new features into the photographic picture of this really existing reality recorded by photographic or video means: geometrically special values, elements of motion, owing to which the realness of this reality is shaken because of the elements alien to it genetically.

This realness of a new reality is created through the combination of two values independent of each other which hitherto did not exist together: the real photographic recording and the real, special geometrical elements. The elements of motion inscribed in this reality, because of its truthfulness, create a new artistic situation (despite a certain logical shaking of its credibleness, doubts cannot be raised as to the realness of this mutual system).
(1980)

Józef Robakowski
MECHANICAL AND BIOLOGICAL REGISTRATION

For many years I have been carrying out experiments on the relationship of my psycho-physical organism to the devices which produced mechanical registration (e.g. film camera, photo camera, TV camera, tape recorder).

The effect of these experiments has been confirmed by the capital significance of these technical findings, for they present the possibility of trans-ferring my psych-physical state, temperamental state and conscious states on to tape.

At last, thanks to my own personal specifics and possibilities, which permit me to cross my own latent thoughts with complicated realistic problems – phenomena – I have the possibility of registering any part of me. They themselves have become my own instruments of penetration into the mysteries of the world and present the possibility of another discovery.

These pieces of equipment are valuable, for through them I can uncover more of what I know, see or feel. When, in a moment of awareness, I can add their nature to mine, there is a special type of link. Then my experience will be deeper and richer.
(1977)

Józef Robakowski
THE STATE OF CONSCIOUSNESS

BY USING THE KNOWLEDGE OF PHYSICAL REALITY, AND ANALYSING IT BY MEANS OF CONTEMPORARY TECHNIQUES (FILM, PHOTOGRAPHY, VIDEO, SOUND…) I WANT TO ATTACK MY HABITS OF PERCEPTION, DESCRIBING COUNTLESS TIMES, 'THE SPHERE OF THE OBVIOUS'.

REALISING THAT IMAGINATION, INTUITION AND PRESENTLY USED MEANS OF DESCRIPTION AND MARKING ARE IMPERFECT, I TURN TO THE METHODS ACCEPTED BY SCIENCE AND TO THE DEVELOPMENTS OF TECHNOLOGY. I SUPPOSE, OR SHOULD I SAY, I AM SURE, THAT THEY WILL GIVE ME A MORE PRECISE WAY OF DESCRIBING REALITY.

LOOKING FOR SENSE IN THE SEEMINGLY ABSURD ASSUMPTION IS THE ESSENCE OF MY WORK.

I have chosen, for the description of the content of reality, a mechanical method, disinterested in its own end, objective by nature, and giving, through its physical factuality, cognition of what is rational – I and the reality. Treating this METHOD as 'the physical reality', I am trying to eliminate, as far as it is possible, the commentary of human philosophy and all which has been brought about by longstanding traditions in the understanding of the aesthetics of art.

Thus, 'A R T' treated as a means of empirical cognition became a method of examining 'one's own suggestion', and the form of its intellectual manipulations revealed quite precisely its weaknesses as well as the weaknesses of those who undertake such examinations.

That is why I reject in my work both the 'live language' (intuitive one) and the specifically codified language as being too stiff, having too few possibilities by subjecting it to definite utilitarian functions – for instance, communication.

I am finding that the social roles engaged by these examinations, only through the motif of suggestion, create a situation where the 'other' person always has a chance (through their interest) to become an observer or even an active participant in the 'process of revealing reality'. That is why the 'thoughtless audience' is absolutely unnecessary here.

(1977)

Józef Robakowski
THE STATE OF CONSCIOUSNESS

Under the pressure of the up-to-date semiological investigations about film, there appears to be a need to describe and interpret the new structural elements of the films being produced by the Warsztat Formy Filmowej – Workshop of the Film Form. Here attempts are being made to develop the techniques and means of description lying outside the theory of literature; hence the revival of interests in the s.c. 'pure cinema'/pure film art, and the efforts to purify film from any possible narrative or descriptive structures, and the methodology of literary poetics.

Again, much attention was given to verify that the s.c. 'substance of the film structure' was based on the characteristics of the fono/photographic recording. Any comparative interpretations were rejected, such as juxtaposing film to painting, music, theatre, poetry, or literary narrative.

Especially valid is questioning the links between film and literature, or stated in another way, of contradicting the very common view that a film event is, by nature, 'literature-bound' – a conception reasonably backed up by many approved theoreticians of film art.

In Warsztat Formy Filmowej, a basic question was raised: CAN WE SPEAK A FILM LANGUAGE?

This question has resulted in many film productions in which the common prejudice of the theory of literature – bound characters of film theory – and the system of signs ascribed to it become a master pattern for all semiotic and linguistic attempts. The linguistic conceptual system has appeared, after investigation, to be an artificial treatment – an operation violating, in a sense, the pure film notation. The notation of film results in a different pattern of signs, outside language. Any analysis of a film event by means of linguistic categories is therefore impossible.

In the programme of the s.c. 'General Semiology', including any activities, operating with signs, film continues to be a signal structure and can be expressed in a different conceptual language.

The investigations evidenced certain linguistic deficiencies, which, however, does not discriminate against the fantastic possibilities of using i) many combinations of phonemes, morphemes, and lexemes that are present in a language, and ii) language not subject to grammatical rules – since nonsensical usage seems to be the procedure for adapting the categories elaborated by the structural linguistics on the grounds of the film semiology.
(1975)

Ryszard Waśko

INTRODUCTION TO THE 'MODELS OF FILM STRUCTURES'

General Remarks

As is known, the constructing of models is a method used in science to simplify problems and thus increase the chance of solving them. There exist two kinds of model. The first, the so-called theoretical model, is a set of simplifying assumptions, and the other, the so-called real model, is the very object or set of objects fulfilling such assumptions (this model is the realisation of the theoretical one). Achieving the real model is possible through constructing a physical relation of objects that would simplify the examined reality but be similar to it in such a way that it may be used to solve the problems concerning this reality.

Logic and the Problems of the Film Subject

The process of acquiring knowledge consists of active procedures of the examining person on some material, e.g. already acquired knowledge, objects given physically or notionally. The activities are described here in so-called 'everyday language' using such expression as 'I assume', 'I accept', 'I change', etc. The operations with notional objects may be expressed in sentences of the type 'if Y then Z', where 'Y' is a description of the objective result of the operation, and 'Z' the knowledge obtained in those conditions. In this way, the relation, the activity of examining in relation to the objects, shows that the examining person does not introduce, himself, any changes. Thus there is the possibility of conducting verifiable, precise operations (also mental ones). Such operations are possible thanks to the use of elements of logic which deal with the analysis of language and such activities as thinking, defining, classifying, etc. Performing activities with the help of elements of logic in 'Models of Film Structures', I was aiming at both coming to know their functioning in the sphere of film subject, and the behaviour of a given film structure using those elements.… One of the purposes of using the theory of models and multitude theory in 'Models of Film Structure' was to enable the introduction of such an activity that would lead to a more precise (objective) cognition (operation) of the analysed object. Using the problems of logic is at the same time an attempt at creating a methodology (of film) for solving, not necessarily all of its problems, but at least some of them. This type of specific methodology (if it were created) would constitute a set of examinations, the result of which would be a more perfect knowledge of the subject, film.

Ryszard Waśko
'BEFORE AND AFTER' – AN EXPLANATION OF MY 'HYPOTHETICAL WORKS'

In my work up until now, and I am thinking about the years 1972–75, I was interested in the mathematical logic of the existence of film. Through the phrase 'Models of film structures' I tried to understand what it was that guided film, what was its structural matter, matter in the logical sense, and not matter in the understanding suggested by P. Gidal in the *Structural Film Anthology*. Hypothetical Film enters the sphere of the abstract understood in a very extreme way. Hypothetical Film does not test, it does not analyse, it does not trouble itself with logical, illogical or material existence of film, on the other hand it suggests the carrying over of a physical system in the direction of an unintelligible unverified reality, hypothetical reality. Hypothetical Film proposal opens – I believe – a new field for discussion which is far greater than the field of film itself (film-fact). I believe that the leaving of the sphere taking film for granted is, at this moment, the most important and interesting problem, a problem which allows us once more to leave the boundaries of what has already become our knowledge (awareness).

Hypothetical Film considers in each of the proposed arrangement its basic value – 1 second – simultaneously with its divisions into lesser qualities. It has been accepted that 'physical time', in which each event has its beginning and end (e.g. projection time), may be lessened to a statistical time, time with abstract and not physical characteristics. These conditions are met by a so-called 'empty (stasis) interval time' existing as an abstract quality in the physical arrangement, through which its projection becomes a hypothetical projection. The 'empty interval time', stays in relation to 'physical time' understood as the denotation of the time of exposure of each separate film frame (as I have already described in my 'Four-dimensional photography'). Physical time (exposure time) may exist even in most extreme qualities, as its own projection; on the other hand in the system proposed by Hypothetical Film it can exist only simultaneously (parallel) with the 'empty interval of time', in the same, 'physical time' also becomes hypothetical projection. The 'empty interval time' stays in relation to 'physical time' understood as the denotation of the time of exposure of each separate film frame (as I have already described in my 'Four dimensional photography').

Physical time (exposure time) may exist even in most extreme qualities, as its own projection; on the other hand in the system proposed by Hypothetical Film it can exist only simultaneously (parallel) with the 'empty interval of time', in the same, 'physical time' also becomes hypothetical projection of physical reality and abstract reality. Hypothetical Film consists of a number of projections considered in the context of the basic quality – 1 second of physical time – reduced to value 'O' (1 second running time of the 'empty interval time').

'Before and After' – a short text on my last work called Hypothetical Film by Ryszard Waśko, Łódź 1979.
R.W.

Originally published in LUX Artists' Moving Image.

A REBELLION À *LA POLONAISE*

Mateusz Werner

In the Soviet Union or Communist Poland, where cultural life was ruled by the totalitarian dictatorship with the help of its political censorship, phrases like 'artistic rebellion', 'aesthetic transgression', 'avant-garde' and 'struggle for freedom of expression' would be used as commonly as they were in France or the US. What they stood for, however, was something completely different. This seems to go without saying – and yet do we *really* keep it in mind while comparing the works of, say, Sergei Eisenstein and D. W. Griffith or Kazimir Malevich and Barnett Newman, or while going into analogies between the artistic consequences of the 'Prague Spring' and the 'Paris May'? These reservations remain in force when a question is asked about a Polish 'New Wave'. Obviously, it would be easiest to reject them by saying that, in a historical sense, no such phenomenon existed, thereby closing the case. Still, why is it worthwhile to keep on asking such questions? Because while probing this topic, we get to what is perhaps the heart of the matter: what was the 'artistic revolt' in a captive world? What did a gesture of radical aesthetic choices stand for in a culture where, as Wisława Szymborska wrote, 'apolitical poems are also political'?

In order to visualise the incongruence of the two worlds and the absurdity of historical analogies, let us consider a trivial and forgotten episode of the early 1960s. The French *Nouvelle Vague* is well-known to have begun as a rebellion of 'film archive rats' under the banner of *Cahiers du Cinema* magazine, scribblers with leftist tendencies, who were familiar enough with the narrative potential of film language to ridicule and compromise the Gaullist 'papa's cinema', which told its petty bourgeois dreams through Hollywood-style formulas. It was about then, at the time when Truffaut, Resnais, Godard and Rohmer scored their first successes at European film festivals, that Poland faced its so-called 'screenwriters' rebellion'. At first glance, it might have looked similar to what was going on in France. A number of excellent writers – among these Jerzy Stefan Stawiński, Józef Hen and Aleksander Ścibor-Rylski, supported by the great film critic Bolesław Michałek, at that time the editor in chief of Poland's most important film weekly, *Film* – refused to obey the Polish cinematic paradigm of the late 1950s, which they had co-founded themselves by writing screenplays for Andrzej Wajda, Jerzy Wojciech Has, Andrzej Munk and Kazimierz Kutz. Was not their switch to directing their own movies a gesture similar to the one made by the fellow filmmakers of *Cahiers du Cinema*? Indeed, the objective was the same: to leave 'theory' for 'practice', to get the cinema into the right hands, and finally to pursue personal 'success'. What an illusory resemblance!

The Polish screenwriters rebelled against artistic ambitions and elevated 'national' themes of the 'Polish Film School'[1] for the sake of a so-called 'cinema for the people', understood as a product adjusted to the needs of a large audience. Instead of historical eposes or 'intellectual struggle', they wanted to produce light comedies of manners, crime films, adventure thrillers. And so they did. What originated was average and – a crucial aspect for the Communist authorities – politically safe film entertainment of the 1960s. There is no evidence that the 'rebellion' was in any way inspired by the authorities. There is no doubt, however, that it did serve well their interest. The Polish Film School's founding legend originated in the political 'thaw' after Stalin's death, and this background – combined with an inconvenient selection of themes touching on unhealed war trauma, but also with a symbolic language, full of loftiness and irony – might at any time have shown its dangerous anti-regime potential. Some might ask why the rebellion's battle call was an affirmation of trivial entertainment, and why it should have been voiced by renowned artists, challenging the same tradition with which they had identified themselves as co-authors of the most successful works by Wajda, Munk and Kutz. It is indeed difficult to understand. And yet understandable, if only one takes into account how attractive the Polish public found at that time the forbidden fruit of consumption, entertainment and customised pleasure which money could buy. Disbelievers may recall what a breakthrough it was for the entire Soviet bloc to see Coca-Cola come onto the Polish market in the 1970s. Well, it was a top-level political decision!

Let us however come back to the 'New Wave'. Should the experts in the field be right when saying that this trend developed a coherent poetics – in which an associative tone of the narration, which imitates the chaotic narration of life itself, is supported by dialogue enlivened by the spontaneity of improvisation, shooting all scenes in an open-air location, using natural light and simulation of a natural background sound – then the first Polish 'New Wave' film was made in 1958, chronologically ahead of the French artists' works. I obviously refer to *The Last Day of Summer* by Tadeusz Konwicki, which won the Grand Prix at the Venice film festival – though, crucially, in the category of experimental films. Extremely private and allegedly the cheapest production in the

Fig. 21 *The Last Day of Summer* (Tadeusz Konwicki, 1958)

history of Polish cinema (the whole film crew consisting of just five people), it is at the same time a proof that limitations build the form of a work of art. Konwicki was a novelist and screenwriter, not a professional director, and in his literary work he had rather followed solid psychological and realistic models. As a writer, he had meticulously observed the poetics of 'social realism' during the Stalin era. His film debut, in turn, became an unexpected explosion of auteurist freedom – freedom from moralism, didacticism, theatrical form and psychological predictability. He created a work in which a simple story of an encounter between a man and a woman (Irena Laskowska and Jan Machulski) at the seaside on a sunny late summer day, and all resulting psychological complications, became a light and subtle metaphorical sketch about overcoming the trauma of the war. In Konwicki's picture, the difficulties faced by people interested in each other and craving intimacy as they try to establish interpersonal relations become a figure of incumbent memories, which carry with them an insurmountable experience. Sand dunes, the cold northern sea, clouds and jet fighters shooting across the sky were natural scenery to create this impression, full of smothered eroticism, played spontaneously, with improvised dialogue in parts. *The Last Day of Summer* was so far ahead of its time that there was no response to it. A ground-breaking movie which appeared by some chance, unexpectedly, and caused no ferment, sowed no seeds of rebellion, founded no school. Konwicki's later works showed a return to rather more conventional forms of film language, as if the author became scared of the loneliness to which he condemned himself through the experimentalism of his proposal. No wonder, since, apart from the non-synchronous sound and black-and-white picture, *The Last Day of*

Summer actually meets all the requirements of the *Dogme*. It was definitely too new, too bold and too different at that time to become a milestone. Time was most unkind to this innovation, though. As we watch the film today, it seems to be only too familiar. It lacks a deformation of reality which, through its extremism, might have preserved the boldness of this innovativeness. The experiment undertaken by Konwicki, partnered by his excellent cameraman Jan Laskowski, which was a risky attempt to capture the momentariness of the 'now', to render the entire freshness and spontaneity of what happens between people at a given moment in time, has become the ABC of filmmaking.

While looking for historical analogies, one may also ask what in the Polish cinema of the late 1950s and early 1960s was an easy object for contestation, whose work came to be synonymous with 'papa's cinema', that is, a disrespectfully located point of reference worth rebelling against? In some respects, Polish post-war cinema was closer to what was going on in Italy than in France. As in Italy, in Poland, the Communists took power in the cultural sphere. The obvious difference was that in Italy they enjoyed an authentic authority, deriving moral legitimacy from their record of anti-fascist struggle, while in Poland their dominant position had been imposed by Soviet tanks. Both countries' filmmaking reflected this ideological domination of the radical left in a triumph of a socially committed poetics: Italy saw a heyday of 'neorealism', while in Poland 'social realism'[2] was decreed as the only correct artistic ideology from 1949 onwards. It is difficult to compare the two trends – 'neorealism' developed with its own dynamics; in the course of free transformations, it created its own language and range of topics, featured a number of prominent artists and outstanding personalities, and originated a couple of masterpieces. This may hardly be said of 'social realism' – based on the political catechism of Commissar Zhdanov and passed on official congresses, it was a state-supported 'Party line' in art. Not a single interesting work originated in this trend, and the only films that went down in history were the ones in which the authors tried to overcome the Zhdanovist canon, like *Winter Twilight* by Stanisław Lenartowicz, Munk's *Man on the Tracks* and Wajda's *Generation*. Therefore, the landmark character of Fellini's *Sweet Life*, Antonioni's *Adventure* or Visconti's *Rocco* and *His Brothers* meant something different in the Italian cinema than, say, Wajda's *Kanal*, Munk's *Heroism* or Kutz's *Cross of Valor*. The purpose of these great Italian pictures, which opened the 1960s, was to overcome their own origins rather than radically reject something foreign and disrespected. Suffice to say that the author of the 'neorealist' manifesto, Antonio Pietrangeli, co-penned Visconti's *Obsession* (*Ossessione*), blocked by fascist censorship, while Fellini wrote the screenplay for Roberto Rossellini's *Open City* (*Roma, città aperta*), whereas Antonioni, also one of Rossellini's screenwriters (*Un pilota ritorna*), started his career by making a number of excellent documentaries (*Gente del Po, Netezza Urbana*). There are also obvious links with 'neorealism' in the case of a younger film-maker, Pier Paolo Pasolini.

Wajda's and Munk's generation suddenly started speaking outright while radically rejecting 'social realism', though what they proposed was simply speaking out these dramas and emotions – generally connected with the period of the German occupation, which had remained a political taboo for a dozen or so years – rather than an aesthetic revolution or reversal of the political message behind the social realist model (a step which Polish cinema in fact could not afford until the 'Solidarity' days). The success of *Kanal* or *Ashes and Diamonds* was proof that it was not only Poles who had waited for the story. Wajda stressed on many occasions that he and his fellow film-makers had been aware that 'if we didn't make these films, nobody would, and they would simply never come into existence'. In other words, the Polish 'social realism' functioned as a cultural 'deep freezer', the result being that the films which should have been made in the mid-1940s were not made until the late 1950s. In this sense, 'social realism' was 'policeman's cinema' rather than 'papa's cinema'. Had it not been for the 'deep freezing' of the Stalinist era and the delayed debut of the Polish Film School, what would probably have developed into 'papa's cinema' by the early 1960s would have been something like a Polish 'neorealism', against which Jerzy Skolimowski or Roman Polański might have ranted and raved.

Is such speculation reasonable at all? Perhaps it is not, and yet everybody does it. For instance, the French critics argue about whether there would have been any *raison d'être* for the *Nouvelle Vague* if something like Italian 'neorealism' had developed in France. The discussion was caused by the sensational discovery of a lost copy of *Le Rendez-vous des quais* by Paul Carpita,[3] a Marseilles worker and pupil of a local Soviet cultural institute, and an enthusiast of Pudovkin, Vertov and Dovzhenko. With money supplied by Marseilles harbour unionists, he made a feature about a local dockworkers' strike during the war in Indochina. Carpita's film is socialist-realistic in form though with some elements of 'bourgeois schmaltz', which would have surely discredited him in the eyes of Stalinist censors. Hence in some views, this is the only example of French 'neorealism'. What if there had been more of them? Would the 'caviar left' of *Cahiers du Cinema* have anything to say?

Let us leave the historical analogies at last. The 'New Wave' phenomenon may indeed be regarded as universal and timeless once we assume that Truffaut's or Godard's films are the focus of an eternal gesture of artistic rebellion and aesthetic transgression. With such an interpretation of the term 'New Wave' – and it is probably one that the originators of this publication feel an affinity with – the work of the Polish avant-gardists becomes an obvious field for interpretation. We are touching here the question of the avant-garde's role in Polish cinema. Did it really call for rebellion? It certainly did before World War II, when groups like START, and then SAF,[4] rebelled against the kitsch and trashiness of mass-market productions, searching for unique form that could bear the burden of social criticism as well. This is particularly evident in the practice – excellent and continuously rediscovered – of Franciszka and Stefan Themerson. After the war, however, the founders of START – Wanda Jakubowska, Jerzy Toeplitz, Aleksander Ford and or Jerzy Zarzycki – themselves formed the film-industry establishment and laid foundations for the poetics of socialist realism. Their rebellious experimentation and artistic ambition were replaced by political dogmatism and formal conservatism. When Stalin died and a political 'thaw' followed, the new field of confrontation was no longer the struggle for a new language of cinema but rather the struggle for remembering the various tragic aspects of war without ideological falsifications and restoring them to the collective consciousness. The dividing line established then survived virtually until the late 1980s: everyone crossing the line of falsehood defined by the censor was a rebel. Only that carried authentic risk and required effort. Everything else was but play. This is, probably, the reason for the avant-garde's marginal role in Polish cinema, its peculiarly private character and limited scope of influence. Though, sometimes, the subversive potential of certain formal solutions may have been greater than could be suspected. One such case was certainly Krzysztof Zanussi's *Illumination* (1972), which could have spawned a new genre: the filmic essay, a bit in the vein of Agnès Varda's late work. The combination of a fictional plot and the intrusion of real-life spontaneity in the shape of non-professional actors, improvised dialogue and unique, lifelike mise-en-scène, and, at the same time, the presence within the narrative of the author's commentary and documentary footage of the actual characters – all that created a superb opportunity for making direct references to reality. The hybrid form may have become the vehicle for a multi-level metaphor that would be outside the censor's reach. Meanwhile, however, outstanding documentalists had entered the stage – Krzysztof Kieślowski, Tomasz Zygadło, Marcel Łoziński – and in the early 1970s they made documentary film the main instrument of social and political criticism. When we watch *Illumination* today, we see clearly how fresh and ground-breaking a formula it offered, how the assumed, fictional, schematic and banal combined in it with the element of transgression, spontaneity and structural openness, in order to reflect, on a deeper level, the fundamental tension between convention and expression that seems the pivotal issue for Zanussi's practice.

Interestingly, after 1989, when practising the political metaphor no longer made sense, the rewarding role of the avant-garde rebel was not taken up by Polish filmmakers either. And the few attempts actually made – like Piotr Uklański's *Summer Love* – were understood neither by the critics nor by the public and went virtually unnoticed. At the 2006 Gdynia Polish Film Festival, the author of this essay witnessed

Fig. 22 *Summer Love* (Piotr Uklański, 2006)

the director's post-premiere meeting with the public, which could serve as the perfect example of a comedy of errors. Uklański, who kept the face of an artist who, despite his lack of filmmaking experience, had seriously aspired to create a regular western, was attacked by disappointed fans of the genre pointing to his alleged failures in constructing the western world. The fans, in turn, were opposed by the less naïve film scholars and critics, who, quoting numerous examples, from Sam Peckinpah to John Hillcoat, of western movies that played with the generic norm in order to enrich the genre, proved that *Summer Love* was simply a postmodern variation on the western and that, when watching the movie, one should simply forget the rigid premises of normative poetics. The whole context of a meta-critical play with the conventions of 1990s Polish popular cinema remained opaque for the audience, which either left the theatre, bored with the lack of fast-paced action, or, understanding that the film was about 'something else', something 'difficult', watched in solemn silence the most overacted, self-parodying scenes with Katarzyna Figura and Bogusław Linda. The press, in turn, concentrated on the hefty cost of hiring Val Kilmer, whose presence on screen was to serve as visible proof that Polish cinema was 'recovering from crisis'. This is precisely the cost of artistic experimentation: a communication breakdown. Who knows whether, from this perspective, Summer Love is not the most radical filmic experiment in Poland after 1989?

Originally published in Łukasz Ronduda and Barbara Piwowarska, eds., Polish New Wave: The History of a Phenomenon That Never Existed (Warsaw: Centre for Contemporary Art, 2008).

NOTES

1   Daniel The 'Polish Film School' went down in history as a trend representative of Polish cinema from the 1950s onwards, in which the authors focused on interpretations of historical and national themes (especially a struggle with post-war trauma), in opposition to 'social realism' and in the wake of the 'thaw' of 1956. The history of this generational formation started with the success of Andrzej Wajda's *Kanal* in Cannes in 1957. The trend's canonical titles include *Kanal* (1956), *Ashes and Diamonds* (1958) and *Lotna* (1959) by Andrzej Wajda; and *Man on the Tracks* (1956), *Heroism* (1957) and *Bad Luck* (1960) by Andrzej Munk. A number of later films made between the 1960s and the 1990s referred to the trend's legacy, e.g. *The Ashes* (1965) and *Man of Marble* (1976) by Wajda, *Dance* (1965) by Tadeusz Konwicki and *Death as a Slice of Bread* (1994) by Kazimierz Kutz. See E. Nurczyńska-Fidelska and Bronisława Stolarska, eds., *Szkoła Polska – powroty* (Łódź: Wydawnictwo Uniwersytetu Łódzkiego, 1998).

2   Social realism (socio-realism), well-known as the Communist regime's doctrine and the 'only correct' form of artistic expression, was introduced in the USSR during the Congress of Soviet Writers in 1934; in Poland, it was imposed after the war in 1949 (in Polish cinema, during the Filmmakers Congress in Wisła). As in other arts, it served Stalinist propaganda and a 'realist' presentation of reality in accordance with the historical materialism doctrine, while suppressing formal experiments and censoring artists who refused to obey the guidelines of the socio-realist approach. In Poland it was retained as the official trend in art until the 'thaw' of 1956.

3   It turned out that it was not the French police who had stolen Carpita's film in 1955, as it was believed, but the French Communist Party activists. This is how the director recounts it: 'Well, the police took the film, and the negative disappeared too. I thought they had burned it all, like they said. But, in reality, it was the Communist Party which took the negative. They hid it. The war in Indochina was over, the Algerian war had begun. The Communist Party's position was ambiguous. The party's deputies had voted full powers to [new Prime Minister] Guy Mollet. They didn't want to bring up this history. I only found this out years later, when the negative turned up in an archive. I went crazy, I was furious when I found out. It wasn't the CP which made the *Le Rendez-vous des quais*, it was us, in Marseilles. It's some story, eh?' David Walsh, 'Three Filmmakers Who Were Silenced', *The International Workers Bulletin*, San Francisco, 3 June 1996.

4   The START Society for the Promotion of Artistic Film (Stowarzyszenie Propagandy Filmu Artystycznego), founded in 1930 by Eugeniusz Cękalski to promote politically committed ambitious artistic cinema. START's work was continued from 1937 by SAF (Spółdzielnia Autorów Filmowych, The Film Authors Cooperative), among whose members were the Themersons.

BIBLIOGRAPHY

Abel, Richard, ed., *French Film Theory and Criticism, Vol. 1: 1907–1929* (Princeton, New Jersey: Princeton University Press, 1988).

Aitken, Ian, *European Film Theory and Cinema: A Critical Introduction* (Edinburgh: Edinburgh University Press, 2001).

Apollinaire, Guillaume, 'L'Espirit nouveau et les poètes', Roger Shattuck, ed., *Selected Writings of Guillaume Apollinaire* (New York: A New Directions Book, 1971) [1917].

Ardizzone, Maria Luisa, ed., *Machine Art and Other Writings: The Lost Thought of the Italian Years: Ezra Pound* (Durham; London: Duke University Press, 1996).

Armatys, Barbara, 'Dorobek publicystyczny i dzialalność społeczna "STARTU" (1930–1935)', *Kwartalnik Filmowy*, no. 1, 1961.

Armatys, Leszek, 'Myśl filmowa i dzialalność artystyczna "STARTU" (1930–1935)', *Kwartalnik Filmowy*, no. 1, 1961.

Balcerzan, Edward, *Bruno Jasieński. Utwory poetyckie, manifesty, szkice* (Kraków: Polska Akademia Nauk, 1972).

Balcuch, Alicja, *Tytus Czyżewski. Poezje i próby dramatyczne* (Wrocław, Warszawa, Kraków: Zakład im. Ossolińskich, 1992).

Banaszkiewicz, Władysław, 'Szkic z zarysu krytyki i estetyki filmowej w Polsce (1910–1913)', *Kwartalnik Filmowy*, nos. 2–3, 1956.

_______ 'Film a początki awangardy artystycznej w Polsce (przyczynki i noty)', *Kwartalnik Filmowy*, no. 4, 1959.

_______ with Witold Witczak, eds., *Historia Filmu polskiego 1895–1929, tom 1* (Warszawa: Wydawnictwa Artystyczne i Filmowe, 1989).

Baranowicz, Zofia, *Polska awangarda artystyczna 1918–1939* (Warszawa: Wydawnictwa Artystyczne i Filmowe, 1975).

Barańczak, Stanisław (aka Barbara Stawiczak), 'Trzy złudzenia i trzy rozczarowania polskiego futuryzmu', *Znak*, no. 10, 1979.

Barnouw, Erik, *Documentary: A History of the Non-Fiction Film* (New York; Oxford: Oxford University Press, 1993).

Bartelik, Marek, *Early Polish Modern Art: Unity in Multiplicity* (Manchester; New York: Manchester University Press, 2005).

Bayley, Stephen, 'Britain Has Become Indifferent to Beauty', *The Observer*, 22 March 2009.

Benson, Timothy, ed., *Central European Avant-Gardes: Exchange and Transformation 1910–1930* (Cambridge: Massachusetts Institute of Technology Press, 2002).

_______ with Éva Forgács, eds., *Between Worlds: A Sourcebook of Central European Avant-*

Gardes 1910–1930 (Cambridge: Massachusetts Institute of Technology Press, 2002).

Berghous, Günter, *Futurism and Politics: Between Anarchist Rebellion and Fascist Reaction, 1909–1944* (Providence; Oxford: Berghahn Books, 1996).

_______ ed., *F. T. Marinetti: Critical Writings* (New York: Farrar, Straus and Giroux, 2006).

Bird, Daniel, *Roman Polański* (Harpenden: Pocket Essentials, 2002).

_______ and Jeremiah Kipp, 'Outsiders, Shamans and Devils, Part 1: A Discussion of Central European New Wave Cinema with Film Writer Daniel Bird', *Slant Magazine*, 2009, http://www.slantmagazine.com/house/2009/03/outsiders-shamans-and-devils-part-1-a-discussion-of-central-european-new-wave-cinema-with-film-writer-daniel-bird/.

Bocheńska, Jadwiga, 'Człowiek przed soczewką', *Film*, no. 4, 1976.

_______ *Polska Myśl Filmowa do roku 1939* (Wroclaw, Warszawa, Kraków, Gdańsk: Zakład Naukowy im.Ossolińskich, Wydawnictwo Polskiej Akademii Nauk, 1977).

Bordwell, David, *Narration in the Fiction Film* (Madison: University of Wisconsin Press, 1985).

Borie, Monique, *Mythe et théâtre aujourd'hui: Une quête impossible? Beckett, Genet, Grotowski. The Living Theatre* (Paris: Librairie A.-G. Nizet, 1981).

Borowski, Wiesław, *Tadeusz Kantor* (Warszawa: Wydawnictwa Artystyczne i Filmowe, 1982).

Bowlt, John, ed., *Russian Art of the Avant-Garde: Theory and Criticism, 1902–1934* (London: Thames and Hudson, 1988).

Brakhage, Stan, *Scrapbook: Collected Writings 1964–1980* (New York: New Paltz, 1982).

Breton, André, *Manifestoes of Surrealism* (Ann Arbor: University of Michigan Press, 1972). Translated by Richard Seaver and Helen R. Lane.

Brooke, Michael, 'Polish Documentaries: *A Walk in the Old Town of Warsaw* (1958)', *Kinoblog*, http://filmjournal.net/kinoblog/category/directors/munk-andrzej/.

Bruszewski, Wojciech, *Rozmowy o sztuce, poznaniu i języku* (Łódź: Warsztat Formy Filmowej, 1973–1974).

Brzyski, Anna, *Modern Art and Nationalism in Fin-de-Siècle Poland*, PhD dissertation (University of Chicago, 1999).

_______ 'Between the Nation and the World: Nationalism and the Emergence of Polish Modern Art', *Centropa*, vol. 1, no. 3, 2001.

Bürger, Peter, *Theory of the Avant-Garde* (Manchester: Manchester University Press, 1984).

Burton, Alan, 'The Emergence of an Alternative Film Culture: Film and the British Consumer Co-operative Movement Before 1920', John Fullerton, ed., *Celebrating 1895: The Centenary of Cinema* (Sydney: John Libbey and Company Pty. Ltd., 1995).

Carpenter, Bogdana, *The Poetic Avant-Garde in Poland, 1918–1939* (Seattle; London: University of Washington Press, 1983).

Carrieri, Raffaele, *Futurism* (Milan: Edizioni del Milione, 1963).

Christie, Ian, 'French Avant-Garde Film in the Twenties: From 'Specificity' to Surrealism', David Curtis, ed., *Film as Film: Formal Experiment in Film 1910–1975* (London: Hayward Gallery, 1979).

_______ and John Gillet, eds., *Futurism. Formalism. FEKS. 'Eccentrism' and Soviet Cinema 1918–1936* (London: British Film Institute, 1987).

_______ *The Last Machine: Early Cinema and the Birth of the Modern World* (London: British Film Institute, 1994).

_______ 'Before the Avant-Gardes: Artists and Cinema, 1910–14', *La decimal musa: il cinema e le alter arts. The Tenth Muse: Cinema and Other Arts. Proceedings of the Vi Domitor Conference / VII International Film Studies Conference* (Udine: Arti Grafiche Fruilane, 2001).

———— 'Film as a Modernist Art', Christopher Wilk, ed., *Modernism: Designing a New World (1914–1939)* (London: V&A Publications, 2006).

Cichla-Czarniawska, Elżbieta, *"Heretyk awangardy" Jalu Kurek* (Lublin: Wydawnictwo Lubelskie, 1987).

Coates, Paul, *Lucid Dreams: The Films of Krzysztof Kieślowski* (Trowbridge, Wiltshire, England: Flicks Books, 1999).

Coniam, Matthew, 'Angel Games: The Early Films of Walerian Borowczyk', Matthew Black, ed., *Necronomicon Book Two* (London: Creation Books, 1998).

Cook, Benjamin and Łukasz Ronduda, eds., *The Films of Franciszka and Stefan Themerson*, a booklet accompanying a DVD of the Themersons' films (London: LUX, 2007).

Crittenden, Roger, *Fine Cuts: The Art of European Film Editing* (Amsterdam: Elsevier, 2006).

Curtis, David, ed., *Film as Film: Formal Experiment in Film 1910–1975* (London: Hayward Gallery, 1979).

Czartoryska, Urszula, 'Franciszka and Stefan Themersons: Visual Researchers, Theory and Praxis', Ryszard Stanisławski, ed., *Stefan i Franciszka Themerson. Poszukiwania wizualne / Stefan and Franciszka Themerson: Visual Researchers* (Łódź: Muzeum Sztuki, 1981).

Czeczot-Gawrak, Zbigniew, *Jan Epstein. Studium natury w sztuce filmowej* (Warszawa: Wydawnictwa Artystyczne i Filmowe, 1962).

———— *Zarys dziejów teorii filmu pierwszego pięćdziesięciolecia 1895–1945* (Wrocław, Warszawa, Kraków, Gdańsk, Łódź: Zakład Imienia Ossolińskich, 1977).

Czyżewski, Tytus, 'Pogrzeb romantyzmu – uwiąd starczy symbolizmu – śmierć programizmu', *Formiści*, no. 4, 1921.

———— 'Mój futuryzm', *Zwrotnica*, no. 6, 1923.

———— a. 'Krajobraz w kinie', *ABC*, 3 October 1932.

———— b. 'Film abstrakcyjny', *ABC*, 19 July 1932.

———— c. 'Film konwencjonalny', *ABC*, no. 290, 1932.

Davies, Norman, *God's Playground: A History of Poland, Vol. 2* (New York: Columbia University Press, 1982).

———— *Heart of Europe. A Short History of Poland* (Oxford, New York: Oxford University Press, 1986).

———— *Heart of Europe: The Past in Poland's Present* (New York: Oxford University Press, 2001).

DeKoven, Marianne, *Utopia Limited: The Sixties and the Emergence of the Postmodern* (Durham: Duke University Press, 2004).

Demetz, Peter, 'Introduction: A Map of Courage', Matthew S. Witkovsky, *Foto: Modernity in Central Europe, 1918–1945* (London: Thames and Hudson, 2007).

Dobson, Terence, *The Film Work of Norman McLaren* (Sydney: John Libbey & Co Ltd, 2007).

Donald, James, Anne Friedberg and Laura Marcus, eds., *Close Up 1927–1933: Cinema and Modernism* (London: Cassell, 1998).

Drury, Shadia B., *Alexandre Kojève: The Roots of Postmodern Politics* (London: Palgrave

Macmillan, 1994).

Dubois, Philippe, 'Photography Mise-en-Film: Autobiographical (Hi)stories and Psychic Apparatuses', Patrice Petro, ed., *Fugitive Images: From Photography to Video* (Bloomington: Indiana University Press, 1995).

Durgnat, Raymond, 'Borowczyk and the Cartoon Renaissance', *Film Comment*, January–February, 1976.

Dusienberre, Deke, 'The Other Avant-gardes', David Curtis, ed., *Film as Film: Formal Experiment in Film 1910–1975* (London: Hayward Gallery, 1979).

Dyer, Richard, *The Matter of Images: Essays on Representation* (London: Routledge, 2002).

Eagle, Herbert J., 'Power and the Visual Semantics of Polański's Films', John Orr and Elżbieta Ostrowska, eds., *The Cinema of Roman Polański: Dark Spaces of the World* (London: Wallflower Press, 2006).

Eberhardt, Konrad, 'Poezja konkretu', *Ekran*, no. 20, 1958.

Elder, Bruce R., *Harmony and Dissent: Film and Avant-Garde Movements in the Early Twentieth Century* (Ontario: Wilfrid Laurier University Press, 2008).

Epstein, Jean, 'On Certain Characteristics of Photogénie', Richard Abel, ed., *French Film Theory and Criticism, Vol. 1: 1907–1929* (Princeton, New Jersey: Princeton University Press, 1988) [1924].

Foster, Hal, *Compulsive Beauty* (Cambridge, MA: Massachusetts Institute of Technology Press, 1993).

Fullerton, John, ed., *Celebrating 1895: The Centenary of Cinema* (Sydney: John Libbey and Company Pty. Ltd., 1995).

Gabbard, Glen O. and Krin Gabbard, *Psychiatry and the Cinema* (Washington, DC: American Psychiatric Publishing, 1999).

Garztecki, Juliusz, 'Andrzej Pawłowski', *Ty i ja*, no. 6, 1963.

Gidal, Peter, 'Theory and Definition of Structuralist/Materialist Film', *Studio International*, November 1975.

Gilbert-Lecomte, Roger, 'The Alchemy of the Eye: Cinema as a Form of Mind', Phil Powrie, 'Film-Form-Mind: The Hegelian Follies of Roger Gilbert-Lecomte', *Quarterly Review of Film and Video*, vol. 12, no. 4, 1991.

Giżycki, Marcin, '…Zaciekła praca eksperymentatorska (O filmach Franciszki i Stefana Themersonów)', *Iluzjon*, no. 3, 1983.

________ a. 'Irzykowski, Kuczkowski and the Tradition of "Visionary Film" in Poland', *Afterimage*, vol. 13, autumn, 1987.

________ b. 'The Films of Stefan and Franciszka Themerson', *Polish Art Studies*, no. VIII, 1987, Lux Centre: http://www.luxonline.org.uk/articles/the_films_of_stefan_and_franciszka_themerson(1).html.

________ a. ed., *Walka o film artystyczny w międzywojennej Polsce* (Warszawa: Państwowe Wydawnictwo Naukowe, 1989).

________ b. 'Film w kręgu polskiej awangardy dwudziestolecia międzywojennego', Ryszard Kluszczyński, ed., *Film awangardowy w Polsce i na świecie* (Łódź: Łódzki Dom Kultury, 1989).

________ *Awangarda wobec kina: Film w kręgu polskiej awangardy artystycznej dwudziestolecia międzywojennego* (Poznań: Wydawnictwo Małe, 1996).

________ 'Canis de Canis, czyli Feliks Kuczkowski', Giżycki and Bogusław Żmudziński, eds.,

Polski Film Animowany (Warszawa: Polskie Wydawnictwo Audiowizualne, 2008).

_______ 'The "Red Wall of Surrealism": Experimental and Animated Film After the Thaw', Kamila Wielebska and Kuba Mikurda, eds., *A Story of Sin: Surrealism in Polish Cinema* (Cracow-Warsaw: Korporacja Ha!Art, 2010).

Godzic, Wiesław, 'Stefana Themersona myślenie o filmie', *Kino*, no. 12, 1986.

Goldberg, RoseLee, *Performance Art: From Futurism to the Present* (London: Thames and Hudson, 2001).

Grabowski, Ignacy, 'Najnowsze prądy w literaturze najnowszej. Futuryzm', *Świat*, no. 40, 1909.

Gunning, Tom, 'Loie Fuller and the Art of Motion', *La decima musa: Il cinema e le altre arti. The Tenth Muse: Cinema and Other Arts. Proceedings of the VI Domitor Conference / VII International Film Studies Conference* (Udine: Arti Grafiche Fruilane, 2001).

Haltof, Marek, *Polish National Cinema* (Oxford; New York: Berghahn Books, 2002).

_______ *The Cinema of Krzysztof Kieślowski: Variations on Destiny and Chance* (London: New York: Wallflower Press, 2004).

Hartwig, Julia, *Apollinaire* (Warszawa: Państwowy Instytut Wydawniczy, 1961).

_______ ed., *Guillaume Apollinaire. Listy do Madeleine* (Kraków: Wydawnictwo Literackie, 1976).

Hawkins, Joan, *Cutting Edge: Art-Horror and the Horrific Avant-Garde* (Minneapolis: University of Minnesota Press, 2000).

Helman, Alicja, Karol Lubelski and Władysław Banaszkiewicz, eds., *Z Dziejów Awangardy Filmowej. Materiały z sesji 'Awangarda filmowa lat dwudziestych'*, Sosnowiec, 10–12 March, 1975 (Katowice: Uniwersytet Śląski, 1976).

_______ with Alina Madej, eds., *Film polski wobec innych sztuk* (Katowice: Uniwersytet Śląski, 1979).

Hendrykowski, Marek, *Andrzej Munk* (Warszawa: Biblioteka 'Więzi', 2007).

_______ *Andrzej Munk* (Poznań: Wydawnictwo Naukowe UAM, 2011). Translated by Peter Langer.

Horn, Tadeusz, 'Kino przyszłości', *Kino-Teatr*, nos. 22–23, 1927.

Hulten, Pontus, ed., 'Cinema', *Futurismo & Futurismi* (Milan: Gruppo Editoriale Fabbri, 1986).

Insdorf, Annette, *Double Lives, Second Chances: The Cinema of Krzysztof Kieślowski* (New York: Hyperion, 1999).

Irzykowski, Karol, 'Człowiek przed soczewką. Czyli sprzedane samobójstwo', *Pion*, nos. 24–25, 1938 [1908].

_______ 'Śmierć kinematografu', *Świat*, no. 21, 1913.

_______ 'Futuryzm a szachy', *Ponowa*, no. 1, 1921.

_______ 'Kultura murzyńska w Polsce', *Ilustrowany Kurier Codzienny*, no. 37, 1922.

_______ a. 'Likwidacja futuryzmu', *Wiadomości Literackie*, no. 5, 1924.

_______ b. 'Awangardzistom, utarcie nosa', *Wiadomości Literackie*, no. 10, 1924.

_______ c. *Dziesiąta Muza. Zagadnienia Estetyczne Kina* (Warszawa: Wydawnictwa Artystycne i Filmowe, 1977) [1924].

Jakimowicz, Andrzej, 'Kronika Polskiej awangardy 1912–1957', *Przegląd Artystyczny*, no. 1, 1958.

Janicka, Bożena, 'Man and Ape', Bożena Janicka and Andrzej Kołodyński, eds., *Chełmska*

21. *50 lat Wytwórni Filmów Dokumentalnych i Fabularnych w Warszawie* (Warszawa: WFDiF, 2000).

Janiski, Stanisław, 'Rozmawiamy z J. Lenicą i W. Borowczykiem', *Film*, no. 31, 1957.

Jarosiński, Zbigniew and Helena Zaworska, eds., *Antologia polskiego futuryzmu i Nowej Sztuki* (Wrocław, Kraków: Zakład im.Ossolineum, 1978).

Jasieński, Bruno, a. 'Kieszeń od kamizelki źródłem plagiatu. Rewelacyjne odkrycia pana Irzykowskiego', *Ilustrowany Kurier Codzienny*, no. 37, 1922.

_______ b. 'Kina krakowskie', *Zwrotnica*, no. 3, 1922.

Jaworski, Stanisław, *Awangarda* (Warszawa: Wydawnictwa Szkolne i Pedagogiczne, 1992).

Jodorowsky, Alexandro, 'Vers l'éphémère panique ou Sortir le théâtre du théâtre', Fernando Arrabal, ed., *Le Panique* (Paris: Union générale d'éditions, 1973).

Karabasz, Kazimierz, 'Rok przełomu – rok startu', *Kamera*, no. 1, 1970.

Karcz, Danuta, 'Stefanii Zahorskiej walka o treść', *Kwartalnik Filmowy*, nos. 1–2, 1962.

Keller, Sarah and Jason N. Paul, eds., *Jean Epstein: Critical Essays and New Translations* (Amsterdam: Amsterdam University Press, 2012).

Kieślowski, Krzysztof, *Kieślowski on Kieślowski*, ed. Danusia Stok (London: Faber and Faber, 1995).

_______ 'The Sunday Musicians', Kevin Macdonald and Mark Cousins, eds., *Imagining Reality* (London; Boston: Faber and Faber, 1996).

Kluszczyński, Ryszard, 'Awangarda – sztuka nowa i antysztuka', *Przegląd Humanistyczny*, no. 3, 1986.

_______ a. ed., *Film awangardowy w Polsce i na świecie* (Łódź: Łódzki Dom Kultury, 1989).

_______ b. 'The Eighties: From Specificity to the New Tradition – Avant-Garde Film and Video Art in Poland', *Undercut*, no. 18, 1989.

_______ 'Awangarda i status artystyczny kina', Kluszczyński and Grzegorz Gazda, eds., *W kręgu zagadnień awangardy III* (Łódź: Wydawnictwo Uniwersytetu Łódzkiego, 1990).

_______ *Awangarda. Rozwazania teoretyczne* (Łódź: Łódzki Dom Kultury, 1998).

_______ a. *Zbigniew Rybczyński albo kino jako wideo* (Warszawa: Instytut Kultury, 1999).

_______ b. 'Od konceptualizmu do sztuki hipermediów. Rozważania na temat modelu sytuacji estetycznej w sztuce multimedialnej', Krystyna Wilkoszewska, ed., *Piękno w sieci. Estetyka a nowe media* (Kraków: UNIVERSITAS, 1999).

Kolesnikoff, Nina, *Bruno Jasienski: His Evolution from Futurism to Socialist Realism* (Waterloo, Ontario: Wilfrid Laurier University Press, 1982).

Kołtoński, Aleksander, 'O futuryzmie jako zjawisku kulturalnem i artystycznem', *Krytyka*, no. 42, 1914.

Konigsberg, Ira, 'Avant-Garde Cinema', *The Complete Film Dictionary* (Harmondsworth: Penguin Reference, 1997).

Konwicki, Tadeusz, *A Minor Apocalypse* (New York: Farrar, Straus, Giroux, 1983).

Kostrzyński, Rafał, 'Poznajcie Stefana', *Przekrój*, 26 January 2010.

Kowalczykowa, Alina, *Programy i spory literackie w dwudziestoleciu 1919–1939* (Warszawa: Państwowa Akademia Nauk, 1981).

Kowalczyk, Izabela, 'Feminist Art in Poland', ed. Katy Deepwell, *nparadoxa*, no. 11, October, 1999.

Kowalski, Alfred, 'U tworców polskiego filmu. Rozmowa z Anatolem Sternem', *Świat Filmu*, no. 2, 1937.

Krakowski, Piotr, *O sztuce nowej i najnowszej* (Warszawa: Państwowe Wydawnictwo Naukowe, 1981).

Kuc, Kamila, 'A Cruel Imagination: Roman Polański's Short Films', Kamila Wielebska and Kuba Mikurda, eds., *A Story of Sin: Surrealism in Polish Cinema* (Kraków: Ha!Art, 2010).

Kucharczyk, Jan, 'Pierwiastki filmowe w twórczości literackiej Tadeusza Peipera i Jalu Kurka', *Kwartalnik Fimowy*, no. 1, 1965.

Kuczkowski, Feliks, 'Wspomnienie o filmie przyszlości', typescript in the collection of the Archive of Polish Cinematheque, Syg.A.129, Warsaw [1955].

Kurek, Jalu, 'Kino – zwycięstwo naszych oczu', *Głos Narodu*, 2 March 1926.

_______ 'O nowe drogi w kinematografii. Jeszcze o filmie artystycznym', *Kino dla Wszystkich*, no. 6, 1927.

_______ 'O filmie "artystycznym" i "stosowanym"', *Kino dla Wszystkich*, no. 56, 1928.

_______ 'Uwagi o filmie', *Linia*, no. 3, 1931.

_______ a. 'Objaśniam OR', *Linia*, no. 5, 1933.

_______ b. 'Filmowy nóż w brzuchu', *Światowid*, no. 50, 1933.

_______ c. 'Nogi dziewczęce. Polska awangarda filmowa', *Światowid*, no. 26, 1933.

_______ 'Wspomnienia ze "Straży Przedniej" (Z dziejów filmowej awangardy krakowskiej)', *Kwartalnik Filmowy*, no. 3, 1961.

_______ *Chora fontanna* (Kraków: Wydawnictwo Literackie, 1971).

Kwiek, Paweł, 'Dokument obiektywny o człowieku', 1976, unpublished essay available in the Centre for Contemporary Art, Documentary Department.

Kyrou, Ado, 'The Marvelous Is Popular', Paul Hammond, ed., *The Shadow and Its Shadow: Surrealist Writings on the Cinema* (San Francisco: City Lights Books, 2000).

Lahoda, Vojtěch, ed., *Local Strategies – International Ambitions: Modern Art and Central Europe 1918–1968* (Prague: Artefactum, 2006).

Lawder, Standish D., *The Cubist Cinema* (New York: New York University Press, 1975).

Lawton, Anna, ed., *Russian Futurism Through Its Manifestoes, 1912–1928* (New York; London: Cornell University Press, 1988).

Lemann, Jolanta, 'Poglądy filmowe Anatola Sterna w dwudziestoleciu międzywojennym (na przykładzie publikacji i działalności społecznej)', Alicja Helman and Alina Madej, eds., *Film polski wobec innych sztuk* (Katowice: Uniwersytet Śląski, 1979).

Lenica, Jan, 'Film i formy narracji wizualnej', *Projekt*, no. 6, 1970.

Lentas, Beata and Małgorzata Ogonowska, eds., *Bruno Jasieński. Poezje zebrane* (Gdansk: słowo/obraz/terytoria, 2008).

Levi, Pavle, *Cinema by Other Means* (Oxford: Oxford University Press, 2012).

Lewicki, Bolesław, 'Klub filmowy "Awangarda"', *Kwartalnik Filmowy*, nos. 1–2, 1962.

Lintz, Edward, 'Difficiles Nuage: Gertrude Stein, OuLiPo and the Grammar of the Avant-Garde', Dietrich Scheunemann, ed., *European Avant-Garde: New Perspectives* (Amsterdam: Rodopi, 2000).

Lipski, Jan Józef, 'Tytus Czyżewski', Irena Maciejewska, Jacek Trznadel and Maria Pokrasenowa, eds., *Literatura polska w okresie międzywojennym*, vol. 3 (Kraków: Wydawnictwo Literackic, 1993).

Lista, Giovanni, *Futurism and Photography* (London: Merrell Publishers Limited, 2001).

Lourie, Richard, ed., *My Century: The Odyssey of a Polish Intellectual* (Berkley: University of California Press, 1988).

Malevich, Kasimir, 'Art and the Problems of Architecture: The Emergence of a New Plastic System of Architecture: Script for an Artistic-Scientific Film', Oksana Bulgakova, ed., *Kazimir Malevich: The White Rectangle: Writings on Film* (Berlin; San Francisco: PotemkinPress, 2002) [1927].

Malinowski, Jerzy, 'Janusz Maria Brzeski i Studio Polskiej Awangardy Filmowej. Program kin studyjnych', *Kraków*, May 1975.

Malkiewicz, Jan Krzysztof, 'Kolorowy eksperyment', *Ekran*, no. 5, 1957.

Marinetti, Filippo Tommaso, 'The Founding and Manifesto of Futurism' [1909], 'Destruction of Syntax – Imagination Without Strings – Words-in-Freedom' [1913], Umbro Apollonio, ed., *Futurist Manifestos* (London: Thames and Hudson, 1973).

______ 'List', *Zwrotnica*, no. 6, October 1922.

______ with Bruno Corra, Emilio Settimelli, Arnaldo Ginna, Giacomo Balla and Remo Chiti, 'The Futurist Cinema', Umbro Apollonio, ed., *Futurist Manifestos* (London: Thames and Hudson, 1973) [1916].

Markov, Vladimir, *Russian Futurism: A History* (London: Macgibbon and Kee, 1969).

Marszałek, Rafał, 'Maszyny na rykowisku', *Jan Lenica w Kwancie* (Warszawa: Centrum Klubowe Politechniki Warszawskiej 'Riwiera-Remont', 1976).

Martin, Marianne W., *Futurist Art and Theory* (Oxford: Clarendon Press, 1968).

Mayakovsky, Vladimir, *Pro Eto: That's What* (London: Arc Publications, 2008). Translated by George Hyde and Larissa Gureyeva.

Mazierska, Ewa, 'Międzywojenna myśl o filmie', *Dialog*, no. 2, 1991.

Mertins, Detlef and Michael W. Jennings, eds., *G. An Avant-Garde Journal of Art, Architecture, Design and Film*, 1923–1926 (London: Tate, 2010).

Michalewicz, Kazimierz, 'Z dziejów myśli filmowej w Polsce w latach 1919–1929', *Kwartalnik Filmowy*, nos. 1–2, 1962.

Miczka, Tadeusz, 'Literatura odnowiona kinem', *Film na Świecie*, nos. 325–326, 1986.

______ 'Cinema as Optic Poetry: On Attempts to Futurise the Cinematograph in Poland of the 1920s and 1930s', *Canadian Slavonic Papers*, no. 40, March–June 1998.

Mikołajczyk, Antoni, *The Real and the Evasive* (Poznań: Arsenal Gallery, 1995).

Moassi, 'Awangarda filmowa w Krakowie. "Or" Jalu Kurka i "Europa" Franciszki i Stefana Themersonów', *Nowy Dziennik*, 12 June 1933.

Moore-Gilbert, Bart, *The Arts in the 1970s: Cultural Closure* (London: Routledge, 2002).

Morrison, James, *Roman Polański* (Urbana: University of Illinois Press, 2007).

Motte, Warren F., Jr., 'Introduction', *Oulipo: A Primer of Potential Literature* (Dalkey Archive Press, 1998).

Murphy, Robert, *The British Cinema Book* (London: British Film Institute, 2009).

Nowell-Smith, Geoffrey, *The Oxford History of World Cinema* (Oxford: Oxford University Press, 1996).

Nurczyńska-Fidelska, Ewelina and Bronisława Stolarska, eds., *Szkoła Polska – powroty* (Łódź: Wydawnictwo Uniwersytetu Łódzkiego, 1998).

Olszewski, Lechosław, 'The Activity of the Film Form Workshop as an Example of Art Strategy Towards the Polish Authorities in the 70s', *Artium, Questiones*, vol. IX, 1998.

O'Pray, Michael, ed., *The British Avant-Garde Film: 1926 to 1995* (Luton: University of Luton Press, 1996).

______ *Avant-Garde Film: Forms, Themes and Passions* (London: Wallflower Press, 2003).

Ostrowska, Elżbieta, 'Knife in the Water: Polański's Nomadic Discourse Begins', *The Cinema of Roman Polański: Dark Spaces of the World*, John Orr and Elżbieta Ostrowska, eds. (London: Wallflower Press, 2006).

Ottinger, Didier, ed., *Futurism* (London: Tate Publishing, 2009).

Owen, Jonathan L., *Avant-Garde to New Wave: Czechoslovak Cinema, Surrealism and the Sixties* (London; New York: Berghahn Press, 2013).

_______ 'An Island Near the Left Bank: Walerian Borowczyk as a French Left Bank Filmmaker', *Beyond Borders: Polish Cinema in a Transnational Context*, Michael Goddard and Ewa Mazierska, eds. (Rochester, NY: Rochester University Press, 2014).

Peiper, Tadeusz, a. 'Futuryzm (Analiza i krytyka)', *Zwrotnica*, no. 6, 1922.

_______ b. 'Punkt wyjścia', *Zwrotnica*, no. 1, 1922.

_______ 'Kamedułom sztuki', *Gazeta Lwowska*, nos. 19–21, 1924.

Petro, Patrice, ed., *Fugitive Images: From Photography to Video* (Bloomington: Indiana University Press, 1995).

Piotrowski, Piotr, *Dekada* (Poznań: Obserwator Publishers, 1991).

_______ 'Modernity and Nationalism: Avant-Garde Art and Polish Independence, 1912–1922', Timothy O. Benson, ed., *Central European Avant-Gardes: Exchange and Transformation 1910–1930* (Cambridge: Massachusetts Institute of Technology Press, 2002).

_______ *In the Shadow of Yalta* (London: Reaktion Books, 2009).

_______ *Art and Democracy in Post-Communist Europe* (London: Reaktion Books, 2012).

Poggioli, Renato, *The Theory of the Avant-Garde* (Cambridge; London: The Belknap Press, 1968).

Polański, Roman, *Roman by Polański* (London: Heinemann, 1984).

Polit, Paweł, ed., *Themersonowie i awangarda* (Łódź: Muzeum Sztuki w Łodzi, 2013).

Prodeus, Adriana, *Themersonowie. Szkice biograficzne* (Warszawa: Świat Literacki, 2009).

Prus, Bolesław, 'Widziadła', *Pion*, no. 15, 1936.

Przylipiak, Mirosław, 'Amongst the Statues', Tadeusz Sobolewski, ed., *Polska Szkoła Dokumentu. Wojciech Wiszniewski* (Warszawa: Polskie Wydawnictwo Audiowizualne, 2008). Translated by Aneta Uszyńska.

Pytasz, Ewa and Marek, 'Poetycka podróż w świat kinematografu, czyli kino w poezji polskiej lat 1914–1925', Helman and Miczka, eds., *Szkice z teorii filmu* (Katowice: Katolicki Uniwersytet Lubelski, 1978).

Rees, A.L., *A History of Experimental Film and Video* (London: British Film Institute, 1999).

Rees, A.L., Duncan White, Steven Ball and David Curtis, eds., *Expanded Cinema: Art, Performance, Film* (London: Tate Publishing, 2011).

Richardson, Michael, *Surrealism and Cinema* (Oxford: Berg, 2006).

Robakowski, Józef, *Video Art* (Lublin: Labyrinth Gallery, 1976).

Romin, Seweryn, 'Śmierć sztuce', *Kino-Teatr*, no. 11, 1929.

Ronduda, Łukasz, 'Polish Analogue Video: The History of Polish Video Art, from the 1970s and 80s', Catherine Elwes and Chris Meigh-Andrews, eds., *Analogue: Pioneering Video from the UK, Canada and Poland* (London: Electronic and Digital Art Unit, 2006).

_______ and Florian Zeyfang, eds., *1, 2, 3… Avant-Gardes. Film/Art: Between Experiment and Archive* (Warsaw: Centre for Contemporary Art, 2007).

_______ and Barbara Piwowarska, eds., *Polish New Wave: The History of a Phenomenon That*

Never Existed (Warsaw: Centre for Contemporary Art, 2008).

______ *Polish Art of the 70s* (Warsaw: Centre for Contemporary Art, 2009).

Ryłko, Stanisław, 'Poprawki do polskiego rodowodu Apollinaire'a', *Miesięcznik Literacki*, no. 4, 1971.

Sacharewicz, Jolanta, 'O wciąż tajemniczym Apollinerze. Ostatni wywiad z Anatolem Sternem pani J. Scharawicz', Anatol Stern, *Dom Apollinaire'a* (Kraków: Wydawnictwo Literackie, 1973).

Sady, Małgorzata, 'The Themersons and Film Experiment', *Animator*, festival catalogue, 7–12 July 2009, Poznań.

Samosionek, Tomasz, 'Rozmowa z Wojciechem Bruszewskim', *Zeszyty Artystyczne*, no. 7, 1994.

Sandall, Roger, 'Seven Polish Shorts', *Film Quarterly*, vol. XV, fall, 1961.

Sexton, Jamie, 'Hell Unltd', *Screenonline*, http://www.screenonline.org.uk/film/id/440480/index.html.

Šimičić, Darko, 'The Case of Dada: Searching Through the Archipelago of the Avant-Gardes in Central Europe', Vojtěch Lahoda, ed., *Local Strategies – International Ambitions: Modern Art and Central Europe 1918–1968* (Prague: Artefactum, 2006).

Simpson, Patricia, et al., eds., *Labyrinth* (Hatfield: University of Hertfordshire, 2003).

Skaff, Sheila, *The Law of the Looking Glass: Cinema in Poland, 1896–1939* (Athens: Ohio University Press, 2008).

Słonimski, Antoni, 'Bezczelność producentów tandety', *Wiadomości Literackie*, no. 44, 1928.

Sloniowski, Jeanette, 'It Was an Atrocious Film: George Franju's *Blood of the Beasts*', Barry Keith Grant and Jeannette Sloniowski, eds., *Documenting the Documentary: Close Readings of Documentary Film and Video* (Detroit: Wayne State University Press, 1998).

Śniecikowska, Beata, *'Nuż w Uhu?' Koncepcje dźwięku w poezji polskiego futuryzmu* (Wrocław: Universytet Wrocławski, 2008).

Sontag, Susan, *Styles of Radical Will* (New York: Farrar, Straus and Giroux, 1969).

Stanisławski, Ryszard, ed., *Stefan i Franciszka Themerson. Poszukiwania wizualne/Stefan and Franciszka Themerson. Visual Researchers* (Łódź: Muzeum Sztuki, 1981).

Steegmuller, Francis, *Apollinaire, Poet Among the Painters* (London: Penguin Books, 1963).

Stern, Anatol, a. 'Emeryt merytoryzmu', *Skamander*, no. 17, 1922.

______ b. 'Kino', *Skamander*, no. 28, 1922.

______ c. 'Przeróbki literackie na ekranie', *Kinema*, no. 17, 1922.

______ a. 'Malarstwo a kino', *Skamander*, nos. 29–30, 1923.

______ b. 'Polska "Myszeis" kinematograficzna. Uwagi o naszych recenzentach, reżyserach, aktorach, scenariuszach, krytykach, miłośnikach i wrogach kina', *Skamander*, no. 28, 1923.

______ 'Uwagi o teatrze i kinie', *Reflektor*, no. 1, 1924.

______ 'Pomóżcie nam tworzyć film polski', *Kino dla Wszystkich*, no. 84, 1929.

______ *Wspomnienia z Atlantydy* (Warszawa: Wydawnictwa Artystyczne i Filmowe, 1959).

______ *Bruno Jasieński. Utwory poetyckie* (Warszawa: Czytelnik, 1960).

______ *Bruno Jasieński* (Warszawa: Wiedza Powszechna, 1969).

______ *Dom Apollinaire'a* (Kraków: Wydawnictwo Literackie, 1973).

Sterno-Wachowiak, Sergiusz, *Miąższ zakazanych owoców: Jankowski, Jasieński, Grodziński* (Bydgoszcz: Wydawnictwo Małe, 1985).

Stok, Danusia, *Kieślowski on Kieślowski* (London; Boston: Faber and Faber, 1993).

Strachocki, Janusz, 'Spotkanie z futurystami', *Świat*, no. 38, 1959.

Stypułkowska, Krystyna, 'Apollinaire w krytyce polskiej międzywojennego dwudziestolecia', *Przegląd Humanistyczny*, no. 4, 1961.

Suleiman, Susan Rubin, *Subversive Intent: Gender, Politics, and the Avant-Garde* (Cambridge, MA; London: University of Harvard Press, 1990).

Świeżyński, Wacław, 'Film dokumentalny', Jerzy Toeplitz, ed., *Historia filmu polskiego*, vol. 3 (Warszawa: Wydawnictwa Artystyczne i Filmowe, 1974).

Szkuta, Magda, 'Cracow', 'Warsaw', 'Poznań' and 'Łódź', Stephen Bury, ed., *Breaking the Rules: The Printed Face of the European Avant Garde 1900–1937* (London: The British Library, 2007).

Sztaba, Martyna, 'Z archiwum T. Rozmowa z Jasią Reichardt', *Przekrój*, 4 March 2013.

Taras, Katarzyna, *Witkacy i film* (Warszawa: Oficyna Wydawnicza Errata, 2005).

Tisdall, Caroline and Angelo Bozolla, *Futurism* (London: Thames and Hudson, 1976).

Toeplitz, Jerzy, 'Wczesne poglądy o filmie jako sztuce', *Iluzjon*, no. 3, 1984.

Trzupek, Jan, 'Wprowadzenie', *Andrzej Pawłowski 1925–1986* (Katowice: Galeria Sztuki Współczesnej BWA, 2002).

Turowski, Andrzej, 'Dadaistyczne konteksty', *Awangardowe Marginesy* (Warszawa: Instytut Kultury, 1998).

Tyler, Parker, *Underground Film: A Critical History* (Harmondsworth: Penguin, 1974).

Versari, Maria Elena, 'The Central European Avant-Garde of the 1920s: The Battleground for a Futurist Identity?', Vojtěch Lahoda, ed., *Local Strategies – International Ambitions: Modern Art and Central Europe 1918–1968* (Prague: Artefactum, 2006).

Walley, Jonathan, 'The Material of Film and the Idea of Cinema: Contrasting Practices in the Sixties and Seventies Avant-Garde Film', *October*, no. 103, Winter, 2003.

Warnier, Robert, 'Sensacyjna hipoteza Polska na temat Apollinaire'a', *Życie Literackie*, no. 423, 1960.

Waśkiewicz, Andrzej K., ed., *Anatol Stern. Wiersze Zebrane*, vol. 1 and 2 (Kraków: Wydawnictwo Literackie, 1986).

Wat, Aleksander, 'Wspomnienia o futuryzmie', *Miesięcznik Literacki*, no. 2, 1930.

_______ *Mój Wiek* (London: Polonia Book Fund, 1977).

Ważyk, Adam, 'Guillaume Apollinaire', *Wiadomości Literackie*, no. 1, 1928.

Werner, Mateusz, 'A Rebellion a la Polonaise', Łukasz Ronduda and Barbara Piwowarska, eds., *Polish New Wave: The History of a Phenomenon That Never Existed* (Warsaw: Centre for Contemporary Art, 2008).

White, John J., *Literary Futurism: Aspects of the First Avant-Garde* (Oxford: Clarendon Press, 1990).

Whoopee, 'O prawdziwe kino. Co widzimy na ekranie, a co jest istotą sztuki filmowej', *ABC*, 16 March 1930.

_______ 'Bez aktorów. Wizja przyszłości', *ABC*, 16 August 1932.

Wielebska, Kamila and Kuba Mikurda, eds., *A Story of Sin: Surrealism in Polish Cinema* (Kraków: Ha!Art, 2010).

Witkovsky, Matthew S., *Foto: Modernity in Central Europe, 1918–1945* (London: Thames and Hudson, 2007).

Wróblewska, Hanna, 'Antoni Mikołajczyk – rzecz raz jeszcze w natusze światła', *Exit*, no.

2, 1994.

Wyszyński, Zbigniew, 'Krakowska awangarda filmowa lat trzydziestych', *Kino*, no. 12, 1975.

Zagrodzki, Janusz, a. *Janusz Maria Brzeski, Kazimierz Podsadecki 1923–1936. Z pogranicza plastyki i filmu* (Łódź: Muzeum Sztuki, 1981).

______ b. 'Outsiders of the Avant-Garde', Ryszard Stanisławski, ed., *Stefan i Franciszka Themerson. Poszukiwania wizualne / Stefan and Franciszka Themerson: Visual Researchers* (Łódź: Muzeum Sztuki, 1981).

Zahorska, Stefania, 'Krytyka wobec modernizmu', *Praesens*, no. 1, 1926.

______ a. 'Film abstrakcyjny', *Wiek XX*, no. 8, 1928.

______ b. 'Treść czy abstrakcja', *Wiek XX*, no. 13, 1928.

______ 'Film eksperymentalny', *Kino Teatr*, no. 10, 1929.

______ 'Drogi rozwojowe filmu', *Miesięcznik Literacki*, no. 5, 1930.

______ 'Zagadnienia formalne filmu', *Wiadomości Literackie*, no. 52, 1931.

______ 'Polski film dobry', *Wiadomości Literackie*, no. 52, 1932.

______ 'W obronie polskiego filmu', *Wiadomości Literackie*, no. 17, 1933.

______ 'Dwie polskie krótkometrażówki', *Wiadomości Literackie*, no. 3, 1936.

Zoller, Maxa, 'KwieKulik' Open Form Film: Polish Expanded Cinema?', A.L.Rees, Duncan White, Steven Ball and David Curtis, eds., *Expanded Cinema: Art, Performance, Film* (London: Tate Publishing, 2011).

Żurowski, Maciej, 'Apollinaire w czterdziestolecie smierci', *Przegląd Humanistyczny*, no. 6, 1958.

ONLINE MATERIALS

Bird, Daniel and Jeremiah Kipp, 'Outsiders, Shamans and Devils, Part 1: A Discussion of Central European New Wave Cinema with Film Writer Daniel Bird', *Slant Magazine*, 2009, available at http://www.slantmagazine.com/house/2009/03/outsiders-shamans-and-devils-part-1-a-discussion-of-central-european-new-wave-cinema-with-film-writer-daniel-bird/

Brooke, Michael, 'Polish Documentaries: A Walk in the Old Town of Warsaw (1958)', Kinoblog, available at http://filmjournal.net/kinoblog/category/directors/munk-andrzej/

Checefsky, Bruce, 'Apteka. Reconstruction', Filmoteka Muzeum, available at http://artmuseum.pl/pl/filmoteka/praca/checefsky-bruce-pharmacy

Libera, Zbigniew, 'How Artists Are Tamed! Zbigniew Libera and the Polish Press 1980–2005', a lecture given at University of Michigan School of Art & Design, in partnership with the Center for Russian and East European Studies, 19 January 2006, available at http://www.youtube.com/watch?v=UFCVAzB2J8w

Giżycki, Marcin and Ignacy Szczepański, 'Obliczenia Rytmiczne. Reconstruction' Filmoteka Muzeum, available at http://artmuseum.pl/pl/filmoteka/praca/gizycki-marcin-szczepanski-ignacy-jalu-kurek-or-obliczenia

'Stefan and Franciszka Themerson', LUX Centre, available at http://luxonline.org.uk/artists/stefan_and_franciszka_themerson/index.html

The Themerson Archive, available at http://www.themersonarchive.com

Zarębski, Piotr, 'Europa 2', Filmoteka Muzeum, available at http://artmuseum.pl/pl/filmoteka/praca/zarebski-piotr-europa-ii

FILMOGRAPHY

Intimate Rites (Zbigniew Libera, 1984)

Summer Love (Piotr Uklański, 2006)

Changements de rues (Paul Gilson, 1930)

The Adventures of Gerard (Jerzy Skolimowski, 1970, UK/Italy/Switzerland)

Allegro vivace (Antoni Radzinowicz, 1965, Poland)

L'Amour braque (*Limpet Love*, Andrzej Żuławski, 1985, France)

Anémic Cinema (Marcel Duchamp, 1926, France)

Apteka (*Pharmacy*, Franciszka and Stefan Themerson, 1930, Poland)

Ars Amandi (*The Art of Love*, Walerian Borowczyk, 1983, France)

Au Pair Girls (Val Guest, 1972, UK)

Ballada f-moll (*F-Moll Ballad*, Andrzej Panufnik, 1945, Poland)

Ballet Mécanique (Fernand Léger, 1924, France)

Berlin: Symphony of the Big City (Walter Ruttmann, 1927, Germany)

La Bestia nello spazio (*The Beast in Space*, Alfonso Brescia, 1980, Italy)

La Bête (*The Beast*, Walerian Borowczyk, 1975, France)

Beton (*Concrete*, Janusz Maria Brzeski, Kazimierz Podsadecki, 1933, Poland)

Bykowi chwała (*Glory to the Bull*, Andrzej Papuziński, 1971, Poland)

Był sobie raz (*Once Upon a Time*, Jan Lenica and Walerian Borowczyk, 1957, Poland)

Calling Mr Smith (Franciszka and Stefan Themerson, 1943, UK)

Cérémonie d'amour (*Love Rites*, Walerian Borowczyk, 1988, France)

Cet obscur objet du désir (*That Obscure Object of Desire*, Luis Buñuel, 1977, France)

Un chien andalou (Luis Buñuel and Salvador Dalí, 1929, France)

Chinatown (Roman Polański, 1974, USA)

The Chronicle of a Summer (Jean Rouch and Edgar Morin, 1961, France)

Cinq minutes du cinéma pur (*Five Minutes of Pure Cinema*, Henri Chomette, 1926, France)

Coalface (Alberto Cavalcanti, 1935, UK)

Colour Box (Len Lye, 1935, UK)

Colour Studies of Chopin (Eugeniusz Cękalski, 1944, USA)

Une Collection particulière (*A Particular Collection*, Walerian Borowczyk, 1974, France)

Contes immoraux (*Immoral Tales*, Walerian Borowczyk, 1974, France)

Cul-de-Sac (Roman Polański, 1966, UK)

Czarodziej (*The Sorcerer*, Tadeusz Makarczyński, 1963, Poland)

Deep End (Jerzy Skolimowski, 1970, West Germany/UK)

Le Depart (Jerzy Skolimowski, 1967, Belgium)

Der gelbe Klang (*The Yellow Sound*, Vassily Kandinsky and Arnold Schönberg, 1911,
    Germany)

Diabły (*Devils*, Kazimierz Urbański, 1963, Poland)

Diagonal Symphony (Viking Eggeling, 1924, Germany)

Le Dictionnaire de Joachim (*Joachim's Dictionary*, Walerian Borowczyk, 1965, France)

Die glückliche Hand (*The Hand of Faith*, Vassily Kandinsky and Arnold Schönberg, 1913,
    Germany)

Dom (*House*, Jan Lenica and Walerian Borowczyk, 1958)

Drama in the Futurist Cabaret No.13 (Victor Kasyanov, 1914, Russia)

Drobiazg melodyjny (*Moment Musical*, Franciszka and Stefan Themerson, 1933, Poland)

Dzieci oskarżają (*The Children Accuse*, Edward Skórzewski and Jerzy Hoffman, 1956,
    Poland)

Dzieje grzechu (*The Story of Sin*, Walerian Borowczyk, 1975, Poland)

Dwaj ludzie z szafą (*Two Men and a Wardrobe*, Roman Polański, 1958, Poland)

Elementarz (*The Primer*, Wojciech Wiszniewski, 1976, Poland)

Emmanuelle 5 (Walerian Borowczyk, 1987, France)

L'Encyclopédie de Grand-Maman en 13 volumes (*Grandmother's Encyclopedia in 13
    Volumes*, Walerian Borowczyk, 1963, France)

Entr'acte (René Clair, 1924, France)

L'Étoile de mer (Man Ray, 1928, France)

The Eye and the Ear (Franciszka and Stefan Themerson, 1944-45, UK)

Europa (*Europe*, Franciszka and Stefan Themerson, 1932, Poland)

Flirt krzesełek (*Flirting chairs*, Feliks Kuczkowski, 1916, Kraków, Polish territories)

Frustration (José Bénazéraf, 1971, France)

Gdzie diabeł mówi dobranoc (*Where the Devil Says Goodnight*, Kazimierz Karabasz and
    Władysław Ślesicki, 1956, Poland)

Gdy spadają anioły (*When Angels Fall*, Roman Polański, 1959, Poland)

Gips – romanca (*A Plaster Romance*, Kazimierz Urbański, 1960, Poland)

Goto, l'île d'amour (*Goto, Island of Love*, Walerian Borowczyk, 1968, France)

Le Gros et le maigre (*The Fat and the Lean*, Roman Polański, 1961, France)

Hamleś (*Little Hamlet*, Jerzy Skolimowski, 1960, Poland)

Harivari (Antoni Radzinowicz, 1967, Poland)

Heroïnes du mal (*Three Immoral Women*, Walerian Borowczyk, 1979, France)

Igraszki (*Games*, Kazimierz Urbański, 1962, Poland)

Interno di un convento (*Behind Convent Walls*, Walerian Borowczyk, 1977, France)

Les Jeux des anges (Walerian Borowczyk, 1964, France)

Kapelusz (*Hat*, Janusz Majewski, 1961, Poland)

Kilka opowieści o człowieku (*A Few Stories About Man*, Bogdan Dziworski, 1983, Poland)

Kineformy (*Kineforms*, Andrzej Pawłowski, 1957, Poland)

Kobiety pracujące (*Working Women*, Piotr Szulkin, 1978, Poland)

Kopalnia (*Coal Mine*, Natalia Brzozowska, 1947, Poland)

Kostka cukru (*A Cube of Sugar*, Jacek Bławut, 1986, Poland)

Lampa (*The Lamp*, Roman Polański, 1959, Poland)

Le Locataire (*The Tenant*, Roman Polański, 1976, France)

Lody ruszyły (*The Ice Is Moving*, Jerzy Bossak, 1947, Poland)

Ludzie z pustego obszaru (*People from an Empty Zone*, Kazimierz Karabasz and Władysław Ślesicki, 1957, Poland)

Mackbeth (Roman Polański, 1971, UK)

Majdanek, cmentarzysko Europy (*Majdanek: The Cemetery of Europe*, Aleksander Ford, 1944, Poland)

La Marge (Walerian Borowczyk, 1976, France)

Materia (*The Matter*, Kazimierz Urbański, 1962, Poland)

Miasteczko (*Little Town*, 1956, by Jerzy Ziarnik, Poland)

Moje miejsce (*My Place*, Marcel Łoziński, 1986, Poland)

Moja ulica (*My Street*, Danuta Halladin, 1965, Poland)

Moonlighting (Jerzy Skolimowski, 1982, UK)

Muzykanci (*The Musicians*, Kazimierz Karabasz, 1960, Poland)

Nagrodzone uczucie (*Love Required*, Walerian Borowczyk, 1957, Poland)

Na srebrnym globie (*On the Silver Globe*, Andrzej Żuławski, 1976/1988, France)

Nie płacz (*Don't Cry*, Grzegorz Królikiewicz, 1972, Poland)

Niewinni czarodzieje (*Innocent Sorcerers*, Andrzej Wajda, 1960, Poland)

Niedzielny poranek (*One Sunday Morning*, Andrzej Munk, 1956, Poland)

Night Mail (John Grierson, 1936, UK)

The Ninth Gate (Roman Polański, 1999, Spain/France/USA)

Nóż w wodzie (*Knife in the Water*, Roman Polański, 1961, Poland)

Obliczenia Rytmiczne (*O.R., Rhythmical Calculations*, Jalu Kurek, 1934, Poland)

On Zabił, Ty Zabiłeś, Ja Zabiłem (*He Killed, I Killed, You Killed*, Mieczyslaw Szczuka, 1925, Poland)

O slavnosti a hostech (*The Party and the Guests*, Jan Němec, 1966, Czechoslovakia)

Ostatni dzień lata (*The Last Day of the Summer*, Tadeusz Konwicki, 1957, Poland)

Paragraf Zero (*Article Zero*, Włodzimierz Borowik, 1957, Poland)

Il Perfido Incanto (Anton Giulio Bragaglia, 1918, Italy)

Perdu... (Rostandre aka Walerian Borowczyk, 1958, Poland)

La petite marchande d'allumettes (*The Little Match Girl*, Jean Renoir, 1928, France)

Poemat symfoniczny "Bajka" Stanisława Moniuszki. Koncert w Klubie Fabrycznym Zakładów "Ursus" (*Stanisław Moniuszko's Symphonic Poem Fairy-Tale: A Concert in the Ursus Tractor Factory Club*, Andrzej Munk, 1952, Poland)

Possession (Andrzej Żuławski, 1981, France)

Postava k podpírání (*Joseph Kilian*, Pavel Juráček and Jan Schmidt, 1963, Czechoslovakia)

Powódź (*Flood*, Jerzy Bossak, 1947, Poland)

Primary (Richard Leacock and the Maysles Brothers, 1960, USA)

Przekroje (Janusz Maria Brzeski, 1931, Poland)

Przygoda Czlowieka Poczciwego (*Adventure of a Good Citizen*, Franciszka and Stefan Themerson, 1937, Poland)

Rain (Joris Ivens, 1928, Netherlands)

Repulsion (Roman Polański, 1965, UK)

Ręce do gory (*Hands Up!*, Jerzy Skolimowski, 1967/1981, Poland)

Le Rhythme Coloré (Léopold Survage, 1914, France)

Rien Que Les Heures (*Only the Hours*, Alberto Cavalcanti, 1926, UK)

The River (Pare Lorentz, 1937, USA)

Rondo (*Rondo*, Janusz Majewski, 1958, Poland)

Rosemary's Baby (Roman Polański, 1968, USA)

Rynek (*Market Square*, Józef Robakowski, 1971, Poland)

Le sang des betes (Georges Franju, 1949, France)

Le Sang d'un Poète (*Blood of a Poet*, Jean Cocteau, 1930, France)

The Seashell and the Clergyman (Germaine Dulac, 1928, France)

Shadows (John Cassavetes, 1959, USA)

Słodkie rytmy (*Sweet Rhythms*, Kazimierz Urbański, 1965, Poland)

Somnambulicy (*Somnambulists*, Mieczysław Waśkowski, 1957, Poland)

Song of Ceylon (Basil Wright, 1934, UK)

Spacerek staromiejski (*A Walk in the Old City of Warsaw*, Andrzej Munk, 1958, Poland)

Ssaki (*Mammals*, Roman Polański, 1962, Poland)

Szczurołap (*The Rat Catcher*, Andrzej Czarnecki, 1986, Poland)

Szkoła podstawowa (*Primary School*, Tomasz Zygadło, 1971, Poland)

Stolarz (*The Carpenter*, Wojciech Wiszniewski, 1976, Poland)

Szpital (*Hospital*, Krzysztof Kieślowski, 1976, Poland)

Success Is the Best Revenge (Jerzy Skolimowski, 1984, UK)

Suita warszawska (*Warsaw Suite*, Tadeusz Makarczyński, 1946, Poland)

Sweet Movie (Dušan Makavejev, 1974, Canada/France/West Germany)

Tam i tu (*There and Here*, Andrzej Pawłowski, 1957, Poland)

Le Théâtre de M. et Mme. Kabal (*The Theatre of Mr. and Mrs. Kabal*, Walerian Borowczyk, 1967, France)

Trzecia część nocy (*Third Part of the Night*, Andrzej Żuławski, 1971, Poland)

Turksib (Viktor Turin, 1929, Soviet Union)

Uwaga chuligani! (*Look Out, Hooligans!*, Edward Skórzewski and Jerzy Hoffman, 1955, Poland)

Vita Futurista (Arnaldo Gina, 1916, Italy)

Vynález zkázy (*The Fabulous World of Jules Verne*, Karel Zeman, 1958, Czechoslovakia)

Wanda Gościmińska włókniarka (*Wanda Gościmińska: A Weaver*, Wojciech Wiszniewski, 1975, Poland)

Warszawa 1956 (*Warsaw 1956*, Jerzy Bossak and Jarosław Brzozowski, 1956, Poland)

What? (*Che?*, Roman Polański, 1972, Italy/France/West Germany)

Z miasta Łodzi (*From the City of Łódź*, Krzysztof Kieślowski, 1968, Poland)

Zanim opadną liście (*Before Leaves Fall*, Władysław Ślesicki, 1964, Poland)

Zombi 2 (*Zombie Flesh Eaters*, Lucio Fulci, 1979, Italy)

Zwarcie (*Short Circuit*, 1935, Franciszka and Stefan Themerson, Poland)

Życie codzienne (*Everyday Life*, Piotr Szulkin, 1975, Poland)

Życie jest piękne (*Life Is Great*, Tadeusz Makarczyński, 1957, Poland)

Žvahlav aneb šatičky slaměného Huberta (*Jabberwocky*, Jan Švankmajer, 1971, Czechoslovakia)

Marcuse, Herbert 112
Marinetti, Filippo Tommaso 33–4, 38, 43, 46, 52n.n.39,42, 54n.73, 58
Marker, Chris 101–2
Markowski, Andrzej 71, 72
Mayakovsky, Vladimir 13, 43, 50n.24, 58
Maysles Brothers, David and Albert 75–6
McLaren, Norman 39
Meissner Ryszard 120
Méliès, Georges 87
Menken, Marie 83
Metzger, Radley 112
Miczka, Tadeusz 32–4, 38, 47–8
Miłosz, Czesław 65
Mitry, Jean 83
Modinari, Aldo 33
Moholy–Nagy, László 13, 25
Morin, Edgar 76
Mrożek, Sławomir 100
Munk, Andrzej 70–2, 81n.14, 156, 157–9, 162n.1

Němec, Jan 89
Newman, Barnett 155
Norwid, Cyprian Kamil 68, 80n.6

Panufnik, Andrzej 68–70, 80n.6
Papuziński, Andrzej 78–9
Partum, Andrzej 121
Pasolini, Pier Paolo 112, 159
Pawłowski, Andrzej 2, 84–5
Peckinpah, Sam 161
Péret, Benjamin 99
Picasso, Pablo 11, 33
Pietrangeli, Antonio 158
Piotrowski, Piotr 2, 4, 5n.1, 52n.43
Podsadecki, Kazimierz 8, 17, 51n.26
Polański, Roman 86–9, 93–103, 106–9, 113–14, 159
Pollock, Jackson 86
Połom, Janusz 119–21, 124, 134
Prauzel, Andrzej 121
Pudovkin, Vsevolod 159

Queneau, Raymond 102–3

Rees, A.L. 2, 4, 7, 11, 38–41, 49n.5
Reichenbach, François 83
Renoir, Jean 89
Resnais, Alain 101–3, 156
Richter, Hans 12, 13, 17, 24, 34
Robakowski, Józef 119–20, 122–4, 128–32, 135n.n.5,14, 140–1, 149–50
Rohmer, Eric 156
Rossellini, Roberto 35, 158–9
Rouch, Jean 76
Różycki, Andrzej 115n.5, 119–2-, 130
Ruiz, Raúl 110
Rybczyński, Zbigniew 119–20, 126–9, 135n.5

Schmidt, Jan 89
Schönberg, Arnold 33, 50n.20
Ścibor–Rylski, Aleksander 156
Scott, Sir Walter 101, 107
Skolimowski, Jerzy 2, 4, 88, 95–113, 159
Skórzewski, Edward 73–4
Ślesicki, Władysław 73–4, 76, 81n.26
Sollers, Philippe 110
Sontag, Susan 112, 121
Sowiński, Zdzisław 119
Stalin, Joseph 1, 12, 16, 72, 84, 91, 98, 103, 156–7, 159–60, 162n.2
Stawiński, Jerzy Stefan 154
Stern, Anatol 9, 14–5, 32, 34–40, 43–8, 51n.30, 52n.45, 53n.n.58,61, 54n.77, 57–8, 133
Strzemiński, Władysław 13
Survage, Léopold 33
Švankmajer, Jan 100
Szczepański, Ignacy 40, 49n.4
Szczerek, Janusz 121
Szczuka, Mieczysław 8, 11–15, 27, 36, 57–8, 84
Szulkin, Piotr 77–9

Tanner, Alan 83
Tashlin, Frank 112
Themerson, Franciszka 2–4, 7–9, 12–13, 15–28, 31–3, 36–40, 43, 47, 49n.4, 51n.28, 52n.55, 58, 84, 88, 160, 162n.4